The nonprofit sector in France

Johns Hopkins Nonprofit Sector Series

edited by Lester M. Salamon and Helmut K. Anheier
Institute for Policy Studies, The Johns Hopkins University

Manchester University Press is proud to be publishing this important new series, the product of the most comprehensive comparative analysis of the global nonprofit sector ever undertaken. The growth of the sector between the public and the private, known variously as the nonprofit, voluntary or third sector, is one of the most significant contemporary developments in societies throughout the world. The books in this series will cover the development and role of this sector in a broad cross-section of nations, and also provide comparative, cross-country analyses.

Johns Hopkins Nonprofit Sector Series 3

THE NONPROFIT SECTOR IN FRANCE

Edith Archambault

Manchester University Press

Manchester and New York

distributed exclusively in the USA by St. Martin's Press

Copyright © Lester M. Salamon, Johns Hopkins Comparative Nonprofit Sector Project 1997

Published by Manchester University Press
Oxford Road, Manchester M13 9NR, UK
and Room 400, 175 Fifth Avenue, New York, NY 10010, USA

Distributed exclusively in the USA
by St. Martin's Press, Inc., 175 Fifth Avenue, New York
NY 10010, USA

British Library Cataloguing-in-Publication Data
A catalogue record for this book is available from the British Library

Library of Congress Cataloging-in-Publication Data
The nonprofit sector in France
        p.   cm. — (Johns Hopkins nonprofit sector series)
    Includes bibliographical references and index.
    ISBN 0–7190–4903–2. — ISBN 0–7190–4904–0 (pbk.)
    1. Nonprofit organization—France.   I. Archambault, E.
II. Series: Johns Hopkins nonprofit sector series.
    HD2769.2.F7N66   1997
    338.6—dc20   95–33689
                                                                                            CIP

ISBN 0 7190 4903 2 *hardback*
     0 7190 4904 0 *paperback*

First published 1997

01 00 99 98 97   10 9 8 7 6 5 4 3 2 1

Typeset in Great Britain
by Northern Phototypesetting Co Ltd, Bolton
Printed in Great Britain
by Bell & Bain Ltd, Glasgow

CONTENTS

Contents

TABLES AND FIGURES

Tables

Figures

SERIES EDITORS' FOREWORD

This book is one in a series of monographs on the voluntary or nonprofit sector throughout the world that have resulted from the *Johns Hopkins Comparative Nonprofit Sector Project*, a major inquiry into the scope, structure, history, legal position and role of the nonprofit sector in a broad cross-section of nations.

Launched in May 1990, this project has sought to close the glaring gaps in knowledge that have long existed about the thousands of schools, hospitals, clinics, community organizations, advocacy groups, day care centres, relief organizations, nursing homes, homeless shelters, family counseling agencies, environmental groups and others that comprise this important sector. Though known by different names in different places, these organizations are present almost everywhere, albeit to widely differing extents. More than that, there is significant evidence that they are growing considerably in both scope and scale as faith has declined in the capability of government to cope on its own with the interrelated challenges of persistent poverty, environmental degradation and social change. Indeed, we seem to be in the midst of a global "associational revolution" that is opening new opportunities for organized private action and placing new demands and responsibilities on private not-forprofit groups. As a result, it has becoming increasingly important to understand what the scope and contours of this nonprofit sector really are, and what its potentials are for shouldering the new demands being placed upon it.

The *Johns Hopkins Comparative Nonprofit Sector Project* was conceived as a way to meet this need, to document the scope, structure, revenue base and background of the nonprofit sector, and to do so in a way that not only yielded solid and objective information about individual countries, but made it possible to undertake cross-national comparisons in a systematic way. For this purpose, we identified thirteen countries representing different religious and historical traditions, different regions of the world, and different levels of economic development. Included were seven advanced industrial societies (the US, UK, France, Germany, Italy, Sweden and Japan), five "developing" societies (Brazil, Ghana, Egypt, Thailand and India), and one former Soviet bloc country (Hungary). In each of these countries we recruited a local associate and undertook a similar set of information-gathering activities guided by a common definition, a common classification scheme and a common set of data-gathering forms and instructions. The result, we believe, is the first systematic attempt to put the nonprofit sector on the social and economic map of the world in a solid and empirical way.

The present volume reports on the results of this in France. Written by our French local associate, Professor Edith Archambault, the book presents the first systematic analysis of the French nonprofit sector ever. Using a broad range of quantitative and qualitative information, Dr Archambault shows how nonprofit organizations have grown from political obscurity to a veritable economic force that now represents one of the socially and economically most vital parts of French society. Of special interest in the French case is the long-standing hostility to voluntary organizations that was one manifestation of the French Jacobin tradition (such organizations were formally outlawed between the French Revolution and 1901) and the striking support such organizations have recently received from government as a byproduct of the dramatic governmental decentralization that took place in France in the 1980s. Professor Archambault concludes her book with an account of current trends and developments in the French nonprofit sector. She shows that the challenges facing the nonprofit sector are at the heart of significant changes underway in French society that range from greater political decentralization and a more heterogeneous population to basic economic restructuring.

From its outset, the *Johns Hopkins Comparative Nonprofit Sector Project* has been a collaborative effort among an extraordinary group of scholars with support from a wide array of funders and advisors. The team of local associates – Martin Knapp and Jeremy Kendall in the UK, Edith Archambault in France, Paolo Barbetta and Pippo Ranci in Italy, Helmut Anheier, Eckhard Priller and Wolfgang Seibel in Germany, Éva Kuti in Hungary, Tadashi Yamamoto and Takayoshi Amenomori in Japan, Leilah Landim in Brazil, Lawrence Atingdui and Emmanuel Laryea in Ghana, Amani Kandil in Egypt, Amara Pongsapich in Thailand, Sven-Erik Sjöstrand, Filip Wijkström, and Thomas Lundström in Sweden – has worked together at every stage to perfect the infor-mation-gathering forms, develop the basic definitions and classi-fication scheme and interpret the results. To all of them, we owe a deep debt of gratitude.

Thanks are also due to the numerous individuals who served on the International Advisory Committee to this project, to the mem-bers of the national advisory committees we formed to oversee the work, to Richard Purslow of Manchester University Press for the crucial encouragement he has provided in bringing this work to publication, and to the foundations, corporations and govern-ment agencies throughout the world that provided support to make this work possible.

It was more than 150 years ago that the Frenchman Alexis de Tocqueville identified the "art of associating together" as the mother of all science. Today we appear to be in the middle of an extraordinary explosion of associational activity as new forms of organized citizen action are taking shape and expanding their role in widely disparate parts of the world. Our hope is that the series of monographs of which this volume is an important part will help make this process of change more visible and more under-standable and thereby contribute to its success. We are convinced that important values hinge critically on this result.

L.M.S.
H.K.A.
Baltimore, Maryland
January 1996

Chapter 1

TERRA INCOGNITA:
THE FRENCH NONPROFIT
SECTOR

In France, as in most other countries, the increasing importance of
the role of nonprofit organizations in the everyday life of citizens
and the involvement of those organizations in many recent policies, at national or local level, contrast with its relative official
invisibility in the country's institutional landscape. As in many
other countries, statistics on the sector as a whole are simply not
kept. And while such terms as *économie sociale, tiers secteur, secteur
sans but lucratif* may be cited occasionally by specialists or employees of nonprofit organizations, they are not used in general dis-
course.

1.1 Growing awareness of the third sector

Why is it so important to know more about the nonprofit sector, in
empirical as well as in analytical terms? Generally speaking,
because the third sector is able to reconcile private initiative and
common interest on public matters. In the specific case of France,
since the 1960s we can observe an increase in the economic and
social importance of this sector which is simultaneously at the root
and a way of expression of cultural and social change. In fact, we
can see that all new social movements embodied their ideology in
nonprofit institutions: feminism, ecology, defence of human rights
and peace, defence of sexual or ethnic minorities, antiracism, concern for Third World development. For instance, on this last point,
most French professions have now a voluntary homologue "without borders", involved either in emergency control or in Third

1

World development: *Médecins sans frontières and Médecins du Monde* are the first and the most famous, but pharmacists, architects, engineers, agronomists without borders are also examples of this concern.

Similarly, the recent increase in the cultural level of the French population (Donnat, 1994; Donnat and Cogneau, 1990) is of course a consequence of a higher level of education, but it is also the cause and a consequence of the flourishing of culture nonprofit organizations such as music ensembles, chorales, amateur performing arts centers, film clubs, volunteer radio stations, historical societies and socio-educative and popular education associations. Social tourism also developed cultural activities according to the slogan "Don't tan stupid". All those organizations acted for the democratization of culture. New forms of sociability can be found in culture and recreation nonprofit organizations, as well as in neighborhood organizations or multipurpose rural centers.

In more traditional fields, private schools and nonprofit organizations delivering health care and social services have also expanded during recent decades to cope with human needs. Their economic activity cannot be neglected. We can cite: hospitals, emergency medical or out-patient services, home hospitalization, residential care facilities and services for the handicapped, the elderly, children and adults in need, day care services, relief, assistance and income support organizations. In those sectors, nonprofits created new jobs during a period of growing unemployment and they developed an important economic activity as a consequence of their social role. The same process can be observed when nonprofit organizations tackle economic activity in sectors overlooked by standard enterprises in order to provide temporary jobs and better qualifications for unskilled young people, former delinquents or drug addicts.

Last, a better knowledge of the nonprofit sector is required when the limits of the welfare state are emphasized by authors from different schools of thought and when the recent Decentralization Acts (1982–83) provoke a major reappraisal of the respective roles of central and local governments and of public and private entities in the provision of human services. The slowing down of economic growth, together with the upward trend of unemployment since 1974, is at the origin of the financial crisis of the welfare state; social welfare spending grows rapidly while social contributions stagnate. Simultaneously the legitimacy of the welfare state is questioned by those who point out the growth of an inefficient bureaucracy, the lack of initiative or even the disincitement to work of recipients of public assistance, the partitioning of social policies, the inadequacy of general rules in specific cases and, finally, the slowness of statutory services to cope with new social needs and new forms of poverty. Decentralization is a way to bring government nearer the citizen; in this sense, it fights the shortcomings of the welfare state; after a millennium of centralization, it is a hallmark of change in French behavior, as we will see later. But local authorities, in charge of new powers, are in search of private partners; they contract out many tasks and for social and cultural concerns, nonprofit organizations are chosen as partners.

1.2 Lack of information

Despite these reasons to improve the knowledge of the nonprofit sector, it has remained a "terra incognita" overlooked by official statistics and by researchers and considered as insignificant. With the exception of some data on membership, which interested sociologists, and on the annual creations of new nonprofits recorded by the Ministry of the Interior no reliable data existed on this sector before this study began (Archambault, 1984). A major objective of the Johns Hopkins Comparative Nonprofit Sector Project was to fill the gap in basic statistical data about the nonprofit sector in the twelve countries involved in the project (Salamon and Anheier, 1992a). As a result of this research in France, we found that the nonprofit sector is not as insignificant as previously assumed. With a turnover of more than FF. 200 billion, the size of the nonprofit sector is comparable to such activities as transport or textile industries. And it is surprising to learn that employment in social services nonprofit organizations, the main subsector, is 300,000 employees, i.e. exactly the same as employment in the motor car industry, one of the most conspicuous sectors in terms of industrial employment.

1.3 A broad definition: social economy

What precisely do we mean by the "nonprofit sector"? Of course, in a comparative approach, we have to agree on a definition to ensure that the same thing is meant in each country. The most common and rather recent term in France is *économie sociale* or "social economy". Legal status is the main criterion for membership in the social economy. It includes four distinct components (Archambault, 1993).

- *Cooperatives*, governed by a 1947 general status of cooperation Act (revised in 1985). Cooperatives are numerous in agriculture, entailing the participation of four out of five farmers. This component also includes large cooperative banks such as *Crédit Agricole, Crédit Mutuel* or *Banques Populaires*, created initially on the principle of collective self-help to serve the credit needs of low-income groups. Despite this origin, the cooperative banks increasingly operate like regular banks.
- *Mutuals* are heirs of the oldest part of the French nonprofit sector. Mutual societies, governed by a 1955 mutual societies code, supplement the social security scheme on a voluntary basis for health insurance. Beyond insurance, mutual societies provide health and welfare services, including medical clinics, day care hospitals, pharmacies, nursing homes and social service centers for the elderly and handicapped. In addition, mutual societies serve as *de facto* social security agencies, providing compulsory social security for civil servants, teachers, students and farmers.

    Other mutual insurance companies, subject to the General Insurance Code, operate on a nonprofit basis and hold about 35 per cent of automobile policies and 25 per cent of other property policies.
- *Associations* represent the most important and the most diverse component of social economy. Most of them are declared associations subject to the 1901 Act, which defines an association as "a convention according to which two or more individuals permanently put in common their knowledge or activity with an aim other than the share of profit". In a country ruled by civil law, the 1901 Act proposes the most liberal and flexible status under French Law, the closest to common law agreements. That

is why this legal status is adopted by nonprofit organizations of very different size and operating in diverse activities. Despite this mainstream status, some associations remain undeclared and some others prefer to become "public utility" associations, a more favorable status but granted following a two-year application procedure (cf. chapter 3).

- *Foundations* enjoy the same privileges as public-utility associations. They have no membership but they rely on an endowment. They are governed by very recent Acts (1987, 1990). For a long while, the state was suspicious of foundations and that is why there are very few foundations in France compared to other European countries of similar size, such as the UK, Germany or Italy.

1.4 The common definition of the comparative project

Social economy with its four components should be compared to the project's common definition of the nonprofit sector. Widely divergent historical, religious, cultural and political traditions among nations make it difficult to compare nonprofit sectors cross-nationally. To facilitate such comparisons, a common definition identifies the key features that nonprofit organizations share in virtually all countries; five criteria have been identified as the most important (Salamon and Anheier, 1992a).[1] Using these criteria, the nonprofit sector can be defined as a collection of organizations that are simultaneously:

- *Formal*, i.e. institutionalized to some extent. In some countries, institutionalization is signified by a formal charter of incorporation; in others by a simple registration. But institutional reality can also be demonstrated in other ways: having regular meetings, officers or rules of procedure, or some degree of permanence. Purely *ad hoc*, informal or temporary gatherings of people are not considered as part of the nonprofit sector under this definition. Otherwise the concept of third sector becomes far too amorphous and ephemeral to grasp and examine.
- *Private*, i.e. institutionally separate from central or local government. Nonprofit organizations are neither part of the gov-

ernmental apparatus nor governed by boards dominated by government officials. This does not mean that they may not receive significant government support either in money or in kind, or that government officials cannot sit on their boards. The key here is that nonprofit organizations are fundamentally private institutions in basic structure.

- *Nonprofit distributing*, i.e. not returning profits generated to their members or directors. Nonprofit organizations may accumulate profits in a given year, but the profits must be plowed back into the basic mission of the agency, not distributed to the organizations' members or governing board. In this sense, nonprofit organizations are private organizations that do not exist primarily to generate profits. Rather, they have some "public interest" purpose and are *not primarily commercial* in operation and purpose. This differentiates nonprofit organizations from the other component of the private sector: private businesses.
- *Self-governing*, i.e. equipped to control their own activities. Nonprofit organizations have their own internal procedures for governance and are not controlled by outside entities.
- *Voluntary*, i.e. involving some meaningful degree of voluntary participation, either in the actual conduct of the agency's activities or in the management of its affairs. This does not mean that all or most of the income of an organization must come from voluntary contributions, or that most of its staff must be volunteers. The presence of some voluntary input, even if only a voluntary board of directors, suffices to qualify an organization as in some sense "voluntary".

To be considered as part of the nonprofit sector under this definition, an organization must make a reasonable showing on *all* five of these criteria. What is more, to keep the scope of this comparative project within manageable limits, we added two further restrictions: the organizations included in the project had to be nonreligious and nonpolitical.

- *Nonreligious*, i.e. not primarily involved in the promotion of religious worship or religious education. Religiously affiliated nonprofit service organizations are included in the project, but not the congregations, synagogues, mosques, or churches where religious worship takes place. Such religious institutions

are properly part of the nonprofit sector but were excluded
from the analysis here to keep the project manageable.

- *Nonpolitical*, i.e. not primarily involved in promoting candidates for elected office. Organizations that engage in advocacy
activity to change government policies on particular topics (e.g.
civil rights, the environment) are included in the project, but
political parties and other organizations devoted principally to
getting people elected to public office are not. Here, again, such
organizations are properly part of the nonprofit sector, but they
were excluded from the analysis here to keep the effort manageable, and because they lay outside our principal area of
interest.

For the purposes of this project, therefore, only organizations that
fit these seven criteria are included. Even so, this includes an
immense variety of types of organizations. In particular, we developed a classification system, the International Classification of
Nonprofit Organizations (ICNPO), to group these organizations
systematically (see chapter 4).

1.5 Applying the common definition: the nonprofit
sector in France

When we examine how the seven criteria listed above can fit the
social economy organizations, we have to exclude many types of
organizations and also to include some which are not considered
as part of the social economy.[2]

Some criteria are common to both concepts: social economy
organizations are *nonreligious* and *nonpolitical*; more basically, they
are *formal*,[3] *private* and *self-governing*. The 1980 charter of social
economy[4] lays down as a principle that the organizations are independent from government, at the central or the local level. So
some associations which are in fact quasi-governmental agencies
have to be excluded. Examples include the *Association pour la Formation Professionnelle des Adultes*, which works in continuing education, and the *Institut National de la Consommation*, the main
umbrella group for consumer protection. At the local level, many
para-municipal associations exist in many towns: created and run
by officials, they circumvent public law regulations, avoid public

accountability, and escape civil service requirements. According to both definitions, these entities have to be excluded from the social economy and from the nonprofit sector.

The *voluntary* criterion is also a communality in the comparison of the nonprofit sector and the social economy. In the social economy, it is often restricted to a volunteer board of directors, which characterizes all social economy organizations. But the voluntary component may be more important in associations.

So the main difference between the two concepts relies on the *nonprofit distributing* criterion. In all social economy organizations, profit is not the aim of the organization and remuneration of capital in the form of dividends does not exist. But in associations and foundations, the income in excess of expenses is reinvested in the organization, while mutuals and cooperatives either reinvest profits or more commonly distribute them to members and clients in the form of discounted fees or reduced prices. In addition, mutuals and cooperatives are primarily member-oriented and have no public interest purpose, and most of them are primarily commercial. Where the social economy would include cooperatives, the nonprofit sector definition would exclude them as businesses (except school cooperatives and some housing cooperatives which behave like associations). Likewise the entire banking sector and mutual insurance societies, including health supplementary insurance, would *not* meet the nonprofit sector definition principles, but they are included in the social economy. Conversely, health and social care establishments run by mutual societies are not businesses and are included in the nonprofit sector, exactly like the same facilities run by associations.

Conversely, for historical reasons (see chapters 2 and 5), private schools and private higher education are not considered – and do not consider themselves – as components of the social economy. Most of them, however, meet the seven criteria of the definition of the nonprofit sector: certainly, most of the elementary and secondary schools are Catholic, and largely subsidized by government; but they provide education services, they are not primarily involved in the promotion of worship and they are self-governing, so they are part of the nonprofit sector according to our definition.

To summarize, when we apply the core definition to France, the nonprofit sector includes:

- foundations;
- associations, except those which are not self-governing;
- health and social care establishments run by mutuals;
- school cooperatives and housing cooperatives.

The nonprofit sector is part of a larger aggregation of social institutions referred to as the social economy. Mutuals and cooperatives can be considered as "borderline organizations", as we have seen that the two concepts of the social economy and the nonprofit sector are basically compatible.

1.6 Borderline cases

In the following monograph, mutuals and cooperatives are *excluded* borderline cases. We will now insist on some *included* borderline cases:

1.6.1 Borderline cases between the nonprofit and the forprofit sector

In this category we can find social tourism, work councils and *entreprises intermédiaires*, which are specific to France.

- *Social tourism* is specific to France, though versions of it can be found in some European countries with strong socialist traditions. The establishment of social tourism dates back to 1936 when the first "vacation with pay" was introduced by the government. The socialist minister Leo Lagrange instigated a network of holiday villages or camps for working-class families. He also established youth hostels, holiday centers for children and similar facilities. This nonprofit network developed fully after World War II.

  Social tourism could be seen as primarily commercial and competing with standard tourism, but its public interest purpose is also clear: encouraging tourism among low-income people, promoting cultural and sports activities and intermingling working and middle classes. Payment is generally in proportion to income and family burden.
- *Work councils* are another specificity and another type of borderline organization, operating in every enterprise with more

than fifty employees. They could be seen as joint-production committees, but they are self-governing and administered by salaried employees elected from union lists. In addition, they manage only cultural activities or social services, such as libraries, canteens, day care and holiday centers. They are funded by 1 per cent of the total wage bill.

- *Entreprises intermédiaires* are organizations with associative or cooperative legal status. They provide temporary jobs for unskilled young people who have failed schooling, potential or former delinquents, and drug addicts. They seek to produce marketable goods or services in sectors overlooked by ordinary businesses. *Entreprises intermédiaires* are usually operated by former social workers; they are government-subsidized, and fit somewhere between ordinary businesses and adult education agencies. Sheltered workshops perform the same function for handicapped people, and they are commonly considered as part of the nonprofit sector.

1.6.2 Borderline cases between the nonprofit and the public sector

We shall examine now two borderline cases considered as included because they meet the seven criteria of the common definition, i.e. chambers of commerce and the education organizations which are run by them, and peripheral public school organizations.

- *Chambers of commerce*[5] in France are close to the public sector, because they are mainly funded by a specific local tax on enterprises. However, they are private and self-governing despite the presence of officials on the board. They run many nonprofit higher education organizations in the field of management and also in vocational training and continuing education, and all of them are part of the French third sector.
- *Peripheral public school organizations* are those primarily devoted to the defence of public schools and the advocacy of secularity of education since the end of the last century. More recently, these peri-school associations run sports, recreation and cultural activities inside or outside public schools. Despite this linkage with public education, these organizations meet all the

seven criteria of the common definition and are undoubtedly nonprofit organizations. Most of them are part of the two umbrellas, *Ligue Française de l'Enseignement et de l'Education Permanente* and *Fédération des Oeuvres Laïques* (French League of Initial and Continuing Education; Secular Nonprofit Organizations Federation).

When looking at the borders of the nonprofit sector, the scope of this concept becomes more precise. The range of organizations it embraces will be discussed specifically in chapter 4, when we will develop the International Classification of Nonprofit Organization (ICNPO). This classification identifies twelve major groups:

- culture and recreation;
- education and research;
- health;
- social services;
- environment;
- development and housing;
- law, advocacy and politics;
- philanthropic intermediaries and voluntarism promotion;
- international activities;
- religion;
- business, professional associations, unions;
- not elsewhere classified.

1.7 Summary of the principal findings

Background

The *Jacobin tradition* is no doubt the most important feature in the historical background of the French nonprofit sector. This Jacobin tradition means etatism and centralization and is a consequence of a millennial fight by central government against any form of local power or intermediary interest group. During the *ancien régime*, the state fought regional governments and religious minorities; during the French Revolution, corporations, the Church and the congregations; during the nineteeth century, the labor movement and the political associations.

The nonprofit sector ceased to be illegal only at the beginning of the twentieth century and that is why most of the nonprofit organizations are relatively recent.

During the 1960s and the 1970s, the French nonprofit sector grew quickly in a context of state-provided welfare. New concerns, financial public encouragement and favorable regulations explain this growth. The coming of a socialist government and the Decentralization Acts (1982) reinforced this trend. *Decentralization*, which broke a millenary Jacobin tradition, was the major incentive: local governments contracted out health, welfare and cultural services and strengthened the partnership between government and the nonprofit sector.

Overall size

Against the backdrop of its recent origin, the overall size of the French nonprofit sector is rather similar to other European countries. In 1990, its full-time equivalent employment was 800,000 persons, that is exactly the employment figures of the whole transport industry or twice those of France's two largest private employers (*Alcatel* and *Générale des eaux*).

The operating expenditures of the nonprofit sector, at 217 billion FF. ($40 billion) represents the gross sales of the aggregate textile, clothing and leather industries. If we add to the operating expenditures an imputed money value of volunteer work, the figure rises to 37 per cent.

The nonprofit sector is not only large, but also growing. Between 1981 and 1991, nonprofit employment increased by 40 per cent while overall employment remained fairly flat and France has experienced an "associative boom" in the rate at which nonprofit organizations have been created over the two past decades.

Structure

Four subsectors dominate the French nonprofit sector: social services, education, culture and recreation, and health. Together they account for 86 per cent of operating expenditures and nearly 90 per cent of the employment of the nonprofit sector. The two first subsectors, social services and education, represent more than half the nonprofit sector, whatever the yardstick.

In the main subsector, social services, the most important organizations are residential care facilities for people with specific needs, with a quasi-monopoly for the handicapped, drug addicts and children in social difficulty. Employment in this subsector is 300,000, the same as in the motor-car industry.

Conversely, the foundations subsector is very small; this is due to restrictive government regulations, a residue of Jacobin fears about the wealth accumulated in *ancien régime* congregations.

Revenue

The government is by far the major source of revenue of the French third sector; 59.5 per cent of total revenue, including third-party payments from social security to health or social services organizations. Earned income from fees and charges is the second source of income, 33.5 per cent of total revenue, while only 7 per cent comes from private giving.

We can see that there are tremendous variations in this revenue structure according to the subsectors. Only three subsectors are government revenue dominated: education, health and social services, the heart of the welfare state. In these subsectors, government is the principal source of funds reflecting a developing partnership, on a contractual basis, in which the state provides the resources and the nonprofit organizations deliver the services. Earned income is the main revenue for culture and recreation, environment, development and housing, civic and advocacy organizations, and of course, business and professional subsectors.

Private giving is low in France and as a share of household disposable income it is less than 0.2 per cent. In donations, only two fields, international assistance and foundations, provide the bulk of the revenue.

Current trends

Because its growth has been fueled so heavily by government support, the French nonprofit sector is particularly vulnerable to cutbacks in that support, which now seem likely in many subsectors. So, the great challenge for the French third sector is to build a more solid base of private support to guarantee a degree of autonomy from the state. A growing competition from the business sector can be expected, and European integration reinforces this trend.

To compete more fairly with the public and the business sector, nonprofit organizations have to improve the professional training of their staff and volunteers, to meet accountability requirements, and to report more clearly on their activity.

The limited legal capacity of the associations declared under the 1901 Act – the most common legal status in the nonprofit sector – is more and more an obstacle to fundraising, investing, borrowing, buying and selling real estate; in a word, it is an obstacle to normal economic activity and so the widening of the legal capacity of the nonprofit organizations is on the agenda.

Finally, ethical issues are a major challenge for the nonprofit sector: in recent years, some nonprofit organizations have been involved in embezzlement, disguised financing of political parties or the major scandal of AIDS-contaminated blood in the nonprofit blood transfusion system. As public opinion considers that the nonprofit purpose is a guarantee of ethical behavior, these scandals ruin public confidence in the third sector.

1.8 A road map

Following this introduction, chapter 2 explores a brief history of the third sector in France and identifies long-term historical factors that shaped the present sector and its components. Chapter 3 presents a discussion of the legal position of the nonprofit sector and examines the characteristics of the major laws dealing with it, including the relevant parts of the tax law. Chapter 4 draws the contours of the nonprofit sector and presents an analysis of its size, scope and composition, with special emphasis on activities and expenditures and sources of revenue. More detail on some of the subsectors within the third sector is given in chapter 5, including culture and recreation, health and social services, education, civic, environment associations and grant-making foundations. Finally, policy issues are examined in chapter 6 which describes the overall position of government toward the nonprofit sector and identifies the key issues and legislation initiatives that confront the nonprofit sector in France today. Chapter 7 highlights the theoretical implications of this study.

Notes

1   We reproduce here the structural/operational definition of Salamon and Anheier (1993a).
2   For a longer and more precise development, see Archambault (1993) and Archambault in Salamon and Anheier series 4.
3   The formal criterion excludes undeclared associations in most cases.
4   A formal declaration signed by representatives of major nonprofit organizations and umbrella groups.
5   The same applies to chambers of crafts and chambers of agriculture.

Chapter 2

CHURCH, REVOLUTION AND REPUBLIC: A BRIEF HISTORY OF THE NONPROFIT SECTOR IN FRANCE

This chapter traces the history of the nonprofit organizations in France, but it can only be a general survey. French historians have been more interested in the origins of capitalism than in the genesis of the nonprofit sector; as far as the more recent period is concerned, few archives of nonprofit organizations have so far been explored.[1]

The objective of the following exposition is to account for the size, scope and role of the nonprofit sector today. We have identified the major trends and events that have shaped the sector and the organizations it comprises, and have also reported on the historical conflicts which may explain its diversity.

We have identified the three long-term trends which have most strongly influenced the development of the nonprofit sector throughout its millennial history:

- the systematic restrictions on the nonprofit sector imposed by a centralized and interventionist state during the 1791–1901 period;
- the early secularization of the nonprofit sector in an old Catholic country;
- the influence of ideology and of the intellectuals, and especially of utopian socialism and solidarism, on the whole social economy.

2.1 Main themes

2.1.1 Etatism, centralization and the nonprofit sector

Etatism is no doubt the most important feature in French history. As mentioned before, the millennian fight of the central state against any form of local power is at the root of French centralization: fight against feudal order, against urban citizens' organizations during the Middle Ages, fight against regional governments and religious minorities during the *ancien régime*, fight against the Church and its nonprofit organizations and against corporations during the French Revolution, and against the labor movement and political clubs during the nineteenth century. The liberal laws at the end of the nineteenth and at the beginning of the twentieth century mark a turning-point: the nonprofit sector is no longer illegal, but in the growing centralized state, new forms of social or economic concerns are becoming public concerns: economic interventionism, a revival of *colbertisme*, appeared during World War I, developed during the two world wars and after the second one. As in many European countries, a strong welfare state emerged.

Since the 1960s, the trend is more toward *laissez-faire* and private initiative. More attention is being paid to the tradition of Anglo-Saxon countries. The Decentralization Act (1982) is a way to strive toward a more European political structure; decentralization is very recent but it seems to have been a strong incentive to the nonprofit sector development. Reducing the prerogatives of the state government to the benefit of local communities has resulted in a partnership between nonprofit organizations and local authorities.

But decentralization is too recent to have become customary, and the average citizen still considers that it is up to the government to deal with any civic, social or economic problem. Therefore, self-help is not a common reflex when a new problem arises, as Tocqueville consistently remarked a century ago.

The Jacobin tradition is a long-term feature of the French government and society, and it can be observed throughout the last millennium. Louis XI and Louis XIV were Jacobins as well as Napoleon or de Gaulle: this tradition is not only one of the dominant features of the French Revolution.

2.1.2 Secular state and Catholic Church

France has always been a Catholic country: as a nation it begins with the conversion of Clovis, the leader of the Franks, to the Roman Catholic faith. As the "eldest daughter of the Church", the kingdom of France adopted Catholicism as the state religion. Parishes and congregations were at the heart of the most ancient charities: relief to poor families and children; care of sick and elderly people; schools and other education and research organizations. Unlike Germany and Italy, France did not develop a tradition of private action and subsidiarity in spite of the strong influence of the Church. Instead, we can see that very early on, and in any case during the Revolution, the central government replaced the Church in hospitals, asylums and schools.

The consequence of French etatism is a reverse subsidiarity principle: the nonprofit sector whether religious or secular deals with public concerns which are overlooked by the state. The "eldest daughter of the Church" was indeed also the first to emancipate. Since the Enlightenment period, atheism or free thinking grew more quickly than anywhere else. Nowadays France is the European country where religious observances are the lowest (13 per cent of the adult population) and stated atheism the highest (14 per cent).

Throughout the past, other religions were either tolerated or banned. The emigration of most Protestants after the Revocation of the *Édit de Nantes*, the nearly permanent persecution of the Jews and the World War II genocide have lead to the quasi-monopoly of Catholicism. The dominant religion was threatened, not by other religions, but by a growing atheism and by a widespread indifference toward religion in general. Even the very recent rise of Islam in France has challenged French society more than the Church. The competition among religions has not been an incentive to the nonprofit sector, as it has been in Anglo-Saxon countries.

However, the competition between the Catholic Church and an active atheism or anticlericalism was, as in Italy, an essential feature throughout the nineteenth century and still has an impact on the nonprofit sector. Until the turn of the twentieth century when it rallied the Republic, the Catholic Church was opposed to any form of social change and in favor of the monarchy (see 2.3.2).

Moreover, the Republicans were often freemasons, anticlerical and in favor of public, secular schools free of charge. While the Catholic Church was developing a Catholic middle-class-oriented school network, the Republicans, in order to support public education, created nonprofit organizations which federated in the still existing *Ligue de l'Enseignement*.

The "school war" has indeed been constant in France throughout the nineteenth and twentieth centuries. Though declining, it contrasts with the peaceful relationship between the Church and the state in the field of health and social welfare.

Since the disestablishment of the Church in 1905, religion has been a private concern. The principle of secularism is at the root of citizenship and of public education. Some American practices, such as the reference to God in presidential addresses, prayers in public school or the collection of taxes for the Church as in Germany, would be unthinkable in France, for most citizens support secularism. This explains why the French nonprofit sector is, except for religious schools, secular.

2.1.3 The influence of ideology on social economy: utopian socialism and solidarity

A strong socialist tradition is at the origin of the nineteenth-century nonprofit sector. In contrast with the Marxist influence on the labor movement, utopian socialism had more influence on cooperatives, mutual benefit societies and many other associations. Utopian socialism fought etatism and centralization against the mainstream, and was in favor of mutual societies, self-determination and federalism. Saint-Simon, Fourier and, in particular, Proudhon were the most outstanding intellectuals of this trend.

The utopian socialist inheritance and the social Christian tradition are the two contradictory ideological currents which can still be found nowadays in the "Second Left". Their influence on the strengthening of the nonprofit sector has been decisive during the last two decades and is conflicting, within the socialist party, with a more traditional Jacobin Left. The Second Left has been very active in promoting decentralization.

At the turn of the twentieth century, when the modern nonprofit sector and social economy appeared, the official doctrine of the Third Republic, the very basis of its secular ethics, was *solidarity*.

The principle of solidarity among the members of a nation was the rationale of income redistribution; among the members of a professional group, it was the justification of mutual benefit societies.

Obviously, there are strong ideological principles at the root of the nonprofit sector and more generally of the so-called social economy. But ideology, as we are going to show, is always biased and moderated by facts.

2.2 Historical narrative

2.2.1 Origin of the nonprofit sector and early history up to the French Revolution

The Middle Ages

The nonprofit sector in France, as in every European country, traces back to the origin of the nation itself. Linked with the Roman Catholic Church, it is older than the forprofit sector, the "market society", which progressively emerged in the late Middle Ages and at the beginning of the Renaissance (Braudel, 1979). The beginning of France as a nation dates back to the late fifth century: AD 476 marks the end of the occidental Roman empire and Clovis, the first king of France, was crowned and converted to Catholicism in 496.

The main feature of the early Middle Ages (fifth to tenth centuries) is feudalism: the central state was very weak, and the social organization was based on the feudal power for military and security affairs and on the Church for spiritual and cultural concerns. The economy was based on a demesne structure and on serfdom; some peasants were free, but most of them were serfs belonging to a lord and paying him heavy duties and in-kind taxes; in return, the lord protected them against any kind of aggression. The Church, as the owner of very large real estate, was very rich; it also raised a specific tax, the *dime*, which represented one tenth of the peasants' income; the property of the Church was considered the patrimony of the poor. It was not only a theoretical point of view: the poor in the parishes were on a nominative list, the *matricule*. They had a right to receive one third of the gifts to the parishes. At the end of this period, monastic orders also expanded, especially the Benedictine order, and they used to welcome poor and sick people in their convents (Mollat, 1978).

At the climax of the Middle Ages (eleventh to thirteenth centuries), the power of the state was reinforced and the territory of the French kingdom expanded; the central power of the king and of his government conflicted with and overcame step by step the feudal order at the end of the period; serfdom became progressively obsolete and the feudal economy regressed as the urban population and activities increased. During the eleventh century, the communal movement freed the main towns from the landlords' domination and taxation: the organizations of citizens, mainly tradesmen and craftsmen, who during the communal movement had been fighting the feudal power, can be viewed as the ancestors of civil rights organizations; the *bourgeois de Calais*, immortalized by Rodin, are the emblematic figures of those citizens' organizations.

Economic growth took place during this period and international trade developed with the Crusades and during the periodic trade fairs in the northern and eastern towns. Crafts and textile activities developed in the newly freed towns. The population expanded and around 1300 France was by far the most populated country in Europe, with about 15 to 20 million inhabitants (Fourquin, 1977).

Economic prosperity of course was not widespread and the number of poor was still very large. The parishes and the Benedictine convents no longer had the monopoly of charity (Mollat, 1978). Philanthropy was secularized with the rise of royal generosity. King Louis IX, *Saint Louis*, is the best example of this royal concern with the poorest people. Lords following the precept *"noblesse oblige"*, i.e. "Nobility implies duty", were also giving to the poor. In the same period, the newly freed citizens, the newborn *bourgeoisie* competed with the aristocracy in giving. Linked to the guilds, the *confréries de miséricorde* (charitable brotherhoods), ancestors of friendly and mutual societies, first helped the needy members of the organization and, later, any poor or sick person.

Despite this secularization of philanthropy, the role of the Church in charitable organizations remained very important: in every rural parish, the *tables du pauvres* used to provide meals; monastic orders multiplied and specialized. The new mendicant orders, Dominicans and Franciscans, wished to share the fate of the poor; hospitable orders, such as the Knights Templars, created hospitals often called *Maisons-Dieu* or *Hôtels-Dieu*,[2] which welcomed only poor people; other monastic orders created schools for poor children.

The climax of the Middle Ages is characterized by a personalization of charity: every rich person had his poor and competed for this kind of *clientèle*. Cash money supplanted in-kind alms, and philanthropy became more competitive and more institutionalized.

The late Middle Ages (fourteenth and early fifteenth centuries) was a very disturbed period. The Hundred Years War weakened the whole country politically and economically. The Black Death (1348) killed one third of the French population; famines, epidemics and robberies multiplied. The rise of extreme poverty and the decrease of resources created financial difficulties for charitable organizations. In a way, it was a "welfare-church crisis", similar to the welfare state crisis which occurred during the 1980s. The church then tried to shift the responsibility of some charities to laymen and to the emerging central state.

The development of extreme poverty, connected with vagrancy and robbery, frightened the rural as well as the urban population. Everywhere philanthropy became more selective and a distinction was established between bad and good poor people: giving alms was still a duty, but it had to be given to authentic poor who were supposed to make good use of the gift. Priests recommended priorities: the just man rather than the sinner, the relative rather than the stranger (Mollat, 1978).

These two movements, the disengagement of the church and the rise of public safety, explain how the state started to intervene in charities: hospitals concentrated under various kinds of public regulation and became more health- and less shelter-oriented; specialized establishments for victims of the plague, orphans and foundlings multiplied and were run by specialized monastic orders under the supervision of public authorities.

In the late Middle Ages a tendency to control the poor and to confine vagrants and the fringe in workhouses began to appear (Foucault, 1978; Braudel, 1979). This tendency was reinforced during the following centuries and lasted in France until very recently.

Renaissance and classical period (sixteenth to seventeenth centuries)

The Renaissance is a period of demographic and economic growth in France as well as in other European countries, with an opening to the rest of the world. The feudal order was definitely dismissed, the central government reinforced, royal authorities became more organized and established a modern state. The *gold rush*, a consequence of rising international trade, caused inflation, which increased social inequalities: the rich became richer and the poor poorer (Braudel, 1979). The Reformation provoked a thirty-year-long civil war between the Catholics and the Protestants (1562–93). A truce followed the *Édit de Nantes*: the civil rights of the Protestants, including the right to religious observance, were temporarily protected.

During the Renaissance, the medieval guilds (*corporations*) and the brotherhoods (*confréries*) became very powerful and hierarchical: a guild consisted of a master helped by journeymen and apprentices; the fees to enter a *corporation* were relatively high. The guild regulated the quality of the product, with internal control by a corporate police force. Apart from this internal hierarchy, there was also a hierarchy between the guilds themselves; some guilds were oversubscribed and some despised. During the sixteenth century, there were some journeymen's riots against the masters and strikes provoked by the decline of the purchasing power in a period of inflation. The royal authorities intervened in those independent nonprofit organizations to reorganize them, as they had done for charitable organizations. The attitude of the Church towards the *corporations* is also important: it put pressure on them to prescribe moral order in urban areas.

The guilds, which are the ancestors of trade unions and professional organizations, are important institutions in preindustrial civil society and in urban economic activity. As we will show, their importance declined during the seventeenth and eighteenth centuries.

The Renaissance was also a period of secularization of charities. King François I created a "great agency for the poor". This is the first example of public and secular assistance: government trespassed on the Church's domain. In the same period, the royal chaplains were commissioned to control every hospital in the kingdom (Imbert, 1981).

As social differences increased, the fear of the poor grew during the sixteenth and seventeenth centuries, and repressive establishments for vagrants, delinquents and suspect people multiplied, such as the hospitals *La Pitié* in Paris or *La Charité* in Lyon. Foucault (1975) shows that all charitable institutions of the time – general hospitals, insane asylums, schools, workhouses, orphanages – were built on the pattern of jails: supervision and confinement were linked.

The seventeenth century or classical period is the climax of the political, cultural and economic influence of France in Europe. The great Versailles palace is the symbol of the dominant nation supremacy. The central government was based on the principle of "absolute monarchy from divine right" (*monarchie absolue de droit divin*) and local authorities regressed. The bourgeoisie rose with the economic prosperity, linked to the development of road networks and other means of transportation. *Colbertisme* is the French mercantilist doctrine, the beginning of economic dirigism. Colbert was Louis XIV's Minister of Finances; he can be considered as one of the first etatist civil servants who were to become so important in French history. The end of Louis XIV's reign was less glorious; it is a period of financial and social difficulties: many very expensive wars, the building of Versailles and the supporting of a large royal court living grandly, provoked very unpopular rises in taxation. Peasants were impoverished; famines and epidemics reappeared. In the same period, vagrancy and mendicity became punishable.

Two philanthropists are emblematic of this classical period. The first one is Théophraste Renaudot, very well known as the founder of the first newspaper in France. Being also the king's doctor, he was commissioned to control poverty throughout the kingdom. Besides his other private or public activities, he set up, with other physicians, free consulting rooms, free surgery and other home health services for the poor. Those nonprofit organizations contrasted with the hospitals by giving a better quality of medical care and medical innovations. Those charitable consulting rooms conflicted with physicians' guilds and with the faculty of medicine. When Renaudot died (1653) the charitable consulting rooms disappeared. However, they are the matrix of many contemporary nonprofit health organizations (Ferrand-Nagel, 1990).

Another emblematic figure is Saint Vincent de Paul. He created

establishments which still exist nowadays and founded a monastic order, the *Filles de la Charité*, to take care of Parisian foundlings.
The abandonment of children increased very fast during the classical period as a consequence of extreme poverty and of illegiti-
macy. Contrasting with other similar establishments, the
orphanages created by Saint Vincent de Paul did not differentiate
between legitimate and illegitimate children; they were very well
organized, prevented epidemics and provided the children with
education and vocational training. Vincent de Paul collected private and royal funds. When he died in 1660, financial difficulties
appeared. Ten years later the "hospital for foundlings" was state-
approved (*reconnu d'utilité publique*). The royal government made
public subsidies to compensate for the loss of charitable contributions, and thereby controlled the nonprofit institution. This shift
from the private to a quasi-public sphere is very representative of
the evolution of the nonprofit sector in France (Fenet, 1988).

The classical period is also a period of reinforcement of the
Catholic Church, with the Counter-Reformation. Its influence was
very strong in France, especially with the Jesuit order. The Jesuits
victoriously fought Jansenism, which was a kind of French
Catholic puritanism; they also created a large network of schools
for the children of the bourgeoisie and of the aristocracy. These
schools are a still existing part of the nonprofit sector. The reinforcement of a more traditional Catholicism explains the revival of
antisemitism and the departure of French Protestants: in 1685
Louis XIV revoked the *Édit de Nantes* and more than 300,000
Protestants emigrated to England, Germany and America; very
few Protestants stayed in France. The revocation of the *Édit de
Nantes* is certainly at the basis of the French religious homogeneity.

The Enlightenment period (1715–89)

The *siècle des Lumières* marks the end of the *ancien régime* in France.
It was a period of social instability and of cultural effervescence.
The royal power weakened and the principle of absolute monarchy was more and more contested by philosophers like Montesquieu, Voltaire, Diderot and Rousseau. They were influenced
by the English political system and philosophy. They recommended a more democratic government and a more tolerant and
less repressive society, while local governments were reinforcing

and fighting central government. This political weakening contrasted with a relative economic prosperity, based on a progressing agriculture, a rising international trade and a demographic growth despite the beginning of birth control. France was more and more challenged by England for the political leadership and the economic domination of the world. The rivalry between the two nations increased at the end of the period with the French intervention in the American War of Independence.

In the Enlightenment period, civil society was very active and there are early examples of nearly every kind of nonprofit organizations. Besides the inherited health and social institutions, there were flourishing social clubs,[3] learned societies, music or literature circles. Political and philosophical associations, which are the ancestors of civil rights and advocacy organizations, began during the eighteenth century: they fought against slavery, antisemitism, and for religious tolerance and "habeas corpus" in a pre-revolutionary spirit. These organizations were a place for philosophical reflection about individuals, the rights and duties of the state and of the society. They were summarized by the concept of the "social contract" introduced by Rousseau. Public assistance was seen as a part of the social contract: "The state has to grant every citizen a livelihood, food, convenient clothes and a healthy way of life" (Montesquieu, 1748).

This statement of an overall responsibility of the state is very typical of the French way of thinking. It contrasts with the emphasis placed on individual responsibility in Anglo-Saxon countries and also with the flourishing of civil society in that period.

However, one part of civil society was declining and questioning: the corporative system. The guilds grew increasingly closed and resistant to economic and social change, and the first manufacturing innovations took place outside the corporative system. Strict regulations and entry barriers, sometimes monopolies, were checking free competition. Voltaire and the physiocrats denounced guilds as unfair and inefficient, and in 1776 Turgot unsuccessfully tried to suppress them. This was eventually accomplished by the French Revolution.

2.2.2 The French Revolution and the Empire (1789–1815)

Ancien régime *and* Nouveau régime
This period is the great break in French history. Because of its will
to make a clean sweep of the *ancien régime*'s political system and
social order (*"faire du passé table rase"*), the French Revolution is a
turning-point for every specific sector and especially for the nonprofit sector. However, some authors – the most important of them
is Tocqueville (1856) – pointed out that the beginnings of the
French Revolution were to be found in the long-term evolution of
the *ancien régime*; had the revolutionary break not taken place, a
similar evolution would have occurred over a period of a century
instead of a decade.

It is impossible to sum up such an important and restless period
in a few lines. Schematically there are three subperiods:

- 1789–91: liquidation of the *ancien régime* and conquest of civil
  rights;
- 1792–95: climax of instability; civil war and wars against a large
  part of Europe, *Terreur* and final collapse of the Jacobins;
- 1795–1815: during the last decade, rebuilding period of new
  social and political order becoming more and more dictatorial,
  in a context of permanent war. It is also the very beginning of
  industrialization in France.

Beyond the historical events, this period is the matrix of quite a
few durable institutions such as a modern constitution, the Declaration of the Rights of Man (an echo of the American War of Independence), modern taxation, the development of free enterprise,
the definitive secularization of many charitable institutions. It was
also a period of intense intellectual activity; a lot of principles with
short-lived or non-existent practices were put aside, to be applied
decades later. For example, the republican order based on a representative political system, the principles of compulsory, public,
free and secular education and of the responsibility of the government in citizens' welfare.

Décret d'Allarde *and* Loi Le Chapelier
In the nonprofit sector, the French Revolution provoked an important recession and in some cases a collapse. Nonprofit organizations were viewed as intermediary bodies between the individual

and the state; this created a fracture in the unity of the nation. Though privileges had been abolished since the *Nuit du 4 Août* (1789), some of these organizations created privileges for their members. Most of them were appendages of the Roman Catholic Church; since the French Revolution was anticlerical, the will to reduce the Church's and congregations' properties and influence was very strong.

In that context, the most important Acts were the *Décret d'Allarde* (March 1791), suppressing the guilds, and the *Loi Le Chapelier* (June 1791) which forbade any voluntary association except political clubs, with this important rationale: "No one shall be allowed to arouse in any citizen any kind of intermediate interest and to separate him from the public weal through the medium of corporate interests." As a consequence, in the 1789 Declaration of the Rights of Man, the civil right of association is missing.

As mentioned above, guilds had become more and more closed shops and were a brake to free enterprise and fair competition. Therefore the rising bourgeoisie, the main beneficiary of the French Revolution, fought against them as against a form of feudal and medieval survival. In modern words, we could say that the *Loi Le Chapelier*, following the British example, was a deregulation Act. Its aim was to allow modern industrialization and to prevent labor unionism. But it also meant the disappearance of a structure of sociability and training, and of the only organization of mutual assistance outside the family.

The struggle against the Church and the congregations also had important consequences for the nonprofit sector: congregations were expelled and the clergy had to acknowledge the Republic; the property of the clergy and of the congregations was seized and sold to wealthy middle-class people, providing resources to the government. Many schools or charitable institutions had to be closed. The most important ones, namely hospitals, were nationalized and run by the local government. In the same period, the function of hospitals was redefined: they ceased to be shelters for the poor and became mostly health care centers; they also became high level medical schools.

In 1795, a bill organizing public elementary education was voted, but not applied, because of lack of financing. So semi-clandestine Catholic schools continued to exist, especially in the western part of France. Religious associations with sacramental purpose were run by priests who did not acknowledge the Republic. Some congregations became clandestine as well (Vovelle, 1988).

On the contrary, political clubs, the pillars of the revolutionary movement, were encouraged (Furet and Ozouf, 1988). The most important one is obviously the Jacobin club, which was the most radical one. Its members were in favour of the most extreme centralization of the administration. "Jacobin" as an adjective means centralized. Other famous political clubs were the *Feuillants*, the *Cordeliers*, and the *1789 Society*. After 1795, and the decline of the Jacobin clan, clubs became suspect and were hit like other associations by the prohibition of coalitions.

In 1810, Napoleon on one hand softened the *Le Chapelier* Act and on the other hand made the Penal Code a more repressive legislation. "Any association of over twenty persons, whatever their purpose, cannot be created without the government's agreement and must respect the conditions imposed by public authorities." This legislation lasted throughout the nineteenth century, until the 1901 Act. Leaders of unauthorized associations continued to be punishable and were sued by the reinforced repressive system of the Empire.

This period is truly a break in the development of the nonprofit sector. A drastic redistribution of respective responsibility in the private and public spheres, as far as social issues are concerned, took place. The most impressive work in this field was done by the *Comité de Mendicité*, who considered it necessary to eradicate mendicity, which had been punishable since the seventeenth century. Some very important principles were set out by this committee: "The extreme poverty is the fault of the government", therefore "public assistance to the poor is a sacred duty. Society owes poor citizens a support and must either give them work or, if they are unable to work, secure them a livelihood" (Barthe, 1991; Ewald, 1986).

Similarly, in the British laws concerning poor citizens, there is a distinction between the poor who are able to work and those who are not. The responsibility of the government is clearly stated and the eradication of extreme poverty is on the agenda. But no real social policy followed this principle and, at the end of the period, private philanthropy was again called for.

The recession of the nonprofit sector during the periods of the French Revolution and the Empire was prolonged throughout the nineteenth century in a long-term and severe conflict between an omnipotent centralized state and a continuous and diversified trend towards creating associations, despite the fact that they were prohibited. It is the historical root of the backwardness in the French nonprofit sector compared to the American or the British ones.

2.2.3 Industrialization and the world wars

Industrialization spread in France over a longer period than anywhere else in Europe or in North America, and whether or not the concept of "industrial revolution" can be applied to France is to be questioned (Marczewski, 1961; Clapham, 1961).

As mentioned above, France was the first country to practice birth control, in spite of the influence of the Roman Catholic Church. The consequences of this early eighteenth-century behavior is the slower growth of population during the nineteenth century compared with other European countries (Table 2.1).

Table 2.1

Population in France, Great Britain, Germany, Russia and the United States (millions)

	1800	1850	1900	1930	1950
France	27.3	35.8	39.0	41.8	41.9
Great Britain	15.0	22.6	38.7	46.0	50.6
Germany	24.6	35.9	56.4	64.3	69.0
Russia (USSR)	37.0	60.2	111.0	156.0	193.0
United States	5.3	23.2	76.0	122.9	151.7

Source: W. S. Woytinsky and E. S. Woytinsky, *World Population and Production*, New York, Twentieth Century Fund, 1953, p. 44.

Slow industrialization and slow demographic growth explain why rural depopulation appeared very late in France and took place mainly during the twentieth century: 75 per cent of the population lived in rural areas in 1800 and 65 per cent still did so in 1880 (Marczewski, 1961).

This demographic and economic background is important to

explain the evolution of the nonprofit sector during this period of a century and a half. The political context and the relationship with public authorities were also very important. Before the installation of a stable republican government in 1873, France varied between constitutional monarchy (1815–48), bonapartism (the Second Empire, 1852–70) and short insurrectional or republican periods: the 1830 *Trois Glorieuses*, the Second Republic (1848–52) and the *Commune* in 1871. In this political context, every government interpreted in their own way the prohibition on coalitions; they repressed the opponents while authorizing and promoting the nonprofit organizations which were on their side.

The social question and mutual societies

Though less rapid than elsewhere, industrialization and urbanization led to a significant pauperization of the growing working class: hygienists described the bad work and sanitary conditions in factories as well as in housing. In the absence of labor regulations, sickness, work accidents and unemployment led to extreme poverty. Despite the prohibition of coalitions, mutual societies, most of which were linked to a clandestine labor movement, survived in surreptitious networks. They provided money to the unemployed and to the strikers on a mutual aid basis. The survival of these clandestine associations and the fact that some political associations in favor of the Republic bypassed the legislation by creating a lot of associations of less than twenty persons, provoked a hardening of this legislation. The 1834 Act reinforced the 1810 Act and increased the repression of unauthorized associations: like the leaders, the members of such associations became punishable. This new legislation encountered violent opposition; this was the origin of the 1848 Revolution (and provoked the creation of the secret *Sociétés de résistance*).

During the Second Empire period of economic prosperity, the working class grew and began somehow to benefit from economic growth. Though still clandestine, the workers' movement became more and more important.

The authorized nonprofit sector

During the constitutional monarchy period, the Church and the congregations brought their nonprofit organizations back into the open and favored the creation of primary and secondary schools.

This reconstruction was made possible by public compensation for the previous despoiling of property during the French Revolution. Authorized associations such as the mighty *Société philanthropique* inspired by freemasonry flourished; they were run by "persons of distinction", the notables, who created quite a few charitable institutions, such as health centers or meal delivery services (*soupes populaires*). They also controlled some "good" mutual aid societies, that is, those which were not linked to the labor movement.

During this period, there were ideological conflicts about how to solve the *question Sociale*. Non-interventionist authors, such as the economist J. B. Say, thought that "society doesn't have to support its members" and "to give the poor a right to alms is to destroy the ownership right and to favor communism; inequality does not mean injustice" (Say, quoted by Ewald, 1986, pp. 57–9). According to these authors, individuals have to provide for themselves by instituting reserve funds, in order to avoid poverty as well as other risks. The philanthropic society agreed with these principles. Moreover the utopian socialists, Saint Simon, Fourier, Proudhon, Buchez, Blanc and Blanqui, proposed alternative social systems based on mutual help, cooperation and voluntary association.

The utopian socialists' influence

Utopian socialism appeared before Marxism; in France it still has a deep influence on social economy organizations, cooperatives, mutual societies and a great many associations.

The instigators of the French utopian socialists – Saint Simon (1760–1825), Fourier (1772–1837), Proudhon (1809–65) – were influenced by English authors like Owen, or by experiences such as the Rochdale cooperative (Gueslin, 1987; Sawadogo, 1989).

Saint Simon was in favor of an industrial society with a technocratic management to replace control by the owners. The ideal society should be based on associations of free workers, of independent producers, without any hierarchy except for one based on skills. The aim of production is to improve the way of life of the poorest. Business associations will progressively replace the government in all political and social issues except in the field of public safety and defence.

Fourier's utopia is the *phalanstère*, a project very close to the

Israeli kibbutz: 400 families living in the same building in autarky, producing what is necessary and consuming what is being produced. Poverty and wage-earning were abolished. Every decision in the *phalanstère* was taken in general meetings, without representation or delegation (it is the origin of the principle of "one man equals one vote", a very important one in the French social economy organizations).

Proudhon is the theoretician of mutualism and of federalism. Mutualism stands between individualism and communism and restricts the rights to private property ("private property is theft"). Mutual exchange, on the basis of work, substitutes for money exchange: mutual insurance societies, mutual credit banks, shared housing, friendly societies guarantee against the disadvantages of free competition in the economic sphere.

Federalism is a political structure which is consistent with mutualism, as a pluralistic structure. Based on a social contract which balances authority and freedom, Proudhon's federalism advocates the subsidiarity principle and recommends free education, independent from both the state and the Church. Mutualism, self-determination and federalism – the inheritance of Proudhon – remain the main features of the nonprofit sector in France.

The utopian socialists had a more direct influence on this sector during the short-lived Second Republic which voted symbolic and ephemeral civil rights: "universal" suffrage (for men only), freedom to associate, suppression of censorship for the press and of the death penalty, creation of huge workhouses for unemployed people. All these civil rights and institutions lasted less than one year and died out with Napoleon III's coup.

The aborted 1848 Revolution, however, left a deep impression and foreshadowed the evolution of the late nineteenth and early twentieth centuries. More than 1,000 associations and over 400 mutual aid societies were created during the year 1848 alone (Agulhon, 1973).

Their influence was even greater on the very brief Parisian insurrection of the Commune (March-May 1871). At the end of the war against Prussia, Parisian workers and craftsmen revolted against a conservative government and organized an independent local government under the workers' control.[4] The legal government repressed the insurrection in blood and beheaded the socialist movement. This short episode was also an opportunity to reinforce the central government against the local ones. As a punishment, Paris had no mayor until 1977, when Jacques Chirac was elected. Under the influence of Proudhon and Fourier, the communards were in favor of association and cooperation and wanted the fall of the central state; as these ideas were associated with the Commune, they were brought into disrepute.

Charte de la Mutualité *(1898) and solidarity*
The nonprofit sector ceased to be illegal in the late nineteenth century: the punishment for the crime of coalition, which included striking, was abolished in 1864, and associations revived. The Third Republic granted many still-existing civil rights, and after ten years of parliamentary discussion, labor unions were legalized in 1884 – which is very late compared with what happened in other European countries. This historical fact may explain the weakness of French trade unionism: nowadays, the unions are far weaker in France than in any other EC country.

During this period, mutual benefit societies dissociated themselves from labor unionism. They became more middle-class-oriented and some political leaders used the mutual movement against the labor movement. The 1898 *Charte de la Mutualité* consecrated this evolution and legalized the mutual benefit societies. Three kinds of mutual benefit societies were created: free, approved and state-approved (*reconnues d'utilité publique*) mutual societies. They were allowed to work in any area of social protection – sickness insurance, industrial injuries, premature death, retirement compensation – but they had to specialize in risks like any other insurance company; their regulations were lighter or heavier according to their legal status. In fact, collecting the savings of the middle class was not sufficient for mutual benefit societies to grant other allowances than sickness income maintenance and they failed when they tried to build a retirement pension scheme (Gibaud, 1986; Gueslin, 1987).

The same year (1898) marks the very beginning of the public social policy in France, with the vote of a law on industrial injuries and accidents. Before this law, the injured worker had to prove the employer was at fault to receive compensation. According to the new law, the employer had to pay in any case: the professional risk had become a social risk (Ewald, 1986). Moreover, progressive income taxation was introduced, and mutual help societies were legalized in 1898.

This concept of solidarity arose under the influence of Pasteur's discoveries: epidemiology showed that curing somebody from a contagious disease, such as tuberculosis, benefits not only that person but also his or her neighbors and relatives. Solidarity was the official doctrine of the Third Republic, inspired by freemasonry. Under the inspiration of the sociologist Durkheim and the philosopher Bourgeois, solidarity is opposed to individualism and is summed up by the slogan: "Everyone is indebted to his neighbor." A newborn child has duties to preexisting society since he or she has inherited a language, knowledge, skills and tools from that society. Rights counterbalance duties. The rich especially are indebted to the poor: charity, which is a choice, has to be replaced by solidarity, which is a social duty (Zeldin, 1973; Gueslin, 1987; Barthe, 1991). As Durkheim advocated, solidarity and mutualism are a rehabilitation of intermediate bodies, of professional organizations. Solidarity is still a basic principle of social economy and means a feeling of belonging, income redistribution between members and joint responsibility.

Anticlerical revival and the Dreyfus affair

This period of the definitive instalment of the republic in France is also one of anticlerical revival, linked to three conflicts.

First there was the ideological conflict, at the time of the Third Republic, which was between the Catholic hierarchy who were in favor of the monarchy, against the wish of the liberal Pope Leon XIII that they rally the republican state, and the people in power influenced by the freemasonry.

Second, the Dreyfus affair divided France into two clans. Dreyfus was a Jewish captain unjustly accused of being a spy. He was sentenced to banishment after a resoundingly antisemitic trial, although years later he was rehabilitated. During the last years of the nineteenth century, most Catholics and the army were *antidreyfusards* and most republicans, Protestants and Jews, were *dreyfusards*: they denounced the collusion between the army and the Church.

The control of education was the third source of conflict. To establish a republican spirit, the Secretary of Education, Jules Ferry, set up the compulsory, free of charge, lay school, conceived but not carried out by the French Revolution. A network of public primary schools spread throughout France. Republican teachers were fighting against both the regional languages and the clerical influence. For the first time, public secondary schools educated girls and, separately, the male elite. The Jesuits, who were in charge of most private schools, were the first ones to be prohibited to teach, and later on, this measure was extended to all congregations. As far as higher education was concerned, the newly founded public universities had a still-existing monopoly on granting degrees. The Church, of course, resisted this reduction of its educational influence.

The 1901 law

These conflicts between the state and the Church became exacerbated at the beginning of the twentieth century. It is the historical background of the 1901 Act on associations which was also against congregations. What was the situation of associations before the 1901 legislation? Three characteristics can be pointed out:

- an administrative authorization was still a prerequisite for founding an association of more than twenty members, although exceptions were sometimes made.
- the necessary "state approval" (*reconnaissance d'utilité publique*), to make the association a legal entity, was sparingly granted.
- a lot of specific statutes existed: labor unions, foreign associations, political clubs, institutions of higher education, social clubs (*cercles*).

The 1901 Act is the legal consecration of what was already in existence. It defines an association as a "convention according to which two or more individuals permanently share a common knowledge or activity with another aim in mind than sharing profit". When it has been created, an association must be declared at the *préfecture*. Undeclared associations have no legal rights. Declared associations have only limited legal rights: they are not allowed to own real estate or to receive legacies. This limited legal capacity was ordered to prevent the Church from passing off parishes or congregations as associations. "State-approved" associations have full legal capacity and can own real estate and receive legacies. They have to be acknowledged by the *Conseil d'Etat* after a rather long and restrictive procedure.

The freedom to associate, that is free entrance and free exit to and from an association, contrasts with the life-long vows of congregation members, considered as an alienation of individual freedom; it is the reason why congregations were excluded from the benefit of the 1901 Act common law. Congregations had to be authorized by the government, as in the previous legislation. The very anticlerical government of Combes[5] ruined and expelled the congregations, suppressed 2,500 unauthorized Catholic schools which had been created before 1901, and refused authorization to open 11,000 schools or hospitals run by congregations.

The war between the state and the Church ended in 1905 with the still-existing legislation of the disestablishment of the Church: henceforth the Catholic religion was no longer the state religion in France as it had been during the past millennium of monarchic government. The Church and the state were legally separated in France and religion became a private concern. In 1905, specific legislation ruling congregations was ordered and most congregations came back to France.

The advent of "social economy": Le Play and Gide

The end of the 19th century is also a period of experimental employers' philanthropy. Some employers,[6] mainly in the textile industry, built housing for their workers and promoted some kind of retirement funds and family allowances. This philanthropic movement was influenced by the social Catholicism stemming from the *Rerum Novarum* encyclical. For the employers, it was also a way to stabilize and control the workers, since social benefits were lost when the worker went to work in another factory. Le Play was the theoretician of this employers' philanthropic movement and in 1856 he founded the *société d'économie sociale*. With Charles Gide he promoted social economy during the Universal Exhibitions of 1889 and 1900 in Paris. The Catholic feminist movement is close to this movement and is the origin of social workers: at the beginning of the twentieth century, some single middle-class women settled in deprived areas and created "social houses" to provide social and legal services to the poor. They also fought for women's liberation in society and the Church. The establishment despised them. They were very active during World War I as nurses; a lot of women were enrolled (Guerrand and Rupp, 1969).

World War I was a turning-point for the nonprofit sector, with the growing importance of the Red Cross and other emergency and relief organizations. It was also a melting-pot for the various social classes in trench warfare and blood. Growing taxation was accepted to finance the war, but the tax burden was not alleviated after the armistice. It was to provide assistance for war victims, such as war damages or veteran allowances. The recovery of Alsace and Lorraine, lost in 1870 and since ruled by German law, created a new problem: those regions benefited from the German social insurance set up by Bismarck (sickness and industrial injuries insurance; retirement and disability pensions). In 1918, France had no social insurance, except for industrial injuries, and had to choose between specific rules for the two newly recovered regions or the generalization of social insurance. Of course, the centralized government chose the second.

The beginning of a public social insurance scheme
The interwar period was thus the beginning of state social insurance in France, after the German pattern: compulsory sickness insurance, disability and old age insurance for low-income salaried employees. However, the French established family allowances, at the philanthropic employers' suggestion. These were also prompted by a birth-raising policy since the birth-rate in France had been steadily dropping. During the interwar period, it fell below the death rate. During economic growth in the 1920s, there was a manpower shortage due to the death of a lot of young men during the war and to low birth-rate; a flow of immigrants arrived from Italy, Spain, Belgium and Poland: there were 1,400,000 foreigners in France in 1919 and 3,000,000 in 1930, many of whom became French citizens. The French population became more diversified and the immigrants started creating foreign associations to keep up their specific character and culture.

New poverty, the Great Depression and **Front Populaire**
World War I was also a period of dirigism and the beginning of inflation in France while prices had been steady throughout the nineteenth century. Between 1914 and 1920, prices had multiplied by five and the elderly holding government bonds were ruined. This new poverty was a concern for charitable organizations since public income-support programs didn't exist. Other forms of new poverty appeared during the Great Depression.

The Great Depression was less severe than in other industrial countries and it was also belated. The peak of the unemployment rate reached 20 to 22 per cent in 1933 in Great Britain and in the United States. In France it was around 5 per cent in 1936. But the unemployment rate was less significant in France because of the importance of agriculture. Farmers were the main victims of the Great Depression in France as agricultural prices slumped. Social and political tensions were growing; strikes were very long and widespread. Extreme-Right leagues and, on the opposite side, antifascist organizations came up. The 1936 socialist government of *Front Populaire* was the result of these political and social tensions. It raised the wages after the 1936 *Accords Matignon* (general collective bargaining) and regulated the first paid holidays (*congés payés*).

For the first time, the working class enjoyed a vacation. Léo Lagrange, a minister in the *Front Populaire* government, was the instigator of a complex network of holiday camps and villages for the working-class families. He also created youth hostels (*auberges de jeunesse*), and holiday centers for children. This was the origin of "social tourism" in France which is an important part of the nonprofit sector.

Nazi occupation and Resistance
World War II was a period of restriction of the freedom to associate: from 1939, foreigners' associations had to be authorized. This legislation was repealed very late, in 1981, when Mitterrand became President. After the *drôle de guerre* (phony war: September 1939–May 1940), the defeat and the occupation of the German army in May 1940, the authoritarian and pro-Nazi Vichy government of Maréchal Pétain (1940–44) questioned the 1901 Act: every association could be dissolved by an administrative act (1941). The freemasons and many political organizations were dissolved. On the other hand, the Vichy government created a pro-governmental associative network, especially youth organizations. Many forbidden associations were clandestinely reorganized. This clandestine network was a basis for the Resistance movement directed by de Gaulle. At the end of World War II, the 1901 Act was reenacted and all restrictions, with the exception of foreigners' associations, were abolished. The Act would never be seriously questioned again.

Generally speaking, World War II was a very regressive and mortifying period for France. Despite relatively few human losses during the "phony war", civilian casualties were numerous through air bombing and the Jewish genocide approved by the Vichy government. The economy was exhausted by the Germans in kind and money levies. Inflation occurred in spurts during the war and in the postwar periods. Once more, the French population was divided in two: the *pétainistes* and the *gaullistes*, and this division still lingers nowadays. Of course, the *pétainistes'* numbers were larger in 1940 and so were the *gaullistes'* in 1944!

2.2.4 Recent developments (1945–90)

The recent history is characterized by four features: demographic recovery, constant economic growth (lower after 1973), stable republican government participating in the development of European integration and a growing welfare state, unquestioned despite the current financial difficulties.

The demographic recovery was due to a baby boom, longer than in any other European country. Though declining, the birthrate is still higher nowadays than in most European countries. Manpower shortage during the postwar period promoted new immigration flows: Spanish, Portuguese and more and more Maghrebines (Algerians, Tunisians and Moroccans). Immigration flows officially stopped in 1974–75, but clandestine immigration still exists.

A high sustained growth, 5 per cent a year, occurred between 1945 and 1973. This period is characterized by the complete modernization of agriculture with a significant degree of rural depopulation, and the growing participation of French manufacturing industries in international competition, especially after the 1960 Treaty of Rome which created the European common market. This exceptional economic growth gave rise to a higher standard of living for the whole population; economic inequalities are decreasing in the long run. The oil crisis reduced economic growth and unemployment rose dramatically. Unemployment hardly existed before 1965.

In the recent period, the republican government changed from the Fourth Republic (1945–58), dominated by parliamentary power and many political parties, into the Fifth Republic (since

1958) introduced by General de Gaulle, its first President. The presidential power increased and the tendency was toward bipartisanism; it was a steadier political regime than the previous one, and it stood closer to other European countries.

The emergence of a welfare state is the most recent development.

Comprehensive social security

Social security is run by representatives of employers and employees and regulated by the state. Initially intended for the salaried population, the social security scheme previewed an extension to the whole population, which occurred about 1970. A compulsory unemployment insurance scheme run by specific associations, the ASSEDIC (*associations pour l'emploi dans l'industrie et le commerce*), grouped together in the national organization UNEDIC (*Union nationale pour l'emploi dans l'industrie et le commerce*) was created later. From the very beginning, the benefits from social security were an important part of household income: 15 per cent in 1949 and this increased to 34 per cent in 1990. The welfare state is an important reality in France. Regular polls show that French people are attached to the principle of social security.

The creation of the social security scheme called into question the role of the mutual societies, which had been very active in social insurance management since 1930. According to the legislation, they would have to adapt in the direction of mutual aid and management of the social actions of the newly created work councils. It was a wrong estimate and mutual societies are still very active in social protection, for two reasons (Archambault, 1986; Caire, 1984). First, social security sickness insurance reimbursed health expenses of households but the patient's contribution amounted to 20 per cent or 30 per cent. This contribution is covered by mutual societies for their members. Similarly, mutual societies expanded to full-income guarantee in case of sickness, accident or death. Second, the extension of social security to the whole population was slower than planned, which explains why some special social security systems are completely run by mutual societies: it is the case for civil servants, students, self-employed people and above all farmers. The case of the farmers is interesting because it is a specific case of delegation of a public service mission to the nonprofit sector: the Agricultural Mutual Society is a completely autonomous social security, mainly financed by fiscal income. The Agricultural Mutual Society is linked to many associations which are active in rural areas, and subsidizes this associative network.

Mutual societies were not only a complement to social security. They were and still are very active in the field of medical and social prevention: drug and alcoholism prevention, modern birth control, regular medical check-ups, poliomyelitis or tuberculosis prevention, or now AIDS prevention, are fields where mutual societies and associations were first; social security followed. In the postwar period, mutual societies also began to run health and social establishments, mainly for the handicapped and the elderly.

The relationship between social security and the nonprofit sector is complementary rather than competing (see chapter 4).

De Gaulle and etatism

After the victory of the Allies, a provisional government led by de Gaulle reestablished the republican legality, with the idea of sweeping out the old French society and all previous leaders. A Constituent Assembly was elected and a new constitution was voted in 1946. A lot of civil servants were dismissed and the new ones were linked by experience in the Resistance networks. As far as the following generations are concerned, they followed the pattern of the new *Ecole Nationale d'Administration*. These high level civil servants were at the birth of French modernization since many of them became public enterprise managers; many companies were nationalized to reorganize the French economy and sometimes to punish collaborationist and petainist businessmen. French etatism was reinforced in the economic as well as in the political fields. One of the most brilliant of these civil servants was François Bloch-Lainé, the director of the *Caisse des Dépôts et des Consignations*, the main state investment bank. In the 1960s, Bloch-Lainé advocated a vigorous civil society by strengthening the nonprofit sector. Later, he founded the FONDA (*Fondation pour la vie associative*) and was the president of the main umbrella organization of the nonprofit sector, the UNIOPSS (Ullman, 1993).

Work councils and labor unions

The postwar period was the peak of the Communist Party in France; it was also the climax of labor unions, and especially of the main union, the CGT (*Confédération Générale du Travail*), linked to the Communist Party. The modern legislation on employment and work dates back to this period. The work councils (*comités d'entreprise*) were created in 1946: these councils, run by representatives of the labor unions elected by employees on labor union lists, are compulsory when a company has more than fifty employees. They are financed by a 1 per cent wage deduction from the employees. Works councils manage canteens, day care and holiday centers for the workers' children, and social services for the families. Lately they have become very active in the democratization of culture and of the arts. Because of their compulsory character, they are borderline organizations of the non-profit sector.

Catholic revival and decolonization

The postwar period has also been a period of Catholic revival in France, specially concerned with youth, the working class and the peasantry. Many Catholic youth associations, such as *Jeunesse Agricole Chrétienne* (JAC) and *Jeunesse Etudiante Chrétienne* (JEC), were created in the interwar period and were very active in the post-war period. The influence of JAC on the modernization of agriculture was decisive and many leaders of those youth organizations became politicians, labor union or business association leaders. Some priests became workers; those priest-workers, condemned by the Pope, had a great deal of influence on the Catholic youth organizations, especially on the JOC (*Jeunesse Ouvrière Chrétienne*). A concern with the Third World and decolonization is characteristic of most young people involved in this Catholic revival.

In the 1950s, the French colonial empire collapsed. The first Independence War broke out in Indochina. Run by a professional army, it had a moderate impact on the French population, but the defeat of Dien Bien Phu (1954) shocked public opinion. The same year, the Independence War broke out in Algeria; it lasted for eight years. There were 1,500,000 French people then living in Algeria and the whole contingent fought against the Algerian nationalists. This decolonization war had a great impact on the French population, just as the Vietnam War did on the Americans. A lot of organizations, some for the war, others against it, flourished. The economic and political consequences of this war caused the end of the Fourth Republic and are at the root of de Gaulle's come-back.

When he came back to power, de Gaulle changed the constitution in order to establish a more steady political regime. The new and still existing constitution was voted by a large majority and de Gaulle was the first President to be elected. He ended the Algerian War with difficulty and peacefully decolonized the African empire.

Consumer society, 1968 and the aftermath

In the 1960s, when the colonial wars ended, economic prosperity grew and inflation slowed down. Step by step, the working class caught up with the consumption pattern of the middle class.

With the rejuvenation of the population, its enrichment and higher level of education, the end of colonization, the growing participation of women in active life and the change in family patterns, new concerns appeared in society and gave rise to a new kind of association which multiplied in the mid-1960s: environment defence and protection; feminism, notably focused on the fight against birth control restrictions and abortion prohibition; support for international development and Third World countries. This last concern replaced the advocacy of decolonization.

The climax of these new concerns was of course the very brief but extremely important May 1968 movement. In the smoky atmosphere of the "on strike" universities, the students' movements were developing day and night these new topics as well as criticizing the "consumer society" and organization and teaching methods in higher education.[7] Workers, white collar workers and young executives came out two weeks later and a general strike paralyzed the whole economy for one month. The movement ended late in June with an important wage rise after collective bargaining, a bursting-out of the right-wing middle class inspired by de Gaulle and new parliamentary elections. One year later, de Gaulle left power after a negative referendum. Five years later the international oil crisis occurred.

After the events of 1968, the government tried to reintroduce authorization for political extremist associations, but the 1971 Act, voted by Parliament, was cancelled by the *Conseil Constitutionel*, the French supreme court, as being against the constitutional rule which includes the freedom of association.

More traditional nonprofit organizations expanded during this subperiod: health and welfare establishments and services multiplied both in the public and the private sector. Parent-teacher associations had to be represented in national education and developed. The first Secretary of Culture, the famous writer André Malraux, encouraged the creation of the *Maisons de la Culture*, multipurpose culture and art centers, and the *Maisons des Jeunes et de la Culture*, culture and recreation facilities intended for young people; most of these still existing organizations are 1901 Act associations and they benefit from significant public subsidies. The aim of this cultural network was to democratize and decentralize culture, especially the visual and performing arts. However, the public consists mostly of middle-class people and the supremacy of Paris in cultural activity remains.

In 1971, Jacques Delors proposed a bill, voted by a large majority, to promote continuing education. A special tax on the wage bill subsidizes continuing education schemes run by either for-profit, nonprofit or public establishments. Therefore many associations were created in the early 1970s; the competition between establishments benefited mainly private organizations, either nonprofit or forprofit. Nowadays, one employee out of four benefits each year from one form of training or another.

During the 1960s and 1970s, France began to catch up in the development of the nonprofit sector. New concerns, a more active "civil society", financial public encouragement and favorable regulations explain this evolution.

Socialist government and decentralization

This tendency was reinforced in the 1980s. From a political point of view, this period is characterized by two main features, the first long-term Left government and the 1982 Decentralization Act. Periodically in French history, left-wing governments had appeared, sometimes linked to revolutionary movements, but they never lasted more than a few months or a few years. The 1981 election of the socialist Mitterrand as President introduced the first durable alternative. Paradoxically, in this period, we can observe a collapse of the Communist Party, previewing the general collapse of communism in Eastern Europe and the rise of an extreme right-wing party, the *Front National*.

The socialist government encouraged social economy organizations, cooperatives, mutual benefit societies and associations by giving subsidies, fiscal incentives and by allowing tax relief on private giving. They also supported umbrella organizations in order to encourage the awareness of the unity of social economy.

The 1982 Decentralization Act, which breaks a millenary tradition of centralization, is the second main feature. Twenty-two regions have become territorial communities, as the municipalities[8] and the *départements*[9] already were. The state's responsibilities diminished and those of local communities increased. The transfer was progressive and has brought France closer to other European countries. Decentralization stimulated the development of the nonprofit sector: a lot of municipalities and *départements* delegated some economic or social local policies to associations or shared their new responsibilities with the nonprofit sector (Tchernonog, 1992b).

The welfare state crisis: a challenge for the nonprofit organizations

From the economic and social points of view, the post-1973 period in France and elsewhere is characterized by a slower growth rate: 3 per cent average growth after the first oil crisis, 1 per cent after the second oil crisis; but the annual growth rate was never negative.

The slow growth, joined to the arrival on the labor market of large numbers of young people and women, provoked growing and long-term unemployment: the unemployment rate rose from 4 per cent in 1975 to over 10 per cent in 1990.

With less contribution from employers and employees and more unemployment or retirement benefits to pay, the social protection schemes have recorded constant financial deficits. Moreover, many unskilled young people, especially immigrants' children, are in fact excluded from the labor market and from social benefits linked to employment. Most of them have become "new poor" or dropouts.

During previous periods, the underprivileged were mainly the elderly. Nowadays, thanks to social security, to contractual retirement and minimum state pensions, the elderly are well off or at least not poor; the nonprofit organizations have to adjust to new poverty.

In deprived industrial areas, such as the northern *départements* or Lorraine, the nonprofit sector cooperated with local government to provide help and income support to the unemployed new poor. It was the foreshadowing of the minimum income for social integration (RMI) policy, enacted in 1988.

As we will show in chapter 6, this policy is a mixture of welfare benefit paid by the state and an "insertion contract" implying a follow-up of the beneficiary by local communities and/or nonprofit organizations.

The RMI social policy is important for the nonprofit sector, because nonprofit organizations are first considered as vehicles of a public policy. This official acknowledgement follows a long-term *de facto* cooperation between nonprofit organizations and public authorities, especially in employment policy and health and social activities. Associations help employment policy by running, with significant public financing, job training programs, especially for unskilled workers. They also run hospitals or clinics and nursing homes; most of those belong to the public hospital service and have been funded since 1985 by an overall endowment provided by health insurance social security. Other nonprofit health establishments have less regulation and negotiate agreements with social security to benefit third party payments.

As the students' and feminist movements regressed, concern for the environment developed, especially in the mid-1970s. In recent years the ecological movement has become more political. Ecological disasters such as the Amoco Cadiz wreck or Tchernobyl nuclear pollution were powerful incentives.

A new concern appeared with the rise of the immigration problems, the demagogue Jean Marie Le Pen adding fuel to the fire. Massive immigration stopped in 1974, but legal entry is possible for people joining their families. Clandestine immigration continues. According to Interior Ministry figures, there are 4.4 million foreigners (8 per cent) as against 3.5 million according to the 1990 Population census (6 per cent). The reality is somewhere between the two figures. The recent immigrants, especially Algerians, Moroccans, Tunisians and Black Africans, are more different, in ethnic and religious terms, from the French population, than the Spanish, Portuguese, Italians or Poles of the previous immigration flows. Moreover, their French descendants do not look like the average French citizens. Recent immigrants concentrate in some suburbs which have sometimes become drug and delinquency areas. This is the background of the racist tendencies and of the rise, from election to election, of Jean Marie Le Pen's *Front National* political party. Some associations are linked to the *Front National* and their official aim is "national identity defence". According to them, immigration is the root of all current difficulties, unemployment, urban insecurity, drugs and delinquency; their slogan is *"La France aux français"*. To fight racist ideas, some antiracist associations have been created, such as *SOS Racisme*, which mix French *"beurs"*[10] and other second-generation young immigrants. In the meantime, with the disappearance, in 1981, of prior authorization for foreigners' associations, minorities' associations have flourished especially Islamic associations (Kepel, 1987). Their aim is very often to build mosques in urban suburbs: Islam is the second most important religion in France.

The result of the constant tendency of the nonprofit sector to adjust to the changing issues of civil society, plus the encouragement of central and local government, is the association boom of the last two decades. From less than 15,000 in the 1960s, the creation of associations went up each year to reach more than 70,000 in 1992. As we will show in chapter 4, the nonprofit sector is therefore creating jobs; in most industries the number of jobs declined during the last two decades.

With this recent expansion, the French nonprofit sector is bringing France closer to the other European countries in that field, even if historical events have shaped it differently.

2.3 Concluding remarks

This oversimplified survey gives an idea of the very long and deep-rooted history of the nonprofit sector. It took it more than a century to recover after restrictions or prohibitions imposed by the Revolution. However, thanks to its expansion over the last two decades, the nonprofit sector in France is very similar in size to that in other European countries: 4.2 per cent of total employment, 3.3 per cent of GDP regarding operating expenditures (see chapter 4).

2.3.1 The role of the state: from hostility to encouragement

Regarding French history, the theory of an inherent conflict between the state and the voluntary sector fits the 1789–1901 period. During this period, the Jacobin governments, whether republican or bonapartist, had a circumspect attitude toward two opposite currents: on the one hand toward the right-wing corporatist and clerical revival trends, on the other hand toward the left-wing movement, which greatly expanded during the Parisian Commune, with a special focus on the trends praising workers' control or anarchy (Archambault, 1990).

The hypothesis of pacific coexistence turning into extensive cooperation between the state and the nonprofit organizations fits into the recent period after the end of the secular war. It is not for the state a way of saving money, as it was during the last two decades in many industrial countries. During this period, French public welfare expenditures were growing. The result of this delegation of social services by the central and above all local governments to nonprofit organizations is that public financing is by far the main financing of the nonprofit sector: about 60 per cent of the income of the nonprofit sector, as we will show in chapter 4, and even more for health or education subsectors.

In-kind public support has also developed recently as we will show in chapter 6: civil servants or municipal officials have been seconded and very often the nonprofit organizations use public buildings and equipment; the money value could be equivalent to that of volunteer work.

2.3.2 The role of the Catholic Church: from direct management to moral inspiration

As shown above, the nonprofit sector was an important challenge in the recurrent conflict between the state and the Church. It was not the case during the *ancien régime*. The Church is established, it is not a rival for the state: education, health and social services are in fact delegated to the Church. The state controls matters of public interest such as sanitary conditions or safety concerns. Sometimes, in case of "welfare-Church crisis", some public financing is awarded.

During the Revolution, the charitable organizations run by the Church were nationalized and the property of congregations sold to the upcoming *bourgeoisie*. Even with new indemnification, the Church could not afford to rebuild the nonprofit network to such a large extent as before; the Church implicitly chose to concentrate on the subsector of education which is considered the most important by far where the transmission of faith is concerned. The opening of more schools by the Church was also filling one of the gaps in government provisions: the state was unable to organize a republican secular education network before 1881 because finance was lacking.

After the 1905 disestablishment of the Church, the conflict between Catholicism and republican ideology focused on school and became more and more political as we will show in chapter 5. Even nowadays, the position towards private schools is still a sensitive issue between the Right and the Left.

In this conflict, the supporters of private schools argue that there is no freedom of education if parents do not send their children to private schools for economic reasons. Private schools guarantee ideological pluralism. The lay camp answer that private schools are instruments of indoctrination and social segregation, that they are against the 1905 law which says that the state may not subsidize any religion.

Contrasting with this everlasting school war, a peaceful relationship existed between the state and the Church in the health and social welfare areas on a contractual basis with social security or other social funds. The Church progressively ceased to run hospitals or welfare establishments or services directly, and associations replaced it, mainly during the twentieth century. In Catholic hospitals or welfare establishments or services, paid staff replaced volunteer nuns. Some nuns are still active and most of the time they receive wages. Most of the leaders and the staff of health and welfare associations are inspired by social Catholicism. The peak associations in the French nonprofit sector are very representative of this Catholic inspiration. More generally, since the postwar Catholic revival, the French Catholic Church has incited young people to work in every kind of nonprofit association. As we will show in chapter 4, the most important variable correlated with giving and volunteering behavior is the intensity of religious feeling and practice, in France as in the UK and USA.

2.3.3 Other factors

The role of the labor unions and political parties in promoting nonprofit organizations is no doubt weaker in France than in Italy or Germany.

As mentioned before, the labor movement is more recent, less powerful, more fragmented and conflictual than in other European countries. Historical reasons explain this weakness. The link between the *Confédération Générale du Travail* (CGT), the most important labor union, and the Communist party is at the heart of the decrease in membership in both organizations since the 1960s. Moreover, as opposed to the German or Italian unions, the French labor unions have not developed any nonprofit welfare network for their members. The competition between the three main unions, CGT, CFDT (Second Left), and FO (First Left) is ideological. They are advocacy organizations and do not provide services.

Though political clubs in the nineteenth century, either prohibited or authorized, may have been precursors of some of the political parties, the current political parties are not very active in developing the nonprofit sector, except for the socialist party. The link between the socialist party, mutual societies, the *Ligue de l'Enseignement* and other lay nonprofit organizations can be observed from the middle of the nineteenth century.

Undoubtedly, the social movement which has had the most decisive and durable impact on the nonprofit sector is the farming movement, which developed during the interwar and the postwar periods. With a Catholic inspiration and Catholic leaders, close to agricultural cooperatives, this movement is characterized by its powerful business organizations (*Fédération Nationale des Syndicats d'Exploitants Agricoles*, FNSEA; *Centre National des Jeunes Agriculteurs*, CNJA) which developed advocacy, legal service and local development organizations. Very active in the modernization of French agriculture during the 1950s and the 1960s, and in the europeanization during the 1970s, they benefited from the *Crédit Agricole*, the main bank of the social economy financial network. The *Mutualité Agricole* and the *Mouvement Familial Rural* also developed health and welfare nonprofit organizations, family services and socio-cultural clubs in rural areas to prevent depopulation. In the most recent period, such organizations have invested in new projects: the isolated elderly, protection and preservation of environment, social tourism in rural areas and local development. They have been very innovative in such activities. The influence of the farming movement explains the parallel between the geographic distribution of the nonprofit organizations, the density of the rural population and religious observances: the highest levels of rural population density, attendance at church and development of the nonprofit sector are to be found in the western and central regions of France. Those regions were also opposed to the Republic during the French Revolution. It is a long story.

Notes

1 This chapter relies mainly on the work of historians such as Mollat, Agulhon, Gueslin, Vovelle and Zeldin, and social scientists such as Tocqueville and Foucault.
2 Some Parisian hospitals, now public organizations, trace their origins back to the Capetian period: the *Quinze-Vingt* hospital, Saint-Louis hospital, the *Hôtel Dieu*.
3 Some of them were clandestine like the freemasons, who were very active in France as well as in the rest of Europe in the eighteenth century.
4 Marx saw the Commune insurrection as an example of applied communism. The anarchist influence is more obvious.
5 Combes was previously a seminarist, like Stalin.
6 Dollfus in Mulhouse, Schneider in Le Creusot, Belle Jardinière et Cristallerie de Pantin in the Parisian area, Gillet in Lyon, Siegfried in Le Havre (Guerrand and Rupp, 1969).
7 It was the author's first year of teaching and one of her best memories.
8 The smallest local community – 36,000 in France – equivalent to parishes.
9 The 95 intermediate local communities – equivalent to counties.
10 A neologism to designate descendants of Maghrebine immigrants; officially French citizens.

Chapter 3

THE LAW AND THE NONPROFIT
SECTOR IN FRANCE[1]

History, culture, social and political trends find a natural translation in the juridical rules governing a given human society. Historical developments ultimately find reflection in legal structures.
The misunderstanding between the strongly centralized French
state and voluntary nonprofit action in the field thus finds expression in the legal regimes established for the nonprofit organizations. The French legislator has at last accepted this type of
organization, but settled rather strict principles ruling them, starting in the late nineteenth century with trade unions (*syndicats*) and
mutual insurance societies (*mutuelles*), and going on with voluntary organizations (associations), and foundations (*fondations*).

The legal provisions (law of 1 July 1901) and the success of the
associations made this type of grouping the pattern of the nonprofit organizations: they will constitute the main subject of this
chapter.

3.1 Basic principles

Preliminary remarks

One major difficulty met in dealing with comparative law, for countries using different languages and endowed with different law systems, is to find suitable words to translate terms, designating
elements which have no exact or similar counterpart between one
language and another, between one juridical qualification or situation and another, and between one legal system and another.

This will apply for instance to the nonprofit concept, which may also designate the fact of not making profits, or not sharing them among members of an organization, bearing in mind anyway that not making profit, generally, involves by itself an impossible sharing; conversely, making a profit does not lead automatically to sharing it out.

Even when one single language is used, French for instance, the meaning of the expression may not be the same in two different French-speaking countries (Luxembourg and France, Quebec/ Canada and France, etc.); even more, in the bosom of the French system, there may exist a difference in meaning of the word nonprofit, between the French civil law, the French fiscal law, the European Community rules. And according to the circumstances, many French expressions may be necessary to translate nonprofit: *non lucrativité, désintéressement* (in the objectives, in the management), etc. Further developments will emphasize these differences.

The French expression *Économie sociale* (social economy) has also to be carefully considered, and must not be identified with nonprofit activities. One cannot even automatically associate both concepts. It is true that, most often, the nonprofit sector belongs to the field of social economy, but this last concept covers a much larger field.

The social economy relates to *several kinds of economic activities*, whose ties with money are governed in a different spirit and with different rules, from those existing in the capitalistic type of activity. Generally, it means a collective property of an organization's patrimony, a power of management and decision established more on a personal basis than on capital invested, and the non-allotment of the final bonus among the members of the organization. Nevertheless, the social economy acts in the general framework of the market laws.

Finally, historical, cultural and/or political reasons have implied differences from country to country, in the juridical treatment of organizations, in regard to their belonging to a profit or to a nonprofit sector. For instance, in many countries, organizations in general (incorporated or not-corporated) are ruled by *one* well-defined law. These organizations are then generally divided between forprofit and not-for-profit (or nonprofit) ones. Many rules, especially those governing the external relations of these organizations (for instance the corporation, the rights of the juridical entity, the relations with other organizations, with the authorities ...) are the same for both types. They only differ on the ground of their particular aims, their internal organization, and the way they use the possible profits they generate (this involving particular tax treatments).

The traditional legal form provided for nonprofit organizations in France

In the French juridical classification of the organizations, historical and political reasons brought about a different solution from the one described above. For a long time, the only organizations which enjoyed formal recognition were of the *"forprofit"* type: companies, societies (*Société* for the French juridical vocabulary). In the French legal system (French Civil Code, articles 1832ff., the first version of which dates back to the beginning of the nineteenth century), the *Société* is the contract instituted by two or more persons who hold in common property and labour, in order to *share* out the resulting profits or savings (this last word has been added only by the law of 4 January 1978, and obviously this particular aim is not, so far, kept exclusively for the forprofit type).

Other possible types of organizations, especially those not having a profit-making aim, with a few exceptions, had to adjust to the business pattern or not incorporate. This lasted until the late nineteenth and early twentieth century. Gradually, trade unions and mutual benefit friendly societies appeared or received formal legal recognition. Then in 1901, the legislature decided to vote a law granting the *freedom of association*: it created, for this purpose, a type of nonprofit organization, the *association*, which was prohibited from generating profit for its membership, and which had to be *not symmetrical* (as exists in several other countries), *but opposed* to the classical already existing juridical type of organization, the business type (*société* in French). This explains why in France, the main legal form provided by the law for nonprofit organizations is given by the Law of 1 July 1901, relating to the *contract of association*. The first article of this law states that "the Association is the agreement by which two or several persons permanently pool their knowledge or their activity, *for any purpose other than the sharing of profits ...*".

As already emphasized, the wording (dating from 1901) was purposely given this way, to clearly lay down the principle that the association object has to be defined as the *opposite of* the object of the company. And, this newly created body being built on the principle of freedom, its constitution, its by-laws, its corporation etc. follow different rules, simpler than those of the private company.

By this contract, associations obtain the moral personality which allows a distinction between the association and its members. But their juridical capacity is *restricted*. Indeed, the juridical person association enjoys less rights than another person, another moral entity (the private company, for instance), especially in the field of real estate property or of receiving legacies. The associations which are given the label of *reconnaissance d'utilité publique* and subsidiarily those whose exclusive aim is charitable – *associations de bienfaisance* – are, however, and on the contrary, more privileged than other juridical entities on this point, as they can not only receive legacies, but in addition are in many cases exempted from inheritance tax or probate duty.

The long but steady building of the European Community has brought forward the question of the comparison of the French situation with the different member states. By the end of 1991, the EU Commission made out a list of one nonprofit organization in each member state, which would be considered as homologous of the ones existing in each of the other member states (such as the association in France). It is noteworthy here, how on the one hand every country has at least one juridical status of organization answering the criteria of nonprofit, and on the other hand there are no two countries having exactly the same pattern. This explains the difficulty the Commission is experiencing in its endeavour to create the future European body to be called "European association".

Among others, a couple of questions may be raised about definitions. The first deals with the exact juridical meaning of the word profit in the French legal system. Generally, reference is made to a historical decision of the French Supreme Civil Court, *Cour de Cassation*, of 11 March 1914, which had to say whether the *Caisse rurale de Manigod* was an association or a business (*Gazette du Palais*, 1914, 1, 1549), depending on the possible sharing of profits or not. It was decided that the profit, or the benefit, consists of *any pecuniary or material earnings being added to the personal wealth of the partners, of the members of a said organization.*

This first decision, combined with the aforesaid text of the law of 1 July 1901, led French judges, later, to designate definitively the *level* at which profit-making would qualify a given organization as a forprofit or nonprofit one. They generally established that *the profit has to be considered at the members' level*. Thus, a given organization, which makes profits now and then or even permanently, which does not distribute them to its membership as benefits or final bonus sharing, but on the contrary deploys them to match its goals, is eligible to be qualified as a nonprofit one.

This position establishes a difference between the French and other neighbouring juridical systems (Belgium, Luxembourg, Italy), regarding organizations of the association type. In Italy, for instance, *the fact of making profit* (and not only sharing it), is virtually forbidden. In Belgium and in Luxembourg, these organizations (which in certain cases can make profits but cannot share them) are not only called *associations*, but also *associations sans but lucratif* (ASBL, nonprofit aim association). In France, such an expression is a tautology; the compulsory aim of not sharing profits is sufficient by itself to stress that the association is *sans but lucratif*, i.e. nonprofit.

The second question deals with the limitative juridical *nature* of profit. French judges took the opportunity to state that salaries and wages, paid on a normal and usual scale to persons performing a real and well-determined job in the service of an association, were not to be considered as profit or benefit. Nevertheless, because of the possible ambiguities, various rules are recommended by the civil and administrative High Courts, for avoiding too easy possibilities for voluntary leaders, or even for members of associations, to perform paid jobs in it.

More generally, the French legal system admits that any organization of which the constitutional by-laws prohibit any kind of direct or indirect sharing of profit may be considered as a nonprofit organization. Actually, such by-laws would assimilate this type of organization to associations, without omitting organizations of a similar type: foundations (*fondations*), friendly societies and mutual insurance societies (*mutuelles, groupements mutualistes*), unions (*syndicats*). This has particularly important repercussions for the level of taxes imposed, for instance, on the economical activities of a given organization. Except for the associations, other types of organizations either are nonprofit ones in the sense earlier described (workers' or employers' trade unions, for example, or mutual friendly societies), or have a different relation to capital and profit-making from the classical type of company (the cooperatives for instance). These three types, associations, cooperatives and friendly societies, are the components of the social economy.

3.2 Nonprofit status

3.2.1 Legal types of nonprofit organizations

Many terms are used in French to designate various forms of groupings forprofit or nonprofit. It is important to clarify some definitions which contrast with the definition of the common business-type organization, the *société*:

- *Société* (societies and companies). This word may be used, generally, to designate any kind of group of people, notwithstanding their forprofit or nonprofit aim. It is used as a generic word. But its legal definition is on the contrary very precise: in the French *Code civil*, article 1832 gives the name of *société* to those groupings, the aim of which is *the sharing out of profits (or savings)* among their membership. Nevertheless, treaties – and especially the Treaty of Rome, the foundation of the EEC – use *société* on some occasions, and, in the French versions of them, for any legal grouping entity.
- *Association*. Since its creation in 1901, this type of grouping became the paragon of the nonprofit groupings. As emphasized several times in the present survey, the aim of the association – a grouping of physical persons and/or legal entities – can *only* be a nonprofit one.
- *Fondation* (foundations). In contrast to the association, the *fondation* is a *legal entity, a grouping of goods, of estate*, earmarked to well-determined nonprofit aims of public benefit. There was no law ruling its existence and operation until 1987, but only usage custom.
- *Syndicat* (trade unions). This type of organization has been legally admitted since 1884. Its aim can only be to protect the

rights of professions and workers, excluding any kind of profit sharing among the membership (trade unions are considered, since 1901, as a particular variety of association).

- *Mutuelles* (mutual friendly societies) and *sociétés coopératives* (cooperatives) have a different vision as regards capital and profit from that of traditional capitalistic groupings. For this reason, they have some similarities with groupings like associations.

As already stated, these three types of organizations are the components of the French social economy.

3.2.2 The law of 1901

Regulating of nonprofit status
- *The association, an organization linking together freedom of association and profit sharing prohibition*
What follows deals directly with the organization called the association. As mentioned above, its juridical status was defined by the law of 1 July 1901. The French Parliament spent several years before the Act was at last promulgated. The purpose was to grant freedom of association, and altogether to ward off any risk of secret or rebellious groups, or organizations whose too important and immutable patrimonies (*biens de main-morte*) might become a danger for the political or economical peace of the country.

That is the reason why the Law creating the association is a very short text (freedom does not admit too many regulations), and why the association does not enjoy the plenitude of rights, as do other legal entities (physical, or of the business type): they cannot own real estate or buildings, except those which are needed for their operation. On the other hand, there is an immense range of possible aims. Only two are prohibited: unlawful aims, and sharing profits among the membership.

The result of the mingling of these two opposite criteria of the association – freedom and prohibition – is that the real law ruling the life and operation of an association is the constitution, the by-laws, the statutes, which the founders of this organization give freely to it, bearing in mind the two prohibited aims.

On one side, the principle of freedom means that the association has no other special formality to effect, in order to obtain its legal entitlement, than to lodge a declaration at the French department of the *Préfecture*, and to "publish" its existence, that is, to advertise in the *Journal Officiel* its name, place and date of birth, its aims, and the names of its founders. The association is then said to be *déclarée et publiée* (declared and published) but usually it is simply *association déclarée* (declared association). A consequence of the principle of freedom is that an association which is not declared is, nevertheless licit, but exists without a legal entity: it is not a legal person (*personne morale*), but only an informal assembly of members with no legal collective means of action. This memorandum will only deal with declared associations.

There is no corporation formality as for instance in the U.S.A., or control of compliance with the law, as enacted by a judge in Germany. (Attempts to introduce to the French legal system *a priori* controls of this type have been definitely rejected by the *Conseil constitutionnel* in its decision of 16 July 1971 (*Recueil Dalloz*, 1972, note 685): freedom of association was listed as one of the fundamental rights guaranteed by the Constitution to the French people.)

Any preliminary control being fundamentally forbidden by law, the possible offences to law can only proceed from the wording of the declared aims of the association – if obviously illicit – or come later, if and when a third party suffers prejudice because of them (the Ministry of Interior, for instance, head of the public security services). Should the case come before court, and evidence be given, the judges have to decide on the dissolution of the association, on the ground of illegal aims.

On the other side, any possible legal aim may be fixed to an association, provided that it does not give occasion to its founders, leaders and members to share benefits among them either directly or indirectly. Should such a prohibited case occur, and constitute a grievance to any public (fiscal administration, for instance) or private person (a competitor firm, for instance), it has generally to be brought before court. The judges, in considering the evidence, decide on requalifying the wrongly so-called association as a company, and/or the loss of the possible preferential tax treatment which such an organization enjoyed.

What has just been said should not mean that the association is governed by less rules than other types of organizations and citizens of the country. Its specific rules are very few and generally appear in its statutes by-laws. But it is submitted to the general law network of rights and obligations ruling the life of every citizen or resident in France.

Associations, as civil groupings, obey the civil law for their internal operation. Certain of their activities, according to their nature, are regulated by the rules of public law (when they perform a task normally carried out by a public entity – see further, section 3.2.3, *The notion of public benefit*), or the rules of the civil law (for instance, when members undertake certain tasks on a voluntary basis), or on the rules of the market economy, that is to say the commercial law (for business-type activities, if there is no specific civil law to apply). Fiscal and labor laws are linked to the activities, and the ways these activities are carried out; thus the labor law applies to associations as it does to all employers, and the fiscal law (with possible exceptions and exemptions due to the way some activities are managed) as to all other taxpayers.

- *The association, a nonprofit organization, faced with the question of ("business type") economical or commercial activities*
Because of the profit prohibition as emphasized before, there was a question about economic activities, and all the more commercial ones: was "making business" allowed or forbidden to the associations? Several courts at different levels had to give the answer of the law. A series of decisions by the French supreme civil court, the *Cour de Cassation*, have made clear that there is no provision in the law of 1 July 1901 or any other text, for prohibiting such activities, which could not constitute the central aim of an association, but could perfectly well be performed as the accessory or even the principal activity, in the service of the nonprofit goal of the organization.

Because of this widening of associations' scope of activities, and of the aforesaid judges' decisions, associations which develop an economic activity are in practice subject to the overall economic and business regulations, as for instance, among the most important:

– law of 1 March 1984 on prevention of companies' financial

difficulties (*relative au règlement amiable et à la prévention des difficultés des entreprises*);

- law of 25 January 1985 about cases of insolvency and bankrupty (*sur le redressement et la liquidation judiciaires des entreprises*);
- law of 11 July 1985 which allows a certain type of association to issue transferable shares (*permettant à certaines associations d'émettre des valeurs mobilières*);
- *ordonnance* of 1 December 1986 related to pricing and competition (*relative à la liberté des prix et de la concurrence*);
- *circulaire* of the Prime Minister of 10 March 1979 related to the fight against practices contrary to competition in commercial and distribution fields (*relative à la lutte contre les pratiques contraires à une concurrence loyale dans le domaine du commerce et de la distribution*);
- *circulaire* of the Ministry of Economy against paracommercial practices (*relative à la lutte contre les pratiques paracommerciales*).

The same pattern exists for the associations' activities linked with the service of public benefit. Several legal and administrative rules exist, which regulate the reception, the use and the control of public subventions, on the ground of the overall rules governing the use of public funding. Other rules govern ways of carrying out missions of public service, when they are performed by private organizations, as the associations are.

But, speaking of the *aim* of an association, and especially because of the politico-constitutional characteristic of the association, there is practically no *a priori* control mechanism in place, to grant and ensure compliance with nonprofit status. There are two main *a posteriori* controls: the court and the fiscal administration. A slight modification of this situation might perhaps occur for some types of associations, if and when the EEC authorities finally establish an association enjoying a special European status still in project (this project is in consideration at the present time for both a "European association" and a "European company"): in this case, there might be a system of European corporation, more or less symmetrical for both types of organizations, opening the opportunity for some kind of *a priori* control for both of them. This project is far from obtaining the unanimous agreement of French jurists, many of whom are reluctant to admit any possible infringement of the "right of association", since a corporation formality might appear more compelling than a simple declaration.

3.2.3 The notion of public benefit

Many words can be used to depict the missions of organizations serving the public benefit one way or another. Often, these terms have no special juridical meaning, but are used to bring out the type of activity of such organizations: *oeuvre* (charity), *activité d'intérêt général* (general interest activity), *activité d'utilité sociale* (social utility activity), etc.

Nonprofit status and public benefit
In some countries, nonprofit status is restricted to organizations that serve some special public benefit. In France, this is not compulsory: nonprofit status has to be considered from two different points of view.

The first aspect is juridical: organizations of which the aim excludes the sharing of profit among the founders, leaders and members – and which generally (but not always) bear the label of association – enjoy *ipso facto* legal nonprofit status, whether they serve some special public benefit or not. They may even simply serve some immaterial or material needs of their members only. Organizations of this first type are to be found in several groups of the ICNPO: culture, arts, service clubs, civil and advocacy organizations, etc. Although such organizations are supposed to serve only their own membership, many of them are considered to give service to the civil society at large, and, therefore, are eligible to part of the privileged treatments granted by the fiscal authorities as described hereafter.

Organizations of a second type are related to a second aspect: the special treatment French public authorities grant organizations which serve the public interest. Very often, but not exclusively, these types of organizations serve people who do not belong to their memberships; they in some way take a share in missions, which belong to the public responsibility of the state. The special treatment they then enjoy is generally expressed in tax privileges (for their own operation, or for the income tax deduction on their donors' gifts), or public funding. The ICNPO list comprises numbers of such organizations, be they in education and research, in health and social services, in environment care, in development and housing, in civil and advocacy organizations, in philanthropy, international activities or professional and business associations, etc.

Some misunderstanding can arise about the term *reconnaissance d'utilité publique* which is granted to some two thousand French associations (from a total of about 700,000): this very official label is a kind of special recognition by the government (on the *Conseil d'Etat 's* advice) of certain associations at their own request. These associations have to show evidence of the importance of their action, the seriousness of their operation, the quality of their performance, their reputation. Of course, most of them fulfil missions of public benefit, but there is no automatic relation. It should be pointed out that the Government is entitled to withdraw the *reconnaissance d'utilité publique* for serious failures.

In addition to *but non lucratif* (nonprofit), the terms *activité d'intérêt général* (general interest activity) and *gestion désintéressée* (nonprofit management) are used by the fiscal administration to designate those organizations eligible for various tax privileges. The first relates to the public benefit aim of the organization, the second to the nonprofit concept (see the section on taxation, p. 66). Precise criteria are supposed to define both of the terms. They have generally been imposed by law and/or by judges' decisions. On its inspections, the fiscal administration checks that these conditions are respected. Should this not be the case, tax privileges may be cut off on the administration's direction, with a possible appeal before court (*Tribunal administratif, Cour administrative d'appel, Conseil d'Etat*).

The *Conseil National de la Vie associative* (CNVA) – a public body appointed by the Government and composed of leaders and representatives of all sectors of the associations' activities – is considering the possibility of using the term "social utility" (*utilité sociale*), conferred on those associations of which the aims, the operation and the activities are oriented toward the service of public benefit, under special conditions to be discussed with the public authorities.

Freedom of association vs. control through agrément
Mention has to be made here of a very important point dealing

with nonprofit organizations serving the public benefit, which leads us to revise somewhat the impression of total liberalism given by the rules governing the associations. Several of the aims of this kind of organization are only possible if the French administration gives its approval: either an agreement (*agrément*), or an authorization.

The agreement is, first, a kind of official recognition of the quality of activities performed in special fields; but overall and very often, these activities are possible *only* if the organizations carrying them out are agreed (*agréées*): nonprofit travel agencies (*associations organisant des séjours et des voyages*, law of 11 July 1975), hunters' federations (*fédérations départementales de chasse – arrêté du 18 septembre 1975*), youth organizations (*associations de jeunesse – décret du 7 juillet 1977*), fishing and fish-culture organizations (*associations de pêche et de pisciculture – arrêté du 23 mars 1982*), associations active in the field of the environment (*associations de protection de la nature, de l'environnement et du cadre de vie – décret du 7 juillet 1977*), etc.

The authorization equal to an agreement (*autorisation valant agrément*) is necessary especially in the sphere of health and social services, for reasons easy to explain: kindergartens, day nurseries for babies, housing of young workers or elderly people, education of the handicapped or juvenile offenders, etc., in order to control the standard of quality of the activities performed. It ought to be stressed here that these controls are imposed upon the aforesaid activities, and not especially upon the associations, and that the requested standards have a pecuniary counterpart.

In these cases, the administration has a discretionary power of decision: it thus grants a kind of monopoly to perform some activities, that is to authorize (or not authorize) a given organization to fix its aim in the fields concerned and carry out the corresponding activities, and consequently to forbid all others to do so.

On one side, the result is that the state administration keeps a very close control on the agreed organization, and becomes a kind of partner for it: the association becomes a legal entity, half private entity, half part of the public administration; strong conditions of morality and financial solvency are demanded, and similarly for their insurance; special statutes and by-laws have to be accepted by the membership and, in some cases, the President is appointed by a Minister; the books, the activity and the general operation of the grouping are controlled by the controllers of the state administration, and so on.

On the other hand, the agreement opens the door to public funding: for instance, only "agreed sports clubs" are eligible to receive such funds; the agreed associations may receive donations and legacies, even if they are not *reconnues d'utilité publique*; for the centers of agreed management (*centres de gestion agréés*), which help their membership keep their books, there are special tax privileges for the members; more important, the agreement allows some associations to bring actions before court for advocating causes in relation to their aim – a very special exception to the French legal principle that no one is allowed to advocate before court somebody else's cause (*nul ne plaide par procureur*): this is the case with public morality organizations (*associations de défense de la moralité publique – décret du 24 janvier 1956*), consumers' organizations (*associations de défense des consommateurs – loi du 27 décembre 1973*), and environment organizations (*associations de défense de la nature, de l'environnement et de l'amélioration du cadre de vie – loi du 10 juillet 1976*).

3.3 Taxation

It has been made clear before that the nonprofit status, in France, must not be identified with the service of public benefit, even if it is obvious that both of the two concepts, nonprofit and public benefit, are linked in the aims of many associations. Nonprofit is a legal obligation for the members of an organization, which claims the association qualification. And serving some public benefit is one of the most genuine goals of organizations composed of people who do not seek their own interest in operating them.

French tax laws (especially regarding income taxation and value added tax) take into account the two aspects, and therefore grant a special treatment for the organizations which are nonprofit ones (even if they do not bear the title of association) on one hand, and grant also various privileges to those which, in addition, serve some public benefit. The French fiscal legislation grants also partial income tax exemptions to those who make charitable contributions to nonprofit organizations. Finally, the *associations reconnues d'utilité publique* enjoy important tax exemption privileges, especially in matters of legacies and donations.

Notwithstanding the present evolution of French institutions towards real decentralization, France has still a rather strong centralized fiscal administration. All fundamental taxes (income tax on physical persons/corporation tax on legal persons, value added tax, license, apprenticeship tax, tax on wages, capital gains tax, tax on capital) are generally established on a state basis, even if parts of some of them finance local needs. However, local authorities, for reasons of decentralization or of tradition, collect some taxes (land-tax, residential tax, building tax) which, in most cases, are not related to nonprofit tax privileges or exemptions. Therefore, the separate treatment accorded by the authorities will chiefly be considered on the national level.

3.3.1 Tax exemption or privileges established in favour of nonprofit organizations

The doctrine of the French fiscal system is built on the law. Its interpretation is the work of both the fiscal administration and, in the last instance, the fiscal judge, who specifies qualifications and criteria.

Two more or less contradictory principles are the essence of the fiscal law rationale, regarding nonprofit organizations:

- The taxes must be equal for all concerned, and the fiscal administration has to be neutral in regard of all economic agents. Distortions in the tax burden create distortions in the free competition rules, and have therefore to be avoided.
- Nevertheless, privileges have to be granted to those organizations which, on one hand, serve some public benefit, and on the other hand, are managed in a nonprofit spirit.

On this basis, the present fiscal situation is as follows (only income/corporation tax and VAT will be described here, but similar observations can be made about license, residential tax, etc.).

Corporation tax

Article 206–1 of the *Code Général des Impôts* (CGI) enunciates that this tax has to be paid by every organization performing activities in order to make a profit. Therefore, the nonprofit organization must fulfil five cumulative conditions, expressed by judges and/or tax administration:

- It has to be of some social utility, that is, answer to needs which are not normally or sufficiently taken care of by the market.
- The organization's management must give no material direct or indirect profit to its founders, leaders or members.
- The activity performed must remain in the general frame of the organization, and contribute to the achievement of its aims.
- Surplus revenue must not be systematically generated: no business methods, moderated prices, balanced management, etc.
- Potential revenue surpluses have to be reinvested in the organization.

If this list of conditions is fulfilled, there is no corporation tax (of which the common rate is 42 or 37 per cent) on the activities income, but a possible 24 per cent or 10 per cent capital gains taxation on the only patrimonial revenues (real estate, shares).

Articles 256-1 and 256-A of the CGI state that this tax has to be paid by persons (physical or organizations) who, usually or occasionally, deliver non-free-of-charge goods or services. On one side, three groups of organizations may be exempted on the ground of the kind of public service they give, and on the other side, there are criteria for exempting those organizations whose activity is a nonprofit one. Organizations which serve some public benefit, and are therefore exempt:

- social, education, culture and sport sectors, and also philosophical, religious, political, patriotic, civic and trade union-type sectors – for the services rendered to their membership, excluding food and shelter;
- social or philanthropic or medical organizations performing services for the benefit of all people, under a list of conditions (either scale of prices officially confirmed by the authorities or not usually offered by the competitive sector services, help with national medical development, nonprofit aim);
- charities or supporting organizations, to a limit of six a year.

Cumulative criteria regarding nonprofit organizations:

- the organization must be managed and administered by unpaid

people, having themselves, or through intermediary people, neither direct nor indirect part in the financial results of the activity;
- the organization must share no profit of any kind, directly or indirectly;
- the organization's members or their beneficiaries cannot be declared assigns of any share of the assets, but only of possible property or contribution brought into the assets.

VAT

VAT-exempted organizations are bound to pay the tax on wages, a tax paid by all employers some thirty years ago, and presently only by a few professions which are exempt from VAT. This tax is practically unknown in the other European countries. In some cases, paying the tax on wages instead of VAT, above all for associations which hire many employees, proves to be unprofitable, since they are allowed (apart from a few exceptions) neither to choose to be VAT-subjected, nor to deduct VAT paid by themselves for their investment and equipment.

For this reason, associations, and the CNVA especially, try to obtain from the government provision for associations to choose their liability for VAT under possible favourable rates, thus bringing them nearer to their homologous organizations in Europe. But one of the dangers in such a change is that the fiscal administration often links VAT exemption and corporation tax exemption. The associations request the autonomy of each of these taxes.

It ought to be stressed that to be subject to VAT tax payment is not always a bad deal, because firms and individuals who do so are entitled to deduct the VAT tax they have themselves paid on their own purchases: this has considerable and positive repercussions on the association's finances when important investments are made. This also confirms the wish of the associations to request the independence of the VAT rules from those of corporation tax.

3.3.2 Treatment by tax law of charitable contributions to nonprofit organizations

The privileged treatment of charitable contributions to nonprofit organizations is quite a recent phenomenon in France. For a long time until the 1980s, there was only a symbolic exemption on the income tax/corporation tax paid by physical persons or organizations to well-defined associations or foundations. If a rather selected and motivated group of donors did nevertheless give important periodical or one-off gifts, this lack of incentive restrained many donors from giving or giving more for various charitable or humanitarian or public benefit causes.

One has to recall here, that legacies and one-off important donations to *associations reconnues d'utilité publique* (or *associations dont la mission est reconnue d'utilité publique* in the *départements* of Alsace and Moselle, still partly ruled by the "German Empire Law of 1908") are generally probate duty- (or inheritance tax-) exempted, and these associations pay reduced purchase tax on buildings if they are active in the fields of welfare, charity or social service. Since 1933, associations whose only aim is charity or relief, not even *reconnues d'utilité publique*, get the same tax privilege.

The general principle, in matters of possible income tax exemptions, on contributions to nonprofit organizations (associations, foundations) is that these organizations have to serve, one way or another, some public benefit. The interpretation of this principle has often changed in the course of time. At present the following treatment applies.

Regarding private individual persons
All income tax payers can claim the following tax advantages.

- Contributions to associations *reconnues d'utilité publique* or foundations *reconnues d'utilité publique*, up to 5 per cent of taxable income, are entitled to a "tax credit" of 40 per cent of the said contributions on the taxes owed by the taxpayer. The same privilege exists in favour of contributors
  - to the parochial associations of the three recognized monotheistic faiths, Christian, Jewish and Moslem, authorized to receive gifts and legacies;
  - to relief and charitable organizations, and to religious communities, legally recognized for the lay nature of their public benefit activities, having got from the public authorities permission to receive gifts and legacies;
  - to the recognized public churches (*établissements publics des cultes reconnus*) in the three French *départements* of Alsace-

Moselle;
- to those associations only registered and published (*déclarées et publiées*), which open an intermediary account in a *state approved* association or foundation.
• Contributions to all other organizations serving any kind of public benefit – philanthropy, education, welfare, family, humanitarian causes, science, sport, culture, enhancing of artistic heritage, environment, spread of culture, language and know-how – up to 1.25 per cent of taxable income, are entitled to the same "tax credit" of 40 per cent of the said contributions on the taxes owed by the taxpayer (50 per cent up to 520 FF. for organizations serving free meals or helping with emergency housing).

Special provisions of the fiscal law include, among the beneficiaries of these privileges, contributions by individual taxpayers to associations whose aim is to finance election campaigns, or to financial agents, under special conditions and controls, and possible maximum amounts (same conditions as for the organizations mentioned in the second part of the list above: 40 per cent up to 1.25 per cent of the contributor's income). The total of both series of contributions cannot go beyond 5 per cent of the taxable income of a said taxpayer.

It should be stressed that for the income tax exemptions, the French system favors small taxpayers (whose marginal tax rate is under 40 per cent), and conversely penalizes big taxpayers (whose marginal tax rate is over 40 per cent).

Regarding companies and firms
All corporations can claim the following tax advantages:

• Deduction of contributions (up to 0.3 per cent of the annual business turnover) to *reconnues d'utilité publique* associations and foundations (or those whose mission has been given the label *reconnue d'utilité publique)* or to charities (*associations de bienfaisance*) according to the 1933 law. The same privilege for:
  - declared associations which opened an intermediary account in the books of a association or a foundation *reconnue d'utilité publique;*
  - public or private schools teaching art or higher level education, as far as they are nonprofit organizations;

- to the parochial associations of the three monotheistic faiths, authorized to receive gifts and legacies;
- to the recognized public churches (*établissements publics des cultes reconnus*), in the French *départements* of Alsace-Moselle;
- to religious communities (Catholic) and congregations legally recognized, for their lay activities serving the public benefit.
• Deduction of contributions – up to 0.2 per cent of annual business turnover – to other nonprofit organizations serving the public benefit: philanthropy, education, welfare, family, humanitarian causes, science, sport, culture, enhancement of artistic heritage, the environment, spread of French culture, language and know-how, and also:
  - to approved organizations helping the creation of firms;
  - to approved public or private organizations or bodies in the matter of scientific or technical research.

Special provisions of the fiscal law include, among the beneficiaries of these privileges, contributions from nonpolitical organizations (forprofit or nonprofit), to associations whose aim is to finance election campaigns, or to financial agents, under special conditions and controls, and maximum possible amounts.

The total of both series of contributions cannot go beyond 3 per cent of the taxable year business turnover of a said taxpayer. In the books of such a taxpayer, amounts may be brought forward over five consecutive years.

3.3.3 In-kind contributions

The donations are only to be given in cash. There is no provision, so far, for claiming tax exemptions for "in-kind" contributions of products. There may be some special agreements in emergency cases, and for special causes: this remains most exceptional. In the same way, voluntary/benevolent/unpaid people, bringing their help to an organization, as important as it might be, are not entitled to estimate their performance in terms of money, and to deduct the corresponding sums from the income tax they have to pay. Some discussions have taken place on this matter, but we are still very far from any progress.

On the occasion of fiscal audits, the tax control officers may make sure, by the necessary supervision of activities, that a said organization belongs effectively to the category to which it claims it belongs, and which gave to its donors the tax deduction right. If not, the organization is struck off the corresponding rolls, and the contributors are no longer entitled to deduct the exemptions corresponding to their gifts. The limitative lists enumerated here make it relatively easy to dismiss possible defrauders.

3.4 Legal issues: defining the nonprofit border

3.4.1. Religion

The study of the motivations of nonprofit, benevolent, voluntary activities (overall when they are collective and organized in groups, specially when their purpose is to serve other people than those belonging to the group) brings out a series of possible sources of inspiration. Some of these sources are modern, and are explained by the need to answer today's social life problems. Very often, traditional, moral and ethical, and also psychological or social reasons or preoccupation, subtend these answers. Among them, and existing already for centuries, are the motivations provided by religious inspiration, even when lay nonreligious or even antireligious concerns may have replaced some of them.

A rapid survey in France, in fields like charity, relief, organizations caring for the family, children, or elderly people, educational organizations, those active in welfare, etc., will show that several among them, probably the majority were, to begin with either inspired by a religious ideal, a church, a parish, a religious community, or composed of a religious membership. Without asserting that the nonprofit sector is essentially an offshoot of religious activism, or of competition among religious trends (one has to remember that the industrial revolution of the nineteenth and the twentieth centuries has given birth to various impulses of assistance or mutual help, the origin of which was either the working class or the managerial class), it seems important to observe how religion and religious groups (for instance in France, Catholic congregations) today find their place or their stamp in the nonprofit sector and in the service of civil society at large.

As for other situations already analyzed, problems and questions relating to religion on one side, and to religious congregations on the other, have to be separately treated, even if they are closely connected.

Religion

As everybody knows, *churches* and state are legally separated in France. A long and painful process ended in 1905 with the Act of 9 December 1905, on the separation between churches and the state. One of the consequences of this is that in France there is no separate body of ecclesiastical law in the bosom of the French legal system (but these bodies exist as internal private rules governing the life of the members of each faith, and the operation of religious communities, religious entities, based on the application of the respective religious laws, and accepted as such by the members of the different churches: Catholic *droit canonique*, Jewish *loi mosaïque*, Moslem *Ulemas*).

There is no portion of French jurisdiction subject to a particular body of laws on the ground of faith, race or religion. There is ultimately (and in principle) no particular form of religion or denomination enjoying preferential treatment in the law. There *cannot* be any difference, because of the secular structure of the Constitution and of the state, even if, for understandable reasons, the Catholic culture of the legislator shows marks of his affiliation (the great majority of French citizens belong to the Roman Catholic Church). Let us here too remember, that in the field of private international law, the French judge bears in mind the possible application to a person of a foreign law in matter of his/her/its personal status, and, only in this matter, applies generally the corresponding foreign law rules, which may be religious or ecclesiastical (for instance, rules concerning the name, marriage, inheritance, etc.) as long as the said rules do not create problems for the peace and security of the French society, and do not shock the French way of life.

For more than a millennium and a half, the Roman, Apostolic, Catholic religion was the state religion in France. (The Kingdom of France was the Church's eldest daughter.) According to the times, other monotheistic religions (Christian reformed, Jewish) were either tolerated or on the contrary persecuted. From 1790 to 1792, the French Revolution abolished the privilege of the Catholic Church, and suppressed the religious Catholic congregations.

Under Napoleon I, agreements were reached with the Pope, and in 1817 and 1825, the *Restauration* established new ties between the state and the Catholic Church. Famous incidents, especially at the end of the nineteenth century, at last led the French Republican authorities to decide in 1905 that there should no longer exist any tie between the French secular state and the religious bodies active in the country. Nevertheless, the French Law takes care of the ways and means of practising a said religion (the traditional monotheistic already existing ones), and the Interior Minister (*Ministre de l'Intérieur*) is in charge of religions.

Roughly, the 9 December 1905 Act established that special declared associations, created following the specifications of the 1 July 1901 Act (the law on associations), are henceforth in charge of taking care, at the level of local parishes, of the cost and public practice of the different religions recognized by the state (Catholic, Protestant, Jewish, Moslem). Particular rules govern their membership, their operation, their financial management, the administration of their property and their dissolution. These *associations cultuelles* (or, for the Catholic faith, *associations diocésaines*) can federate in wider "unions", taking sometimes the name of *Consistoires* (for the reformed Christian Church and for the Jewish synagogues). They must comply with the rules of the general organization of their respective religions (Catholic, Protestant, Jewish, Moslem). Very often, they are the center of groups of organizations active in welfare, social work, charity, education and culture, etc. They are very often the core and the impulsion center of a private school network.

Nonrecognized religions or sects may also create associations they would perhaps also call *associations cultuelles*: if they do not answer to the precise specifications and obligations of the aforesaid law of 1905, these organizations are legally considered as only associations of the French common law (the law of 1 July 1901). This may be compared to the situation in the United Kingdom: charities generally are recognized and enjoy privileges as long as they refer to some kind of deity; this need not be confined to the Church of England or to other forms of Christianity, but freemasonry and groups not founded on a belief in a deity are excluded.

Last but not least, unlike other declared associations, the *associations cultuelles* enjoy a very wide legal capacity regarding their resources, especially in matters of donations and legacies:

- reduced taxes on the purchase taxes of buildings which are needed for their operations or for those of their charities (as for some of the *associations reconnues d'utilité publique* – active in welfare, charity, social service);
- tax exemption for donations and legacies received;
- land tax exemption on building, etc.

Lastly, these special privileges in favor of the three monotheistic faiths do not seem yet to be granted to other churches, or to the various sects. So far, French administration and French judges have not accepted the extension of tax privileges to this type of religious body.

Religious congregations

Under the pre-Revolutionary regime, congregations could quite freely form themselves without authorization. They were considerably developed on the eve of the French Revolution of 1789, but they were suppressed by the Revolutionary laws of 13–19 February 1790 and 18 August 1792. Napoleon I and the *Restauration* authorized them again under certain conditions. The law of 1 July 1901 on associations states that congregations are a specific category of association: new creations were subject to authorization (the freedom of association did not apply to them and actually there were almost no new creations until 1970), those already existing were legally accepted, but in 1904 those active in education and school were dissolved by decree. During the German occupation, in 1942, the "authorization" was replaced by a "legal recognizance". This law also suppressed the "congregation offence to law" (unauthorized creation of a congregation). There probably exist presently in France between 200 and 250 congregations, comprising some 75,000/100,000 nuns and 6,500/20,000 monks.

The law of 1942 states that a French congregation is operated as a nondeclared association until it receives legal recognizance. At that point, a congregation enjoys more rights and privileges than an *association reconnue d'utilité publique*: it may possess real estate without restriction, and freely receive donations and legacies, directly or through the medium of its members.

On the tax level, *grosso modo*, legally recognized congregations enjoy the same rights as *associations reconnues d'utilité publique*, and the unrecognized enjoy those of declared associations. It has already been said that tax privileges and exemptions are the same as for all nonprofit organizations serving some special public benefit.

This last point relates the congregations to the general national pattern concerning the organizations which are nonprofit and which possibly are active in serving some public benefit. (It is obvious that, in the great majority of cases, congregations show themselves to be nonprofit organizations. They then follow the fate of all nonprofit organizations serving a public benefit.)

3.4.2 Political activities

The whole chapter on possible links between politics and association – in its aims, or in its activities – is a direct consequence of the freedom of association instituted by the law of 1 July 1901. In a democratic state, to achieve a political aim and to act consequently in the framework of legality are two quite licit situations. Most often, political parties are created in the form of an association. Political behavior and activities are allowed to the extent that the by-laws of a said association state that the aim and the activities of it are political. Let us nevertheless remember that some political parties are not declared since no rules compel them to do so: they have no legal entity, but it happens that their notoriety is such that everybody, including official authorities or courts, simply accepts the fact: this is the case of the Communist Party in France.

Seditious and factious groups are not allowed (especially since a 1936 Amendment to the 1901 law). On another side, the association's activities have to be consistent with its declared aims: these are the two limits to an association's activity in matter of politics. The rules are the same, for any kind of nonprofit (and, against all probability, forprofit) organization, and not only for associations. Taking into account these aforesaid remarks, this implies that well defined nonprofit organizations can engage in political activities, for instance in the following ways.

- Active participation in campaign activities, in the framework of general police regulations.

- Active lobbying for legislation with government or parliamentarians.
- Raising money for political campaigns. On this particular and delicate point, because of recent scandals related to methods used by political parties to finance their election campaigns, a series of rules have just been established governing such operations: on one side, public funding will be provided to political parties for their election campaigns following certain criteria, and expenses for campaigns will have to keep under certain maxima, and be controlled; on the other side, new tax-exemption rules were established in favour of those taxpayers who make donations for political campaigns.
- Candidates for political offices holding positions in nonprofit organizations are in principle free to do so. The custom is that in this case, these candidates resign their positions in their respective organizations; they generally also resign when they are appointed to an important official post, or elected to a political official assembly. It may happen that there is no resignation if the nonprofit organization is the political party of the new elect, or if the political office is a minor one.

One last point deserves a short note: the influence of the political parties *on* associations. The major political trends inspire various groupings: some take the shape of workers' unions, cooperatives, friendly societies; several are organized under the association statute and constitute a kind of idealistic, philosophic and also a strategic and tactical base for the corresponding parties. The whole question is rather sensitive, but has been resolved quite sensibly except for the money aspect (see the third point in the list above).

3.4.3 Business activities

Associations and business activities
For many, it might look obvious that the nonprofit aim of a nonprofit organization would not allow such an organization to carry on business activities, the definition of which is directly related to the concept of profit-making. (French Law does not really define business activities: it does not even clearly define an economic activity, but only commercial activity, following the old and

obsolete Code of Commerce. An *acte de commerce* is an action of interposition in the circulation of goods and services in order to make a profit. The tradesman is then the person or entity who carries out permanently as a profession a commercial activity.)

Business activities carried out by nonprofit organizations also raise a major problem, related to fair competition among the economic actors in a given market. Various privileges – legal, administrative, fiscal – granted to nonprofit organizations may lead them to benefit from a lighter burden than the one weighing on the other types of organizations (the forprofit ones). How then to justify the presence in the same market, with the same products and the same services offered, of two types of organizations, one of which is allegedly advantaged by a slighter burden on its production costs?

It is true that, more and more, such competition is met. This is the reason for measures taken by the legislature (an association enjoys less rights than other organizations, it cannot – so far – register in the *Registre de commerce et des sociétés*, it does not benefit from all advantages granted to forprofit organizations to stimulate their economic activity, etc.), or by the tax administration (a nonprofit organization which does not serve some special public benefit and is active on the general business market is subject to the same taxes as any other organization). It ought also to be stressed that, very often, nonprofit organizations which offer products and services do so for non-solvent disadvantaged customers, who anyway would not get their products or services from competing forprofit firms (and the said firms would probably not be interested in offering them products and services as well); sometimes, the products and services they propose may even have no equivalent on the market: they do not offer mercantile goods and services; very often, the nonprofit organizations' means of production cannot reach the profitability level of specialized forprofit organizations: they employ disadvantaged types of workers (handicapped, hard-core social cases, etc.), whose "productivity" is rather negative, and they often need extra educative and supervising staff. In such cases, non-paid voluntary work and tax privileges are not sufficient to balance strict professional work performed in the best conditions of competition. One has therefore to "relativize" this unfair competition objection, even if it is met only once in a while.

Anyway, the law of 1 July 1901, on the associations, which are the prototype of nonprofit organizations, involved no provision and no limits regarding economic or even commercial activities, provided that neither direct nor indirect profit sharing be the aim of the organization and/or take place among the membership.

The question came often before the court, generally asked by rival firms, or creditors of associations. For more than twenty years now, the Supreme Civil Court has issued a series of decisions which are now the law on this subject: in 1970, it stated that an association could carry out permanently commercial activities to achieve its nonprofit goal and ensure the necessary budget for this end (13 May 1970, D. 1970, 644). In 1981, it was asserted that, in court, types of evidence which are used between tradesmen and companies could be used against associations which carry out permanently commercial activities (*Bulletin civil IV*, no. 149, p. 117). In 1985, the answer being that an association can carry out permanent commercial activities, the only question pending was to decide when and at which point an association could be juridically qualified a "tradesman"; this qualification involves consequences on various levels: juridical, tax, and possibly the discussion of the nonprofit aim of the organization.

Associations and business ownership
Following the 1 July 1901 law (article 6), associations are allowed to purchase, own and manage the buildings which are necessary for their operations and meetings, to receive public funding and subscriptions from their members. Public utility associations and some well defined categories are entitled to receive donations and legacies (article 11). Courts have also accepted direct cash gifts to these organizations as licit resources.

The same article 11 states that transferable shares owned by an association have to be registered securities. This has led to the conclusion (with the agreement of the courts) that the declared associations may purchase (and the *associations reconnues d'utilité publique* may purchase or receive free of charge) transferable shares under the form of registered securities. This implies that an association is able to become a partner in a company: in a *société civile* (that is to say another nonprofit) or in a *société commerciale* (a commercial firm). This means, further, that an association may be the senior partner in a company, if it possesses the majority of the shares. In this sense, it may be said that an association is allowed to own a more or less important part of companies active in business.

Associations and business operation
On the level of the common civil law, it was said that, in the framework of the nonprofit aim of an association, this organization was able to carry out business activities. When the association is a partner, a major partner, or even the only partner in a company (the case of the "EURL": *Entreprise unipersonnelle à responsabilité limitée*), the business operation is led through the medium of this company. Many associations which do not wish to create ambiguities between their nonprofit aim and their business-type activities, choose to take a partnership in a subsidiary "daughter" company or companies – of a forprofit type – to which they delegate the performance of business-type activities. The corresponding possible profit thus generated is channeled back to the association, and that money is supposed to help the association carry out the budget of its nonprofit aim.

Such arrangements and developments are rather recent, and take place in the general framework of companies' groups and trusts. An association, according to the type of case, may play either the role of a "mother" organization of a group, or the role of a subsidiary "daughter" company.

Associations, business operation and tax status
On the level of the tax law, the tax status of the associations operating businesses directly, or through "subsidiary daughter company" activities, is a rather complex one and is dependent on the case in point. Regarding corporation tax:

- When an association which carries out business activities directly wishes to obtain or to maintain tax privileges established in favor of nonprofit organizations (especially in the case of corporation tax), it often has to bring evidence to the fiscal authorities that the activities in question are needful, unavoidable, for reaching the nonprofit aim of the organization. It has altogether to comply with the criteria listed by the fiscal administration on nonprofit management, and on the public benefit or the public utility of its activities (cf. 3.3 *Taxation*, pp. 66–73), to get the benefit of tax exemption on corporation tax and VAT.

- When business activities are carried out by a "daughter company", taxes on the company's activity (especially corporation tax) are those imposed on any other company performing the same type of activity. The possible share of profits earned by the company and going to the association is subject to a residual tax only (to avoid a double taxation: this privilege belonged only to mother companies until recently, but it has been extended to mother associations as well). In this hypothesis, in several cases, the fiscal administration questions the nonprofit management or even the nonprofit aim of the association, according to the criteria list enumerated in 3.3 above, and imposes the full taxes on the whole of the associations' revenues, should its conclusions lead it to think that the nonprofit criteria are not strictly respected.

In such cases, the tax control officer bears in mind altogether the following three points:

- the relative extent and the type of businesses in which an association and possibly its "daughter subsidiary companies" are engaged;
- the more or less complementary character of these activities with regard to the aim of the association;
- the way the budgetary needs have to be matched.

It is obvious that genuine business-type activities, having neither direct nor indirect link with the aim of the association, and budgetary needs which might be answered by other means, lead the tax control to deprive the association of any kind of nonprofit tax privileges, for the two reasons expressed below:

- All taxpayers are subject to equal treatment for similar situations and activities.
- Fair competition among firms demands that there be no distortion in the tax treatment of economical actors in the same fields and in the same markets. In this sense, profits generated by activities related to the mission of the organization give the association a better chance to keep the advantage of tax privileges attached to a nonprofit organization, than profits unrelated to the aim of the association. The tax law, on this point as on many others, is more restrictive than the civil law.

What has just been described relates to corporation tax. Other especially complex rules govern the regulations on VAT. On matters of business-type activities directly performed, an association is either VAT-exempted, or pays the VAT on the whole of its economic activities, or on the part which cannot be exempted, because of the nature of these activities, or the way they are carried out (cf. 3.3 *Taxation*). Needless to say, activities carried out by a "subsidiary daughter company" are subject to the VAT payment like those of any other company or individual tradesman or businessman.

3.4.4 Ethics

It is indubitable that ethics have a strong relation with the creation and the operation of nonprofit organizations such as the associations. The mutual influence between ethics and law on the subject is, however, difficult to ignore. The keystone of the "ethical" behavior of the association is precisely expressed in article 1 of the 1 July 1901 law, forbidding any kind of profit sharing among the members of the organization. This legal prohibition is the consequence of the moral basis the creators of the association wanted to give to it, and in turn, this article 1 shaped the rules and usage of the associations's ethical behaviour. But it must be stressed that, for the reasons already given, little is said by legal texts; jurisprudence has added a little more, but a lot remains still vague.

Although what will follow may apply to any kind of nonprofit organization, we will focus on the case of the association, and observe how law, judge and administration "translate" their understanding of the nonprofit organization ethics into rules or decisions, and how, in turn, these rules and decisions illustrate the nonprofit concept.

It has already been said that one way the common law judge and the tax administration used to test the reality of nonprofit sharing was to observe the way and the level at which salaries and compensation for expenses were paid, especially to people who were either founders, administrators or mere members of the association. Thus restrictions all proceed from the interpretation the judge or the administration give to article 1 of the law of 1 July 1901.

Speaking for instance of *executive salaries*: "the association cannot pay a salary to a member of the organization for his activity in the framework of the aims of the association. But the association is entitled to pay wages to *people who are not members of the organization*, for the services rendered by them" (Rép. du ministre de l'Intérieur et de la Décentralisation, Journal Officiel, Débats à l'Assemblée Nationale, 21 mai 1984). This presupposes that there are positively *services rendered*, and that the level of the wages is adjusted to the kind of services rendered. Relatively too high wages might lead to suspicion of a fraud against article 1 of the law of 1 July 1901.

More generally, the question asked is: is it possible to be simultaneously a *member* or a leader or an administrator of an association on one side, and an *employee* receiving a salary on the other? There is no single answer to it.

On the common law level (civil law)

- Members (non-leaders) cannot receive a salary for activities directly linked with the aims of the association (as stated before): this becomes a kind of indirect benefit sharing in the framework of the association contract. But a member is entitled to become an employee of the organization for a "technical" job performed (which could be performed as well for a similar salary in any other concern). (Cour d'Appel de Versailles, 13 February 1987.)
- A principle not expressed in the law but more or less related to a profit sharing prohibition is that leaders and administrators can receive no salary for the offices performed. They can only get reimbursement or compensation for their expenses in the service of their organization (this provision appears in almost all the statutes of French associations).
- The most recent doctrine of the *Conseil d'Etat* judges is that an employee of an association can become a member of the board of directors, without losing his job, provided that this paid job has no link with his non-paid office as an administrator, and that the number of administrators who are also employees of the organization is not "preponderant" in the board (*"Avis" du Conseil d'Etat*, 22 October 1970, *Revue trimestrielle de droit sanitaire et social* 1972, 547, no. 32). Nevertheless, the same doctrine excludes the plurality of offices between the capacity of employee and the posts of Chairman, Vice-Chairman, Secre-

tary-general or Treasurer (*"Avis" du Conseil d'Etat*, 21 October 1987, *Juris-associations*, no. 36, November – December 1988). But very recent court decisions do not even dismiss the idea of this plurality in some cases of an executive salaried office and the office of Chairman (*Cour de cassation*, 26 February 1986 and 17 December 1987, in "Droit social" (Blaise, 1988)).

On the tax law level

- As said before, the tax administration relies on a number of criteria for establishing that an organization has a nonprofit aim and/or is providing a public benefit service. Its main concern is to check that salaries paid match real jobs, that compensations cover real expenses, and that the level of the wages or compensation paid is in accordance with the tasks performed, since these wages or compensation should not actually constitute, directly or indirectly, a kind of particular profit for a member of the board of directors, or a mere member of the organization, or even any other individual (Droit administratif, no. 3A-3151, 15 February 1987).

The question of *fundraising costs* becomes a sensible item for those associations which raise funds, especially when they appeal to the public at large. Many such charitable or humanitarian organizations created in 1989 a joint committee, to establish a "deontology charter" in order to insure their operations' transparency. As important as this question might be for those associations in action in this field, it cannot be said that there were no particular regulations of this matter, which lies at the boundary of ethical principles, technical contingencies and psychological realities. Governmental projects of "framing" this new type of activities for most of the French associations concerned very recently became consistent with a chapter of the law of 7 August 1991. According to it, national appeals or fundraising campaigns have now to be announced beforehand, and records of the utilization have to be audited by the *Cour des comptes*. Anyway, possible litigation on this subject – raised by donors, for instance – can come before the court under the rules of the general common law, and not under the auspices of some special law governing nonprofit organizations only.

On the basis of what was said before, *insider trading and self-*

dealing, in the bosom of an association, does not raise particular problems, except for shelter and food (cf. the case of old people's homes or clinics, for instance). But there must be evidence that this kind of operation takes place *only between the association and its members*. In such cases, no taxes, especially VAT, are imposed on them, and there is no possibility of litigation with external firms offering similar products or services. Regarding taxes, shelter and food follow the general pattern of the business activities (see above).

Discrimination in the selection of clients has to be dealt with, in the following two precise ways.

- The association offers goods or services as any other firm active on the market does, its purpose being to sell its production, which is often the result of the occupation of disadvantaged people (handicapped, etc.): this production is subject to the general economical regulation in matter of trade, and for taxation (or tax-exemption), to the rules which have been described before. Discrimination and selection of clients are very strongly regulated, and generally forbidden except for some products (drugs, exclusive "de luxe" creations, etc.).
- The association has a charitable or humanitarian aim, and selects "negatively" its clients, offering to the most disadvantaged people, or to those belonging to a given category of the population unable to pay the regular market price, services or goods at a very cheap price or even free of charge. There is a general agreement that, on this basis, an association is free to organize its selection according to the criteria it will determine. Here, too, tax-exemption privileges are generally granted to those associations which serve that kind of public benefit, and are of public utility. Indeed, the concerned organizations have to limit their operations strictly to their "special" clients, and not offer their products and services to anyone, according to the rules of fair competition.

To sum up this point, it should be emphasized once again that the central "ethical" behavior of nonprofit organizations lies in the fact that there can be neither the direct nor the indirect possibility of anyone getting a material share of the possible profit generated by the nonprofit organization. Only salaries or charitable help may be envisaged. This nevertheless raises the question of the possible limits imposed ethically and/or legally on the associations in their quest for profit: how far can an association go in this direction? One answer looks clear, and has already been emphasized: the aim of a given association cannot comprise that of making profit, not even for distributing among the members, but only for using it for the most commendable charitable purposes. Making profit is possible and acceptable, when activities performed to reach the organization's goals happen to generate profits, or when making profits is part of an educational or a social process. Here we hit one of the most sensitive points of the "associative philosophy", the "associative morality", to which the bulk of the leaders of the "associative world" are most committed.

3.4.5 Legal trends and debates

Since the nonprofit sector in France is chiefly the sector of associations, the main issues facing the nonprofit sector (today or in recent years) are actually those concerning associations. Issues and developments can be connected with three major concerns:

- The principle of *"liberty of association"*, its legal and ethic relation with the "nonprofit aim" (leading to the original participation of volunteers – benevolent, unpaid people, on the boards and in the action fields, thus justifying the name of "voluntary organization" borne by the association in the UK for instance), the limits of the association as a legal entity (in terms of its limited juridical capacity), or conversely its similarity to other legal persons (in the matter of the liability of the organization, of its board and of its board members, for instance).
- The widening of the scope of the *associations' activities* towards public benefit on one side (making the associations a kind of partner of the public authorities), and "economic and business activities" on the other (making the associations partners and competitors of forprofit concerns),
- *The financing of the associations'* operations and activities, by public funding and various tax privileges, by subscriptions and donations, by business-type revenues.

Significant developments have taken place in these three directions in recent years, chiefly because of the very significant increase in the number of new associations created every year, because of the widening of the aims of these organizations, because of the fact that they henceforth form an irreplaceable and important group of social and economic actors in the state's life. Very often, issues belong to two or three of these directions, for instance in the following matters.

The treatment of charitable donations in tax laws

France was rather late on this point, compared to several other countries, especially the United Kingdom and the United States. Consistent progress was reached in the 1980s, even if there is still a gap to fill with the most advanced countries: many humanitarian and charitable organizations now benefit from the new legal provisions (as they have been summarily described in section 3.3 on taxation) consisting chiefly in income tax-exemptions in favor of donors. As for the organization beneficiary, there are special provisions for privileges, also mentioned above, mainly in favour of *associations reconnues d'utilité publique* and of some welfare and charitable voluntary organizations.

The new provisions have even involved the relatively new need for regulation of those organizations which run nationwide appeals through the modern media (mailings, radio, television, etc.). On one side, the concerned major appeal organizations arrange henceforth among themselves voluntary regulation of their operations, revenues and expenditures (*Comité de la Charte*, Code of deontology in matter of appeals). Also a very recent law makes provisions to control those organizations appealing to the generosity of the public at large (*loi no. 91–772 relative... au contrôle des comptes des organismes faisant appel à la générosité publique*, of 7 August 1991). A law of 23 July 1987, on patronage (*loi no. 87-571 sur le mécénat*), governs donations to foundations, and a more recent one of 4 July 1990 governs companies' foundations (*loi créant les fondations d'entreprise*) and donations to them.

The provisions for chartering or incorporating nonprofit organizations

The liberty of association concept demands that there be neither restraint nor control to the creation of associations. A very few rules exist in the law of 1 July 1901, and in its *décret d'application* as to the statutes' wording, and there is no provision for any kind of incorporation. This has been described in section 3.2.

Nevertheless, because of the development of economic or business-type activities performed by the associations, and of the forthcoming completed European Common Market, there are at present some questions about the opportunity of having, for *some* associations, some kind of registration or corporation.

- Speaking of associations which permanently perform business-type activities, some jurists preconize their voluntary registration in the *Registre du Commerce et des Sociétés*, which is the corporation instrument for tradesmen and for companies – of any form. This might have several advantages for the associations, even if it represents a kind of restraint. One advantage, for instance, is that on the issue of building rental, French Law favors the renting of shop or office premises to corporate entities registered in the *Registre du Commerce et des Sociétés*. In matters of relations with bankers, clients, suppliers, partners or competitors, and more generally in matters of associations' credibility, which suffer from insufficient visibility, such a registration might help the concerned associations.
- Speaking of associations which are preparing for a Europe-wide scope of activity in the framework of the EU completion, it has to be pointed out that the legal treatment of the nonprofit sector (and of the association-type organizations) varies from one country member to another. In some, like Denmark, there is no registration, no chartering, no declaration or publication. In others, like Germany, there is a registration in different places, according to the type of activities to be performed (economic or not economic). In others, like Spain, preliminary administrative authorization is needed. The most recent developments of the EU Commission together with the EU Parliament and the EU Economic and Social Committee led to a project of a "European Association", which is supposed to be a kind of synthesis of the different types existing in the European countries. A Commission regulation is at present being studied, of standard European statutes, possibly to be adopted by existing associations throughout the EU countries preparing for Europe-wide activities, or by newly formed associations forming directly themselves with Europe-wide aims and activities. This may lead to a kind of incorporation of some European associations, in France as well as in other EU member countries.

Restrictions or regulations associated with receipt of government support

The nonprofit aim (and its most likely consequence, the service of some public benefit) made associations the natural partners of the public authorities, nationally or locally, of almost all of the government's departments. This partnership was not put in place without various difficulties, because of the comparative "weight" of the partners and the fact that public money was in question. It gave way to a series of legal and administrative rules aimed at modalities and methods of the associations' cooperation with the public service at large, or with various aims of general interest, or with official regulation by the authorities and the administrative judges of the use made of the public funding.

Tax privileges, attached to the activities of that type of association, have already been described in section 3.3. The general partnership rules may be found in several texts, laws and decisions since the creation of the associations, and more especially since the 1930s. Each government department organizes its own mode of partnership (*arrêtés ministériels, circulaires,* etc.) in the general framework of the law, and from time to time, an official order of the government (*décret, décret-loi, ordonnance, circulaire du Premier ministre,* etc.), draws a synthesis of the situation. Restrictions and regulations describe the way the action by the concerned organizations has to be performed, and the technical and administrative controls attached. Very often, there are restrictions on the wording of the statutes and by-laws of the organization, the way decisions are taken, the way the boards have to be elected or designated, the part of the decision which lies in the hands of the government representative(s) on the organization boards, the methods of spending the public funds.

The following official texts give a good view of the whole question: *Circulaire 2010* of 27 January 1975 from the Prime Minister relating to the relationship between public administrations and general interest associations (*relative aux rapports entre les collectivités publiques et les associations assurant des tâches d'intérêt général*), *Circulaire* of 10 March 1979 from the Prime Minister (JCP 1979, III, no. 48289) on the fight against practices contrary to free competition (*relative à la lutte contre les pratiques contraires à une concurrence loyale*), *Circulaire* from the Prime Minister of 15 June 1988 (JO 7 April 1988, Pp. 4584 & 4585), relating to dealings between central government and associations which benefit from public funding (*relative aux rapports entre l'État et les associations bénéficiaires de financements publics*).

A complex system of *a priori* control is built around the *Ministère des Finances* and all other ministries concerned with the activities of a given association. The use made of public funding justifies also *a posteriori* control by courts, and particularly of those which deal especially with public expenditures made from public funds (*Conseil d'Etat and Tribunal Administratif* for the legal aspects, *Cour des Comptes* and *Chambres Régionales des Comptes* for the use of the money and the bookkeeping). The *Cour des Comptes* is qualified for all problems involving public money and associations (*Loi no. 67-483 du 22 juin 1967, loi no. 82-594 du 10 juillet 1982*). And as said above, a recent law of 7 August 1991 entitles the *Cour des comptes* to carry on some control of the books of the organizations which appeal to public generosity in general.

Lobbying or political activity by nonprofits
This issue has been developed in section 3.4.2 on political activities.

Nonprofit/forprofit competition
This problem becomes one of the major issues regarding activities carried out by nonprofit organizations, especially the associations, because of the economic impact of their economic or business activities, on two main levels: the level of the nonprofit organizations' ethics, the level of the possible unfair competition with the forprofit sector (mainly because of possible tax privileges). On the ethical level, the nonprofit sharing aim raises the question of how far to go on the profit-making way, without altering the very nature of the association (one has to remember here the traditional philosophico-religious contempt in this country for money, identified with dirty money).

On the other level, official legal and governmental texts try from time to time to solve the problem, keeping in mind that there are no provisions for this matter in the law of 1 July 1901 (see above, section 3.2.2), but there is a constant pressure from forprofit firms: they fear this particular competition from organizations which do not follow the "normal ethics" of other market actors, which have an odd attitude to the "profit" aim, and which, sometimes, get the advantage of tax-exemption privileges and unpaid voluntary workers, and are thus supposed to bear a lighter financial burden on their products and services prices.

Among these texts, very often issued under the pressure of the business milieux, are those already cited above in section 3.4.5, p. 87 – particularly on practices contrary to competition in commercial and distribution fields (*the Circulaire du Premier Ministre du 10 mars 1979 relative à la lutte contre les pratiques contraires à une concurrence loyale dans le domaine du commerce et de la distribution*), and also on free pricing and against paracommercial practices (*ordonnance du 1 décembre 1986 (JO du 9 décembre 1986*, p. 14773) *relative à la liberté des prix et de la concurrence*), especially in article 37, al. 2. "*Circulaire du 12 Août 1987 du Ministre de l'Economie, des Finances et de la Privatisation relative à la lutte contre les pratiques paracommerciales* (JO du 23 août 1987, p. 9704 et seq.).

Outside the case of associations delivering goods or services to members or particular populations of the country who would not – or could not – get the same from other firms on the market, this general problem becomes especially acute in the case of associations, whose aim is to offer to the population at large products and services directly comparable to similar ones offered by "ordinary" firms or tradesmen. Many organizations of this kind are organized to help disadvantaged or handicapped people to re-enter – more or less – the "main" stream of social life: they give them a job to perform in their production process, and altogether they bring them the necessary care and attention their physical, intellectual or social condition demands. These organizations bear the generic name of "entreprises intermédiaires", "entreprises d'insertion", "associations intermédiaires", "centres d'aide par le travail". Because of their particular aim, the most convenient structure for these types of organizations is clearly the association (but in some cases, one may also find among them companies – limited, by shares, of cooperative type, etc.).

Their general set-up comprises a production department, which looks more or less like that of any other firm in competition for the same product; and an educational department, which is specific to that type of organization: very often, this department is subsidized by public funding or non-business-type revenues. This additional burden on the normal productive structure and the theoretically somewhat poorer "productivity" of the man-power does not – except in some cases – really create competition. The Courts bear in mind this special situation, and either blame those associations doing harm to the other concerns of the market, or, more often, acquit the accused organization of the offence of unfair competition. Tax administration follows the same route, perhaps a little more drastically against the associations.

To avoid such problems, there are from time to time efforts to transform into private "standard" companies those associations which have succeeded in their integration operation, and subsequently their aim tends to change into that of a normal forprofit organization. Very often, this transformation looks impossible, precisely because of the legal difference existing between the two types of organizations (see above, 3.1 and 3.2).

In other cases, solutions have been sought through the creation, by the associations of "daughter firms", of the commercial type (*sociétés commerciales filiales*), in order to let them, instead of the associations, perform the business-type activities. If this solution looks acceptable from a purely legal point of view, there are nevertheless problems with the fiscal administration, which involves the concerned associations in a group of organizations, and imposes corporation tax on the whole operation – including the nonprofit one. This aspect of the problem is one of the most acute, met by associations in this case.

This general question of business-type activities performed by associations is a permanent ethical concern for the legal authorities, for the specialized jurists, and for the leaders of these organizations. Today, business-type activity has become a "must" for most of the associations, often closely linked to the organizations' key objectives. And ultimately, neither law nor the courts forbid it. The right balance between ethics and needs, between nonprofit and business, between making money and sharing money, between public benefit and private aim is sometimes difficult to reach.

The legal liability of nonprofit boards
The answer to this question lies in two references to the French civil code, and in the jurisprudential constructions of the courts.

On the basis of articles 1382ff. of the French civil code, leaders and board members of any kind of legal entity (company, voluntary organization, association, etc.) are personally responsible for the shortcomings and mistakes performed in their capacity, and they fall under the corresponding penalties. But, on the basis of article 1992 of the same code, the liability of an unpaid board member (as is generally the case in nonprofit organizations) is judged less strictly than that of a paid board member.

It has here to be remembered that up to very recently, there was no penal liability of legal entities as such, and therefore no penal liability of the boards as a body, but only of the leading members of it. This applied to forprofit or to nonprofit boards. Very recent provisions of the law, which has not yet really come into force, establish the new legal principle (for France), of the direct liability of legal entities, consisting chiefly in fines or court-decided dissolution.

Articles 1382 to 1386 of the French civil code have been the foundation on which the courts have built a very important and complex system of rules of liability. Among the many types of possible liabilities concerning board members, and apart from the one created by contracts, one can list the following:

- Civil responsibility. Associations, like all other legal entities, have a general obligation of carefulness and care in their operations and activities toward their members or third parties. Board members can therefore, according to the situation, be considered as responsible by the association, by its members, or by any other people who may be harmed.
- Penal responsibility. If a board member in his/her capacity commits illicit acts, he/she may be sued for them.
- Labour responsibility. Board members are responsible for the application of the labour laws, for instance the payment of all labour taxes for their organization.
- Tax responsibility. Since a law of 1980, leaders and board members of nonprofit organizations are responsible for the tax situation of their organization: statements and schedules, and payment of possible corresponding taxes.
- Board members' liability in case of insolvency and bankruptcy (*cessation de paiements, faillite personnelle*). Since 1967, and above all since 1985, board members of nonprofit organizations are under the same rules as any other type of organization (commercial firms, companies, etc.), as far as they develop economic activities: this involves practically all of the nonprofit organiza-

tions today. The law provides in some cases that penalties can be imposed on the leaders and board members: their personal property may be affected, civil and penal sanctions can be taken against them (they may be banned from leading any organization, fined, etc.). Finally, personal bankruptcy may be declared against a board member, possibly involving very significant fines and imprisonment.

Relations between local or national nonprofits and international and regional bodies

This matter is still the least developed among all those considered in this study, but it is also the one which is likely to experience the most important developments in the years to come, at least in the EU framework, or through the setting-up of "nongovernmental international organizations" (NGIO). Difficulties come from the fact that associations, "voluntary organizations", "nonprofit organizations", "unions", etc. not only bear different names from country to country, but also have different legal and administrative structures. Exact counterparts from one country to another are hard to find, although the nonprofit aim is to constitute a kind of common platform.

- NGIOs have already existed for years, whether their headquarters be in France or elsewhere in the world. They generally have a humanitarian, scientific or cultural aim. Because of differences in national legislation, those whose headquarters are not in France have no legal existence, but if they comply with French rules, they can set up a branch of their nonprofit organization, most generally an association, in France under the auspices of the law of 1 July 1901, and officially presumed independent of the "mother organization". With some exceptions, the same system exists in other countries. To remedy such a situation, the Council of Europe adopted on 24 April 1986 a European Treaty to ensure, under precise conditions, the automatic legal existence, throughout the member states of the Council of Europe, of a said NGIO property registered in its country of origin. For many political and tax reasons, this treaty is not yet in force, as the countries concerned – apart from a few – have not yet ratified it. This treaty will be able to give an important impulse to the action of the NGIO, which presently suffers from lack of liberty of action and of funding of their activities. In the meantime, many NGIOs already have links with international or regional bodies: they very often have an informal seat in some of them, with a "consultative" voice – in the various branches of the UNO (in New York, Geneva, Paris or elsewhere), in the Council of Europe (in Strasbourg). They perform official missions in a humanitarian, scientific, cultural, charitable or educational capacity for these central international bodies, and receive from them part of their funding. The same applies to NGIOs and the EU Commission in Brussels, for which various NGIOs, some of them French, carry out missions and from which they receive some funding.

- The EU is also a source of hope for better European transnational activity on the part of many national associations, which also sometimes suffer from the fact that they are confined inside their national boundaries, henceforth too narrow for their scopes and aims. For years, there has been a project of creating a structure of a "European association", supposed to accord with national legislation in the various countries, and involving ethical and legal characteristics of the present nonprofit organizations existing in the member countries of the EU. Here, the complexity of the problem of harmonizing the various laws on nonprofit organizations creates huge difficulties (see section 3.1, *Basic principles*). By the end of 1991, at last, after years of discussions and studies, the EU Commission issued an outline for a "European association", together with the outline of a "European Company", which has been under consideration for some twenty years already!

- Nevertheless, relations exist between French associations or groups of associations (having generally corresponding aims: welfare, humanitarian, cultural, educational, religious, charitable, scientific, economic, politic, etc.) and their counterparts in Western Europe, and also now in Eastern Europe, and even in extra-European countries, especially in the USA or in the Third World. These relations have, so far, no formal structure, but allow exchanges of ideas and experiences, of manpower, of membership, of know-how, of financial help in cases admitted by local laws, etc.

As said earlier, international bodies, like the United Nations

Organization, or the Council of Europe, or the Commission of the European Community, or the European Parliament, have semi-formal or informal relations with French-based NGIOs, as they have with others, based in other countries of Europe. At last, and especially around the European Community bodies, one can observe the enforcement of associations' lobbies, cooperating in either the humanitarian, the charitable, or the cultural actions of these bodies, or helping accelerate the advent of the European-wide field of the associations' activity.

3.4.6 Concluding remarks

As emphasized before, although this is most often the case, there is no legal basic identification between the two concepts of the nonprofit organization and the association; the aim of the latter has to be a nonprofit one, i.e. must not allow any sharing out of profits among the founders, leaders and members. But organizations which do not bear the label of association might also claim nonprofit status, should they fulfil the required condition of not sharing profits, directly or indirectly, among their membership. *This is the reason why the legal texts, when necessary, always mention nonprofit organizations, and not only associations.* (Let us remember here that foundations, among other groupings mentioned in section 3.1, are also nonprofit organizations, although of a different type.)

Also, freedom of association is neither a cause nor an effect of the nonprofit aim of the association: these two characteristics of the association are both the result of the legislator's intention when the legal entity "association" was created in 1901 (see above, section 3.2.2). Everyone is entirely free to found an association together with other people; the aim of their organization has only to be licit, and allow no profit – direct or indirect – in favour of the founders, leaders and members.

The real consequences of both the freedom of association and the compulsory nonprofit aim of an association are, on one hand, the wide range of possible aims open to associations, especially in public benefit servicing, and, on the other hand, the capacity for receiving voluntary money contributions, and the role open to a specific category of social actors, which makes it the most charac-teristic feature of this kind of organization: the benevolent, unpaid, voluntary people who constitute the membership and the leadership of the associations. The association has not the exclusiveness of such a category of people, but there is no doubt that these people find, through the means of the associations, the best way of expressing themselves and intervening in innumerable sectors of social life at large, especially those regarding the private voluntary service of public benefit.

These aforesaid characteristics have shaped the vocation of the association: easy to constitute, easy to adapt to all situations, the association shows itself as a privileged social type of organization, for answering to and serving all kinds of constantly evolving needs of our society, for providing a framework for the management of new forms of action, forms which differ altogether from those performed in private forprofit economic activity, or from those of the official public action. This is less a phenomenon of subsidiarity, or of solidarity, or of charity, or of religious inspiration, or of friendly and social organization, or of freedom, than a wider phenomenon (comprising each of these aspects), of an independent sector of human individual and/or collective activity, closely related to the nonprofit sector at large. This explains the wide success of this kind of organization: probably today more than 700,000 in France, and new creations every year multiplied.

A word ought to be said about the concept of subsidiarity. In some countries, this word is used to describe the intervention process of a given entity. The principle is that an action has to be carried out at the very level where it has to be done, by the people who belong to that level (for instance, the answer to an individual welfare need in a commune, in a township, has to be first sought after on the spot, in the family, in the neighborhood, among the people or organizations close to the place where the need exists, in its immediate environment). Should this be impossible, the principle of subsidiarity will lead to a search for the answer at a higher level: region, state, etc.

In France, the historical background for ages reversed this process. For a very long time, France has been used to seeing the state (the "welfare state", the "providence state", the "central power", the "top"), as responsible in the first instance for answering all the citizens' and residents' needs: this is the direct consequence of the strong centralization which characterized France for a long time. Should the state show an incapacity for doing so (because of bureaucracy, because of an insufficient understanding of situations at the ground level, because of liaison difficulties between the extensive state machinery and situations at individual level), then the intervention of some "intermediary" entity is required to answer – or at least to help to answer – the given need: welfare, social, cultural, etc. Sometimes, local official authorities (the town council, for instance) are in a position to provide the proper answer, or private individuals, organizations or firms. Relatively often, this is the preferred ground of the associations' intervention. This shows that subsidiarity in France (if ever this concept might be applicable in this country) so far follows the reverse of the process which takes place in other countries like Germany, for instance.

Nevertheless, the processes of decentralization, and of integration of the EU countries in a common unique economical and social system, will probably have an influence on the French centralized tradition, and the concept of subsidiarity will have to be used the way it is elsewhere: from the bottom to the top, and not vice versa.

This will perhaps help to understand the way French associations generally intervene, and the rationale underlying the public funding of many associations' activities by the state's authorities.

Notes

1   This chapter is written by Sami Castro, Ph.D in Law, legal advisor of UNIOPSS (*Union Interfédérale des Oeuvres Privées Sanitaires et Sociales*), the most important umbrella organization for private health and welfare nonprofit organizations.

Chapter 4

CONTOURS OF THE FRENCH NONPROFIT SECTOR

The nonprofit sector today is the result of a long and conflictual history, as seen in chapter 2. These historical developments have been reflected in the steady legal status of the 1901 Act, which unified very heterogeneous nonprofit organizations, as shown in chapter 3. What is the size, scope and composition of the nonprofit sector in France today? What are the main resources of the nonprofit organizations? What do the nonprofit organizations do in France today and how many persons are involved in their activities? Such are the questions which will be answered in the present chapter.

These questions are a great challenge because the nonprofit sector was a "terra incognita" as stated in the introductory chapter. So, to use the full spectrum of available data, to fill the major statistical gaps, and finally to build up the estimates, we needed a coordinated research scheme and a methodology common to the other countries included in the Comparative Project. We will begin by presenting the challenge and the methodology.

4.1 The challenge

For a long while, the researchers interested in the nonprofit sector were sociologists: to associate with others is the practice of a fundamental freedom, which extends in democratic countries. In nonprofit organizations, leadership and initiative are important topics and the change in nonprofits' aims can be viewed as a symbol of social change (Heran, 1988; Forse, 1984; Marchal, 1990).

Consistent with this problem, the surveys conducted by the *Institut National de la Statistique et des Etudes Economiques* (INSEE), the French central statistical office, or by the CREDOC, a public research agency studying the consumption and ways of living, were focused on membership, multi-membership and their evolution, and on the profile of associative members (Heran, 1988; Haeusler, 1988). This statistical evidence is still of great though limited interest.

But the relatively steady state of membership in nonprofit organizations was contrasting with the booming creation of associations – one of the rare reliable figures on association – and in the early 1980s, there was a progressive awareness that the economic dimension of the nonprofit sector was overlooked by everybody: *by the public authorities* which viewed the delivery of many public interest services by nonprofit organizations in the areas of education, culture, sports, health and social services as a prolongation of the public sector monopoly; *by the national accountants*, who recorded in a residual sector – the *administrations privées* (private nonprofit institutions serving households) – the production of some nonprofits as 0.3 per cent of GDP, i.e. nearly nothing (see the mode of delineation below); and *by the nonprofit leaders* themselves, who feared their organizations would be considered as commercial businesses if their economic activity was recorded and who emphasized first their social role.

Despite those behaviors, there was a growing demand for statistical evidence on the size and scope of the French social economy, and especially on its "terra incognita", the associations and the foundations, coming from the new leaders of *Économie sociale* umbrellas: *CNLAMCA, Délégation à l'Economie Sociale*, or a special learned society, the ADDES, *Association pour le Développement de la Documentation sur l'Economie Sociale* (Association to promote evidence on social economy) which was created in 1982 to support the building up of a satellite account (an appendix of the national accounting core framework) on social economy and initiated conferences on this topic. The ADDES first conference in 1983 drew the boundaries of social economy (Vienney and Weber, 1983) and gave a rough estimate of the employment in social economy, 6 per cent of the total labor force (Kaminski, 1983). The ADDES second conference focused on associations, the most important and less recorded part of *économie sociale*. For this conference, we collected and criticized the statistical evidence on associations existing in 1984; let us summarize the main statements:

- number of associations: no reliable figure;
- new associations created every year: reliable data since 1965. As there are no statistics on the disappearing of associations, the number of living associations cannot be deduced;
- reliable data on membership and on socio-demographic characteristics of members;
- associations in national accounting: split in many sectors and the *administrations privées* sector gives underestimated and bad quality data;
- giving and volunteering: no data at all at the moment.

Finally we insisted on the fact that every survey used its own classification and therefore statistical evidence was neither comparable nor cumulative. Then building a unique standard classification of nonprofit organizations was a major issue (Archambault, 1984).

Six years later, when the Johns Hopkins Comparative Project started, this statement was still true. The satellite account of social economy was marking time, because of a lack of interest from INSEE, from the organizations themselves and from the *Délégation à l'Économie sociale*. In 1989, the government asked Claudine Padieu, a high-level statistician, to collect and criticize all the data sources on social economy in France. The Padieu report (1990) made some proposals to improve the French statistical system: elaboration of an official classification of nonprofits, improvements in SIRENE file and launching of organizational surveys. But the advice was not entirely followed.

So it was a great opportunity and also a great challenge to be involved in a comparative project aiming to map and measure the nonprofit sector cross-nationally. Now we can answer with precision the important questions asked of the nonprofit sector since 1975: what is the turnover of the French nonprofit sector? The 1990 Padieu report assumes a guesstimate of 100 billion FF. and the 1993 Chéroutre report assumed "more than 100 billion", but in an interview Marie-Thérèse Chéroutre assumed 150 billion FF. Our figure is more than 200 billion[1] and it can be broken down into its components.

What part of the resources of the nonprofit sector is coming from the state, from the local governments, from social security and what part is coming from private giving, from dues, fees and sales? Nobody dared to advance a percentage, and now we may give such ratios at the group level. The extent of employment in the sector and its full-time equivalent has also been computed.

Of course these data are the result of a grand strategy and a multipurpose approach. So it is necessary to spell out how it was done, where the data come from, how reliable they can be considered, and how they are used as building blocks to construct our big jigsaw puzzle.

4.2 Estimating the French nonprofit sector: methodology

Here we will provide a narrative of our strategy and approach to measure the nonprofit sector. This description focuses on the main issues and the main assumptions. All the precise data sources and the technical computations are described in Appendix A.

The Johns Hopkins Project of mapping and measuring the nonprofit sector cross-nationally began with an agreement on a common definition of the nonprofit sector or third sector.[2] For France, the adoption of this common definition stands aside from the concept of social economy and is larger than the usual meaning of the "associative life" in umbrella organizations such as CNVA, GNA, FNDVA (see chapter 1).

4.2.1 The International Classification of Nonprofit Organizations

To be precise about this definition, and to obtain a clear subdivision of the nonprofit sector, we had to discuss and to agree on a common classification. The International Classification of Nonprofit Organizations (Table 4.1) is the result of this discussion. It is great progress to use a common classification, as we have seen above the drawbacks of ad hoc classifications of associations in the different surveys in France. Of course no single classification system is perfect for all possible purposes; in this classification, we identified the criterion of the economic activity that "the establishment or organization carries out, i.e. the product or the service it generates" (Salamon and Anheier, 1992). This criterion is general and can be applied everywhere; it is consistent with – but more detailed than – the United Nations International Classification of Industries and with the French *Nomenclature d'Activités et de Produits* (NAP), the industries and products classification[3] (which is the French version of the European industrial classification).

Table 4.1

The International Classification of Nonprofit Organizations

ICNPO	ICNPO French adaptation
Major group	
Subgroup	
Group 1: Culture and recreation	**Group 1: Culture and recreation**
1 100 Culture and arts	1 100 Culture and arts
1 200 Recreation	1 200 Recreation
1 300 Service clubs	*1 201 Sports and recreation*
	1 202 Social tourism
	1 300 Service clubs
Group 2: Education and research	**Group 2: Education and research**
2 100 Primary and secondary education	2 100 Primary and secondary education
2 200 Higher education	2 200 Higher education
2 300 Other education	2 300 Other education
2 400 Research	2 400 Research
Group 3: Health	**Group 3: Health**
3 100 Hospitals and rehabilitation	3 100 Hospitals and rehabilitation
3 200 Nursing homes	3 200 Nursing homes
3 300 Mental health and crisis intervention	*3 300 Other health services including mental health and crisis intervention*
3 400 Other health services	
Group 4: Social services	**Group 4: Social services**
4 100 Social services	*4 100 Residential homes*
4 200 Emergency and relief	*4 200 Other social services*
4 300 Income support and maintenance	
Group 5: Environment	**Group 5: Environment**
5 100 Environment	*No subgroups*
5 200 Animal protection	

Group 6: Development and housing	**Group 6: Development and housing**
6 100 Economic, social and community development	6 100 Economic, social and community development
6 200 Housing	6 200 Housing
6 300 Employment and training	6 300 Employment and training
Group 7: Law, advocacy and politics	**Group 7: Law, advocacy and politics**
7 100 Civic and advocacy organizations	*No subgroups*
7 200 Law and legal services	
7 300 Political organizations	
Group 8: Philanthropic intermediaries and voluntarism promotion	**Group 8: Philanthropic intermediaries and voluntarism promotion**
Group 9: International	**Group 9: International**
Group 10: Religion	**Group 10: Religion**
	Empty (see chapter 1)
Group 11: Business, professional associations, unions	**Group 11: Business, professional associations, unions**
Group 12: Not elsewhere classified	**Group 12: Not elsewhere classified**

ICNPO provides a useful compromise between the level of detail that might be ideal for national work and the level that is feasible for comparative work. It has a high level of organizing power proved by the fact that the residual group (not elsewhere classified) was of no use in France. When using this classification in France, we classified – as is commonly done for business enterprises – the individual establishments according to their main activity, and there were few borderline problems, at the sector level. At the subgroup level, available data sources compelled us to suppress some subgroups or to change them as shown in Table 4.1. Appendices C and D give the French version of ICNPO, include a translation and adaptation and illustrate the type of nonprofit activities classified at the major and subgroup level.

4.2.2. Variables and data sources

What were the minimum *variables* and *data* needed to portray the sector in a benchmark year which was decided to be 1990? The number of employees (in full-time equivalent, to take account of the importance of part-time jobs in nonprofits), the wage bill, the operating and total expenditures on one hand; the origin of resources, government, private donative and private non-donative on the other hand, including in-kind revenues.

The *expenditure side* follows this logical sequence, in which operating expenditures are the key data:

1	2	3 = 1 x 2	4	5 = 3: 4	6	7 = 5 + 6
FTE employment	Annual avg. wage	Wage bill	Ratio of wage bill	Operating expenditures	Capital expenditures	Total expenditures

The *revenue side* of the nonprofit sector account makes a distinction between:

– resources from:
    central government
    local government
    social security and other social funds (third-party payments)
– donative private resources from:
    foundations
    business and corporations
    individuals
– non-donative private resources from:
    fees and sales
    membership dues
    investment income

These variables were crossed with ICNPO at the subgroup level to obtain a (16 x 25) matrix describing the cash expenditures and revenues of the nonprofit sector. In-kind revenue and expenditure is of great importance in nonprofit organizations; volunteer work especially is a *sine qua non* condition of the existence and of the activity of associations without employees. It is also important in organizations hiring salaried personnel. So we added an imputed value of volunteers' time on both sides of the working matrix. To fill this matrix was of course a challenging issue. The existing and reliable data that we can directly report were some tens out of about 400 required!

Where could the data come from? National accounts and other official statistics constitute the first and principal way; umbrella organizations could also be viewed as data providers. Another approach is to estimate employment and wage bills as the major piece of operating expenditure in a labor-using service industry. Finally population and organization surveys are a way to obtain tentative ratios to fill the gaps of the matrix. And tentative figures are of course better than no data at all!

The national account approach

In the core national accounts, the nonprofit sector cannot be distinguished. French national accountants follow scrupulously – while other countries do not – the European System of Accounts recommendations, that is:

- nonprofits serving businesses (such as professional or business associations) or nonprofits in which fees are more than 50 per cent of the resources of the organization (social tourism, housing, vocational training, etc.) are recorded in the business sector.
- nonprofits in which public subsidies are more than 50 per cent of the resources are recorded as government sector (private schools, hospitals, the majority of health and social services, etc.);
- nonprofits hiring less than two employees are recorded in the household sector and are considered as pure consumers (senior citizen clubs, parent-teachers local associations, self-help groups, etc.).

The private nonprofit institutions serving households represent the remaining part of nonprofits; they are called *Administrations privées*. They include some private nonprofit and nongovernmental organizations: churches, political parties, labour unions, work councils, consumers' organizations, some youth and cultural associations and charities. According to national accountants, *Administrations privées* constitute the least reliable sector of the whole national accounts. For this sector, the benchmark year is very ancient, 1971, and since 1971 rather rough extrapolations have been done to update the data. Improvement may occur when the 1993 SNA (United Nations System of National Accounts) is applied, but the private nonprofit institutions serving households will still be a residual sector in the new SNA.

Figure 4.1 gives a summary of the treatment of the nonprofit sector in national accounts.

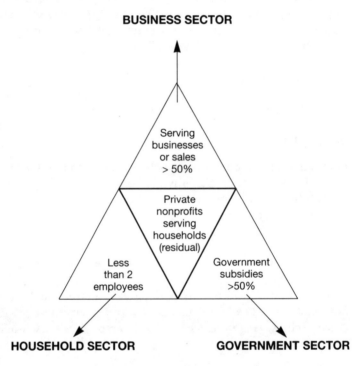

Figure 4.1 The nonprofit sector in national accounts

The big pyramid is the nonprofit sector. The inverse pyramid is the nonprofit sector visible in national accounts.

Fortunately, besides the core national accounts, some *satellite*

accounts[4] exist which constitute a detailed approach of some economic or social fields subject to government policies. We used the
data of the health and education satellite accounts, for both the
expenditure and the resource sides of our matrix.

We also used the results of *official surveys*, regularly conducted
by the Social Affairs Ministry, on private hospitals and on residential facilities for the handicapped, the elderly, children and
adults in need or in danger. In those surveys, nonprofit organizations are isolated from forprofit or public organizations and in this
way we obtained very reliable data.

The umbrella approach

One other data source is umbrella organizations or big organizations. Generally speaking the data from umbrellas are scarce,
incomplete and sometimes inconsistent. Some of them consist of
round numbers which are guesstimates, often overestimated.
However, we used them sometimes and matched them with other
sources. We also obtained directly the accounts of the main emergency and relief charities, such as *Secours Catholique, Secours Populaire, CIMADE, Croix Rouge, Restaurants du Coeur*.

The employment approach

This approach was used to fill the expenditure side of the matrix
when no other data sources were available. We used the data of
the major register on enterprises and establishments, the SIRENE
file run by INSEE. SIRENE is the main file in France: every enterprise when it is created has an identification number which has to
be referred to at every administrative stage; in this way the register is automatically kept up to date. The data included cover name
and address, legal status, economic activity category according to
NAP and number of employees. For associations, SIRENE records
only associations hiring wage-earners, paying VAT or subsidized
by central government. Errors are frequent but data quality is
increasing. We used for associations and foundations the SIRENE
file at the most detailed level (NAP 600) which isolates correctly
culture, sports and recreation, education, research, health, social
services and legal services. After some tidying-up to delete quasi-
public or quasi-business associations, these data were converted
into their full-time equivalent and we computed the wage bill for
every sector. The average annual wage was either reported or

assumed to be 20 per cent less than the wage in private sector (see Appendix A).

The organization approach

Last but not least, the organization approach was privileged to fill the remaining gaps. We conducted *two targeted surveys* with special financing from *Fondation de France*.

A *population survey* on a national representative sample of 2,000 persons over 18 years had been conducted by the *Institut de Sondages Lavialle* in May 1991 on the attitude of French people toward giving and volunteering for the nonprofit organizations. The questionnaire was very close to the similar Gallup survey in the U.S.A. and the classification was ICNPO. This population survey (Archambault *et al.*, 1991) gave the first data in France:

- on the amount of giving and on the volunteering time;
- on the recipient organizations;
- on the socio-demographic characteristics, income and religious practices of givers and volunteers.

With this survey's results, we computed giving and volunteering at the global level. Individual giving was reported on the resource side of the matrix. An imputed value of volunteer time was reported on both sides of the matrix: working hours were multiplied by the average hourly wage in the same sector to obtain this imputed value of volunteering.

To obtain the resource structure of many sectors and subsectors and the ratio of wage bill to operating expenditure, we relied on an *organization survey* conducted in our research team by Viviane Tchernonog (Archambault and Tchernonog, 1994). The questionnaire was designed to be consistent with ICNPO, such that 124 subsectors were proposed to an auto-classification of the nonprofits, and the purpose of the organizations was asked clearly to prevent errors. The questionnaire asked for the following information:

- employment (paid by the organization or seconded by other organizations or public agencies);
- volunteering, with annual number of hours;
- membership dues;
- giving (individual, corporate, foundations);

- fees and sales;
- third party payments from social security and other social funds;
- grants and subsidies (a) from central government
                        (b) from local government (3 levels).

The questionnaire was returned by 3,400 associations. After elimination of the wrong questionnaires or those without any budget, about 2,300 responses were computed to obtain ratios for every sector and subsector to fill the gaps of our matrix. Of course the extrapolation to the whole nonprofit sector of the results of the Tchernonog survey presupposes its relevance and its reliability. What are the strengths and the limitations of this survey?

On the positive side we have to put down the experience of the author, a very professional researcher who previously conducted other important surveys at the local level, on social welfare agencies (*bureaux d'aide sociale*) and on the relationship between nonprofit organizations and local governments (Tchernonog, 1984, 1991). Other assets are the good response ratio for a survey on nonprofits (about 25 per cent), the diversification of the sample all over France and in nearly all the 124 subsectors at the detailed level, the comparability of the structure of the sample and of SIRENE file for employer associations, the value of the data on in-kind inputs (volunteers, seconded jobs, free-of-charge housing or equipment, etc.).[5] Last but not least, the large size of the sample is a guarantee of reliability: ratios rely on hundreds of organizations at group level and on some tens or hundreds at the subgroup level of ICNPO.

On the negative side, we have to report that the representativeness of the sample remains questionable as long as the universe, i.e. the number of organizations, and its structure remains unknown. The absence of coverage of Parisian associations, on purpose, to prevent duplication with umbrella organizations, introduces a bias. The bad quality of the responses on capital expenditures and the absence of distinction between part-time and full-time jobs are other drawbacks. Despite those limitations, the organization approach was a *sine qua non* method to fill completely the 1990 matrix, and therefore nearly all the core tables which are reported in this chapter. The fact that INSEE is currently testing the same organization approach to improve the national accounts of the nonprofit institutions serving households in the new 1993 SNA reinforces our methodology.

To conclude on this point, what can we say on the reliability of our data? Of course, the following tables are *tentative*, but they exist. In a general way and roughly speaking, we can state that:

- Data on expenditures are more reliable than data on revenues.
- Data on the big sectors – the four first in ICNPO – are better than data on the other little sectors, which are more or less guesstimates.
- When two or more data sources gave inconsistent data for the same cell on a table, we have used the lower result, to prevent overestimation and too optimistic comments. It is therefore possible that our data are underestimated.
- We failed to measure the evolution of the nonprofit sector over a decade (1980–90). Because of the lack of data and the impossibility of filling the gaps for the benchmark year 1980, we could only measure the evolution of employment in the nonprofit sector.

4.3 Scope and structure

We will now present a succinct description and analysis of the basic contours of the nonprofit sector. A more detailed analysis of six subsectors will follow in chapter 5, so we will focus here on the overall structure and composition of the nonprofit sector.

4.3.1 The scope and size of the nonprofit sector: key numbers

What is the total budget of the whole nonprofit sector? What is its weight in total economic activity? Such was the recurrent question of the key leaders of the sector and of the representatives of government ministries involved in a partnership with the sector. We evoked the impossibility of building up a satellite account on social economy to answer this question, especially for the associative sector. The main reports in recent years proposed guesstimates, quoted afterwards by the following reports. The Padieu report proposes "a global turnover about 100 billion FF.; health and social services may represent 60 billion FF. The other important subsectors are education and training, then sports, social tourism, culture and recreation" (Padieu, 1990, p. 21). The Chéroutre report quotes "a total turnover of more than 100 billion FF." and quotes for subsector figures coming from previous reports or from the umbrella organizations (Chéroutre, 1993a, p. 33).

According to our methodology, *total operating expenditures* of the nonprofit sector in 1990 represent *217 billion FF.*, more than twice what the nonprofit sector was supposed to be, according to the experts. This figure is consistent with the extrapolation of the results of our organization survey, 235 billion FF.[6] (Archambault and Tchernonog, 1994). It can be compared to the turnover of some industries: electricity, gas and water (218 billion FF. in 1990) or the textile, clothing and leather industry (216 billion FF.). More, the ratio of added value to effective production is much higher in the nonprofit sector than in manufacturing industries.

If we add to operating expenditures a very tentative estimate of capital expenditures, 12 billion FF., we obtain *total expenditures* for the nonprofit sector of *229 billion FF.* Data on investment are either non-existent or of a bad quality.[7] We assumed 4 per cent of operating expenditure when no other data were available. It is very likely an underestimate, but often nonprofit organizations benefit from in-kind support for equipment and facilities. In the present state of knowledge, it was impossible to give a money value for these in-kind resources, but it is a challenge for further research.

In compensation, we were able to assign an imputed value of *volunteer time, 74 billion FF.* The importance of this figure relies definitely on the "shadow wage". We decided to use the average wage in the sector of ICNPO, social security contributions included. This methodology relies on the following assumptions:

- Wage earners and volunteers are substitutes: they do the same job, have comparable skills and have the same productivity.
- If volunteers were salaried, the wage rate would be the same and the social security contribution would be identical.

These assumptions are of course questionable: the paid staff and the volunteers are more complementary than substitute, and if volunteers were on the labor market, equilibrium wage rate would be different, probably lower, and the social security burden would be shared over more contributions. Another "shadow

Table 4.2

The scope and structure of the nonprofit sector: expenditure 1990

Subsector (ICNPO)	FTE employment	Avg. wage (FF.)	Wage BE (FF.1000s)	Ratio of wage BE to OE	Total expenditure (FF.1000s)	Capital expenditure (FF.1000s)	Operating expenditure (FF.1000s)	hours million	Volunteers value per hour (FF.)	imputed value (FF.)	Total operating expend with volunteers (FF.)
1 Culture and recreation	91,320	119.2	10,885	0.283	40,059	1,541	38,518	527.0	58.80	30,988	60,506
2 Education and research	184,332	223.0	41,106	0.765	57,645	3,920	53,725	57.0	110.00	6,270	50,995
3 Health	136,496	149.8	20,447	0.652	33,548	2,196	31,352	32.5	74.00	2,405	33,757
4 Social services	308,367	142.8	44,035	0.703	65,679	3,000	62,679	175.6	70.40	12,352	75,041
5 Environment	5,000	150.0	750	0.500	1,560	60	1,500	111.3	74.00	8,236	9,736
6 Development and housing	37,500	150.0	5,625	0.409	14,312	550	13,762	38.4	74.00	2,694	16,456
7 Civic and advocacy organizations	15,240	180.0	2,743	0.430	6,635	255	6,380	48.9	88.80	4,342	10,722
8 Philanthropic intermediaries and voluntarism promotion	100	150.0	15	0.579	27	1	26	23.4	74.00	1,732	1,758
9 International activities	8,664	140.0	1,213	0.492	2,566	99	2,467	37.1	66.60	2,471	4,938
10 Business and professional associations, unions	15,600	200.0	3,120	0.500	6,490	250	6,240	30.1	98.60	2,968	9,208
Total	802,619	160.5	129,939	0.598	228,521	11,872	216,649	1079.3	70.50	74,468	291,117

wage" could be the opportunity cost of volunteer time, i.e. the wage of the volunteer on the labor market; for using this approach, additional data on the qualifications, age and previous professional experience of the volunteers are necessary and they are not available. A third "shadow wage" should be the average wage of the non-agricultural, or service industries, labor force.

If we add volunteer time imputed value to operating expenditures, we obtain *291 billion FF. This operating expenditure with volunteer time is theoretically the best estimate of the economic size of the whole nonprofit sector* (Table 4.2). The imputed value of volunteer time can be viewed as standing for the added value of the numerous little nonprofits with no paid staff, overlooked by the employment approach. Despite this economic significance, we will focus on the simple operating expenditure which is more reliable because of the uncertainty of imputed value of volunteer time.

Another significant aggregate is the *full-time equivalent employment: 803,000 salaried employees*. This figure has to be compared to others: 950,000 (without FTE) (Padieu, 1989) and 992,500 (without FTE) (SIRENE file, 12/31/91). The nonprofit sector is a labor intensive industry; its labor force is half the labor force of another labor intensive industry, construction (1,600,000 in 1990).

Table 4.3

The third sector in relation to total employment and Gross Domestic Product, 1990

	Employment	Expenditure
Third sector	802,619	216,649
Total economy	19,099,000	6,484,109
Third sector as % of total	4.20	3.34

In order to facilitate international comparison, Table 4.3 presents the nonprofit sector in relation to total FTE employment and to GDP, which are very commonly used yardsticks. But we have to notice that there is homogeneity between the numerator and the denominator for the first ratio but not for the second one: in the numerator of the second ratio, third sector operating expenditures is a sum of final and intermediate expenditures while GDP is a sum of final expenditures. So 4.2 per cent is actually the relative size of the nonprofit sector from the employment point of view, while 3.34 per cent is an overestimate of the relative size of the third sector in terms of GDP (the real figure is about 2.7 per cent). The gap between the relative size in terms of employment and expenditures highlights the fact that nonprofit sector activities are labor-using service industries.

Despite this methodological remark, we notice that contrary to conventional beliefs, the nonprofit sector represents a far more significant component of the French economy than is generally recognized.

4.3.2 The structure of the nonprofit sector

Table 4.4 shows nonprofit employment, by subsector in relation to total employment. We will focus on the first four subsectors, because they represent 90 per cent of total nonprofit employment and also because they can be compared to similar activities in the whole economy. Environment, development and housing, philanthropic intermediaries, correspond to no NAP category; civic and advocacy associations and business organizations are included in a more general activity "counselling, legal services activities" and international activities are compared to employment in diplomatic activities and international organizations.

Table 4.4

Nonprofit employment in relation to total employment by subsector, 1990

Subsector/group	Number of employees		Third sector employment as percentage of total employment
	Third sector	Total economy	
Culture, recreation	91,320	901,147	10.1
Education, research	184,332	1,320,425	14.0
Health	136,496	1,213,022	11.3
Social services	308,367	531,106	58.1
Environment	5,000		
Development and housing	37,500		
Civic & advocacy associations	15,240		
Philanthropic intermediaries	100		
International activities	8,664	25,099	34.5
Business & professional associations, unions	15,600		
TOTAL	802,619	19,099,000	4.20

For the four main subsectors, third sector employment is 10 per cent for culture and recreation, 11 per cent for health and 14 per cent for education and research, and *for social services the third sector is predominant, with 58 per cent of total employment.* So there is a strong contrast between the provision of health services where the public sector is prevalent, and the provision of social services where the third sector is in a quasi-monopolistic position in areas such as handicapped residential facilities. Social services is by far the biggest employer of the nonprofit sector; though France has developed a high level welfare state, private provision of social services coexists with the public supply of social services, with a kind of specialization (see chapter 5).

Table 4.5 presents a more detailed picture of the various sectors, by ICNPO groups. The table presents the amount and share of each group in terms of number of organizations, employment and expenditures.

Table 4.5

The third sector, by subsector, 1990

Subsector/group	Organizations		Annual operating Expenditures		Employment (FTE)	
	Number	%	Amount	%	Number	%
Culture, recreation	71,485	47.1	38,518	17.8	91,320	11.4
Education, research	33,536	22.1	53,725	24.8	184,332	23.0
Health	3,690	2.4	31,352	14.5	136,496	17.0
Social services	25,520	16.8	62,679	28.9	308,367	38.4
Environment	1,200	0.8	1,500	0.7	5,000	0.6
Development and housing	8,730	5.7	13,762	6.4	37,500	4.7
Civic & advocacy associations	3,608	2.4	6,380	2.9	15,240	1.9
Philanthropic intermediaries	14	0.0	26	0.0	100	0.0
International activities	1,240	0.8	2,467	1.1	8,664	1.1
Business & professional associations, unions	2,855	1.9	6,240	2.9	15,600	1.9
TOTAL	151,878	100	216,649	100	802,619	100

"Organizations" means the number of establishments in the SIRENE file, i.e. those which employ at least one salaried person or which pay taxes; that is 151,878 organizations out of a total number of nonprofit organizations which is unknown. The most current guesstimate is 700,000 organizations. Of course, the large organizations are inside the SIRENE file.

Whatever the criterion, the four first ICNPO subsectors, culture. and recreation, education and research, health and social services represent more than 86 per cent of the total: 88.4 per cent of total organizations, 86 per cent of total operating expenditures, 88.9 per cent of total FTE employment. For these four main sectors, there is a contrast between "education and research" which weighs the same according to three criteria (22 to 25 per cent of total) and the three other sectors for which there is a disequilibrium. For "culture and recreation", the sector represents nearly half of the total organizations (47.1 per cent) contrasting with 17.8 per cent of total expenditures and only 11.4 per cent of total employment. Nonprofits in this subsector are mainly run by volunteers: half of volunteer time is spent in "culture and recreation", and the organizations employ only one salaried person on average. The reverse figure is found for health and, to a lesser degree, for social services: few organizations have an important economic activity and are to a larger extent employers. The average employment in health sector is thirty-seven and in social services is twelve. In fact, "social services" is a dichotomic category: we have to distinguish between residential facilities, which follow the health pattern – i.e. a labor-using service industry, with a professional labor force, a high division of labor and the use of heavy equipment – and other social services, which are smaller, more dependent on volunteer work as the paid staff is reduced or nonexistent, and which have few capital expenditures.

In the six little subsectors, three are of some economic importance, especially development and housing (5–6 per cent of the nonprofit sector). This sector is focused on economic activity and has progressed in deprived areas recently, so the share in expenditures is more important than the share in organizations and employment. Civic and advocacy associations and business and professional associations have a similar weight (2–3 per cent); in both cases the share in expenditures is more important than the share in employment as those organizations hire skilled paid staff. International activities and environment organizations are of little economic importance (1 per cent), though their political or symbolic role is much more important. The lowest of the low, philanthropic intermediaries are virtually nonexistent in France, despite the role of *Fondation de France*. We saw in chapter 2 and we will see more precisely in chapter 5 that historical reasons are at the root of the weakness of foundations in France.

Table 4.6 gives a more precise idea of the structure of the non-profit sector and its various subsectors. Average expenditure per organization in the first column is interesting only from a comparative point of view, as the absolute amount means nothing, because of the definition of organizations as recorded in SIRENE file. This table shows that health nonprofits are well above the average, and to a lesser extent social services, business associations and international activities are in the same position, while culture and recreation and environment organizations are below the average. Education and research, and development and housing, are near the average.

Table 4.6

Structure of the third sector, by subsector, 1990

| Subsector/Group | Average expenditure per organization | |
	Amount	As % of average size of all organizations
Culture, recreation	538,826	37.8
Education, research	1,602,010	112.3
Health	8,496,477	595.7
Social services	2,456,074	172.2
Environment	1,250,000	87.6
Development and housing	1,576,403	110.5
Civic & advocacy associations	1,768,293	124.0
Philanthropic intermediaries	1,850,481	129.7
International activities	1,989,516	139.5
Business & professional associations, unions	2,185,639	153.2
TOTAL	1,426,296	100

To have a more precise idea of the absolute amount of average expenditure per organization, we can refer to Tchernonog's survey, which splits employer and non-employer associations and gives a good idea of the wide dispersion of expenditures among nonprofit organizations (Table 4.7 and 4.8).

Table 4.7

Dispersion of expenditure of employer nonprofit organizations, by subsector

ICNPO	Employer NPOs	Number	Average expenditure	1st decile	1st quartile	Median	3rd quartile	last decile
3, 4	Health, social	166	2,453,553	87,676	255,897	82,157	2,432,193	5,142,372
1	Culture	102	1,185,283	64,883	147,000	371,198	1,461,406	3,528,047
1	Sports	113	585,727	31,820	92,608	245,049	625,984	1,842,227
1	Recreation	11	2,329,000	40,654	75,075	187,700	823,624	9,051,098
2	Education	26	3,508,460	66,423	408,720	1,114,280	3,458,576	11,282,174
5, 7, 9, 10	Protect of interests	23	475,747	104,830	200,668	363,127	544,660	818,926
6	Eco activities	42	1,841,613	74,101	228,830	715,587	1,715,000	3,741,255
	TOTAL	483	1,675,089	56,824	150,700	492,255	1,711,865	3,674,570

Source: Enquête LES-CNRS Université Paris auprès des associations – 1991

Table 4.8

Dispersion of expenditure of non-employer nonprofit organizations, by subsector

ICNPO	Non-employer NPOs	Number	Average expenditure	1st decile	1st quartile	Median	3rd quartile	last decile
3, 4	Health, social	366	65,268	2,957	6,017	20,723	51,358	118,219
1	Culture	369	53,096	2,917	7,871	22,726	56,199	107,596
1	Sports	436	83,242	4,408	12,350	35,250	84,140	186,552
1	Recreation	183	50,240	2,804	7,700	17,160	46,600	145,500
2	Education	56	44,544	3,181	5,409	15,656	52,015	131,761
5, 7, 9, 10	Protect of interests	273	23,946	1,062	2,438	7,800	21,513	49,190
6	Eco activities	60	81,395	7,348	13,782	33,202	70,993	206,887
	TOTAL	1,743	58,907	2,562	7,000	20,542	55,461	129,041

Source: Enquête LES-CNRS Université Paris auprès des associations – 1991

Those tables show that employment is a very good criterion of the size of the organization according to expenditure. The average expenditure of employers' organizations is twenty-eight times the average expenditure of non-employers' organizations. This fact strengthens the legitimacy of the employment approach for measurement. We remark that for both categories, the dispersion of expenditures is very high, but higher for employers than for non-employers, as the interquantile ratio shows it:

(ratios)	D9 D1	Q3 Q1
employer NPOs	65	11
non-employer NPOs	50	8

At the subsector level, we can see that the survey's classification splits up culture, sports and recreation/social clubs, including social tourism. This last category has a higher expenditure than the average as the other two are far below. Conversely, health and social services are in the same category, which lowers the average expenditure of this category, in comparison with Table 4.6.

Finally we have to remark that the structure of expenditures by subsector changes dramatically when the imputed value of volunteer time is added to operating expenditures (Table 4.9). First, we have to consider that the imputed value of volunteer time is directed mainly towards "culture and recreation" (42 per cent), then, far below, towards "social services", "environment", "education", "civic and advocacy". No category benefits from less than 2 per cent of total volunteer time. Volunteer time in the four main categories is 70 per cent. We can see the great involvement of volunteers in environment associations, where the volunteers are frequently highly qualified and spend more time a week than in any other category (Archambault *et al.*, 1991).

Table 4.9

Operating expenditures by subsector with or without imputed value of volunteer time

Subsector/group	Annual operating expenditures		Imputed value of volunteer time		Operating expenditures with volunteer time	
	Amount	%	Amount	%	Amount	%
Culture, recreation	38,518	17.8	30,988	41.6	69,506	23.9
Education, research	53,725	24.8	6,270	8.4	59,995	20.6
Health	31,352	14.5	2,405	3.2	33,757	11.6
Social services	62,679	28.9	12,362	16.6	75,041	25.8
Environment	1,500	0.7	8,236	11.1	9,736	3.3
Development and housing	13,762	6.4	2,694	3.6	16,456	5.6
Civic and advocacy associations	6,380	2.9	4,342	5.8	10,722	3.7
Philanthropic intermediaries	26	0.0	1,732	2.3	1,758	0.6
International activities	2,467	1.1	2,471	3.3	4,938	1.7
Business & professional associations, unions	6,240	2.9	2,968	4.0	9,208	3.2
TOTAL	216,623	100.0	74,468	100.0	291,117	100.0

When adding the imputed value of volunteer time to operating expenditures, we obtain quite a different structure. The first four main categories' weight is 82 per cent instead of 86 per cent,

121

"social services" is always in first place (25.8 per cent instead of 28.9 per cent), "culture and recreation" takes second place (23.9 instead of 17.8 per cent), "education and research" becomes the third instead of the second category (20.6 per cent instead of 24.8 per cent) and the relative decrease is important too for "health" (11.6 per cent instead of 14.5 per cent). The relative position of small categories becomes more important when including volunteers: environment, civil and advocacy, international activities, philanthropic intermediaries, business and professional associations, with the exception of development and housing which is downgrading.

4.3.3 Evolution of the nonprofit sector

It would have been of the greatest interest to fulfill the same matrix as for the benchmark year 1990, for another benchmark year, 1980 for instance. As mentioned before, it was impossible to fill the gaps for such a remote year, so we failed to measure the evolution of the nonprofit sector in a decade. However, we can obtain a very rough idea of this evolution by the change in employment in the third sector over the decade 1981–91. The data come from the SIRENE file; 1981 is the first year of existence of this file. We could not compute the full-time equivalent for the year 1981, so, for 1981 and 1991, Table 4.10 gives employment without FTE, for the third sector and for the total labor force. We can assume that the change in FTE employment is roughly the same as the change in total employment.

Table 4.10

Change in employment in the third sector, 1981–91 (without FTE)

	1981	1991	Percent change 1981–91
		Actual	Actual
Third sector	710,847	992,505	39.5
Total labor force	21,716,000	22,204,500	2.2
Third sector % of labor	3.3	4.5	36.6

Despite these methodological warnings, the evolution is striking: *employment in the third sector progressed rapidly (40 per cent) over the decade*, that is an annual mean growth rate of 3.4 per cent, while total employment was stagnant, with a global growth of 2.2 per cent over the decade, that is 0.2 per cent per year. As a consequence, the share of the nonprofit sector in the total labor force was growing from 3.3 per cent in 1981 to 4.5 per cent in 1991. This trend was reinforced in recent years as the labor force in associations was about 1,300,000 in January 1994, according to the SIRENE file, while the total labor force decreased during the same period. In recent years, the nonprofit sector benefited from the employment policy: many of the new employment creations in the third sector are assisted jobs, for instance jobs with an exemption from social security contributions or state paid part-time jobs (*contrat emploi-solidarité*).

Table 4.11 offers a very partial development of employment by subsector, 1981–91. Employment in the SIRENE file is divided between the identified NAP activities, i.e. the first four categories, the category "counselling, legal services activities" where the ICNPO categories "civil and advocacy" and "business and professional associations" are combined, and a residual category "other, not elsewhere classified". Despite this very rough subdivision, we can see that the contribution of the subsectors to the growth of third sector employment is very different according to the subsectors. First we should notice that the decrease of the NEC category is due to a better accuracy of the SIRENE file about the associations' principal activity. The consequence of this decrease is an increase in all other categories, which is a statistical artefact. In addition, we have an actual increase or decrease of employment: we have a dramatic increase in "social services", 123 per cent during the decade, that is 8.4 per cent annual average growth rate; "culture and recreation" employment grew by 68 per cent (5.3 per cent per year) and "civic, advocacy and business associations" grew by 53 per cent (4.4 per cent). A little below the average of third sector, "education and research" grew by 31 per cent (2.7 per cent per year). As for employment in health services, it decreased by 14 per cent during the decade (that is to say, 1.5 per cent per year).

All these variations have to be observed with caution. The SIRENE file was new in 1981 and some of its errors were corrected over time but others still exist. In principle, the SIRENE file only records employment paid by the organization itself, which excludes seconded jobs, paid by the state or by local government.[8] This principle is not always observed. Despite these methodological remarks, the growth of third sector employment, and therefore the growth of operating and total expenditures of this labor intensive industry, cannot be disproved.

Table 4.11

Change in third sector employment, by subsector, 1981–91

	Employment			
Subsector/group	1981	1991	Percent change	Change as percent of total growth
Culture, recreation	96,449	161,630	67.6	170.6
Education, research	115,134	150,515	30.7	77.6
Health	113,734	150,515	−14.4	−36.4
Social services	168,848	376,639	123.1	310.6
Civil & advocacy associations	28,765	44,065	53.2	134.2
Business & professional associations, unions				
Philanthropic intermediaries				
Environment				
Philanthropic				
International activities	187,917	162,316	−13.6	−34.4
Other				
TOTAL	710,847	992,505	39.6	100

In conclusion, *the size of the nonprofit sector in France is about 3–4 per cent of the total economy* according to the criterion. Social services, education and research, culture and recreation, and health are, respectively, *the four main sectors, representing about 90 per cent of the whole nonprofit sector.* As all those industries are highly labor intensive, *the wage bill represents some 60 per cent of operating expenditures* (and if we include the imputed value of volunteer work, the share of labor in operating expenditures with volunteer work rises to 70 per cent).

Of course the economic size and scope of the nonprofit sector do not wear out the meaning of its existence. Taking volunteer work into account is a way to be interested in its sociological significance. The analysis of support of the third sector is another way to study the relationship with public authorities, corporations, donors and members.

4.4 Sources of support

After describing the expenditure side, we will now present an analysis of data reporting on the revenue side of the matrix. We first examine the overall importance of the three major sources of funds, public, private-commercial and private-donative (Table 4.12). This classification is clear and commonly agreed, even if it is not as simple as it seems, as we will show later.

Table 4.12

Sources of revenue of the nonprofit sector in France

Source	Amount	%
Public	129,612	59.5
Private-commercial	72,982	33.4
Private-donative	15,407	7.1
TOTAL	218,001	100.0

4.4.1 Overall importance of the three major sources of funds

Table 4.12 shows the large preponderance of public resources in France and the very low level of private-donative revenue. This overall structure has of course historical roots: in a country where the state is responsible for public interest, if citizens associate to provide public goods, the government has to pay to acknowledge that they do the job of government, whatever the form of the subsidy, grant, contract or third-party payment. Conversely, more than half of the population (57 per cent) is not concerned with giving to the nonprofit sector and corporate giving is very rare and very low compared to Anglo-Saxon behavior. We have to analyze the various forms and origins of public and private revenue.

For *public resources*, there is no equivalent in France of statutory transfers: public transfers are either discretionary or contractual but they are not decided by law. Third-party payments can be easily isolated; they come mainly from social security and also from other social funds and they are focused mainly on social services and health organizations. Grants and contracts cannot be separated: generally speaking, the great majority of associations receive some kind of public support, as an acknowledgement of their social role; the amount is symbolic for small organizations while the large organizations receive the greatest part of public money, on a more and more contractual basis, with reciprocal commitments. Large associations receive also the quasi-totality of third-party reimbursements.[9] We were able to split up grants and contracts according to their origin (state or local government).

Private-commercial resources include fees and charges paid directly by members or clients in exchange for some kind of service. Sometimes fees are the counterpart of the cost of the service, for example in elderly residential homes, but very often they represent only a part of the cost or even a symbolic payment as a counterpart of third-party payments or other public support. In French nonprofit hospitals, social security pays 70 to 100 per cent of the bill, according to the social position of the patient and the severity of the illness, and the remaining part is charged to the patient and is often reimbursed by mutual insurance. In nonprofit schools, fees are very low in comparison to the United States or the United Kingdom: some 3,000–5,000 FF. per year. Moreover, in many nonprofit organizations, fees vary according to the client's declared income, in application of the principle of solidarity: it is the case for social tourism, day care facilities, housekeeping services for the elderly or the handicapped, etc. Sales refer to the income from the sale of goods and services that are not directly related to the primary mission of the organization.[10] In nonprofit accounts, sales are not easy to isolate from fees and charges and we obtained a mixed category: fees, charges and sales.

Membership dues are isolated. They represent a guarantee of independence for the organization and their share in total resources is declining with the size of the organization (Archambault and Tchernonog, 1994). The meaning of membership dues is different in member-oriented and in public-serving organizations. In the former, they can be viewed as the outright purchase of a package of services; in the latter, membership dues are either the price of giving voice to a cause or the cost of lobbying for the interests of a group. For the most general interest-oriented organizations, the dues are purely and simply donative. That is why membership dues to *associations reconnues d'utilité publique* are tax-deductible, exactly like donations.

Investment income is the revenue of investment property. It is a minor flow in France because of the restrictions on declared associations ownership and because of the minor role of foundations.

Finally, *private-donative revenue* comes either from individuals, from corporations or from grant-making foundations. Federated giving could not be isolated and is not important in France, with the exception of the unique Telethon, 360 million FF. in 1993 (see chapter 6). Individual giving goes first to health, then to education, social services, international aid and professional organizations. It is interesting to note that religion, which is outside our field, receives less in France than health, approximately the same amount as education, as France is no longer a religious country (Anheier *et al.*, 1994 and Archambault and Tchernonog, 1994).

Corporations, or the few corporate foundations, give mainly to education, culture and sports and recently to humanitarian or environment organizations. Is corporate giving really giving? If they support sports or a humanitarian cause, corporations expect some advertising return, and it can be seen as publicity expenditure. In the case of education, it is a quasi-tax as corporations have to pay a percentage of their wage bill in apprenticeship tax or training tax, but they can choose the school in the first case and a training organization in the second case which receive the money.

Lastly, in France, grant-making foundations are virtually nonexistent and only *Fondation de France* and *Fondation pour la Recherche Médicale* have a role in funding associations.

Table 4.13 presents a summary picture of nonprofit sector revenue in both absolute and relative terms. The relative size is shown both without and with in-kind contributions. We will first examine the structure of the revenue without and then with in-kind resources.

Government is, as said before, by far the main source of revenue for the third sector with 130 billion FF., 59.5 per cent of cash revenue. The breakdown of the three components, central government, local government and social security is interesting. With 59 billion FF., grants and contracts from *central government* come first; more than half of this money goes to education and research organizations, mainly in the form of the payment of teachers. Social security, with 39 billion, comes second and pays as a third party for health and social services almost exclusively. *Local government* is the coming partner since the Decentralization Act (1983) (32 billion FF., 15 per cent of total cash revenue). Of the three levels of local government, it is the smallest, the commune, which is the most active in financing the nonprofit sector, especially culture, sports and recreation – the main target – then education, and local development and housing. The *département* is specialized in social policy and is therefore a funder of social services. The region is less important.

Table 4.13

Sources of third sector revenue, 1990

	Amount	Percentage of total	
		Excluding in-kind	With in-kind
Cash			
Government	129,612	59.5	44.3
central government	58,649	26.9	20.1
local government	32,398	14.9	11.1
social security	38,565	17.7	13.3
Private contributions	15,407	7.1	5.3
individuals	8,235	3.8	2.8
foundations	911	0.4	0.3
corporations	6,261	2.9	2.2
Private earnings	72,982	33.4	25.0
sales and fees	57,700	26.5	19.8
dues and assessments	13,799	6.3	4.7
investment income	1,194	0.5	0.4
other cash revenue	289	0.1	0.1
Total cash revenue	218,001	100	74.5
In-kind			
Government	–		–
Individual	74,468		25.5
Corporate	–		–
Total in-kind revenue	74,468		25.5
TOTAL REVENUE	292,469		100

Private contributions are low in France compared to other countries: 15 billion FF., 7 per cent of total cash revenue. Of this total, individual contributions represent 8 billion, corporate giving 6 billion and foundations redistribution less than 1 billion.

Private earnings represent one third of total cash revenue, 73 billion FF. The main part by far is sales and fees, 58 billion. Dues and assessments represent an amount equivalent to direct contributions, 14 billion. Investment income is very low, 1 billion and other cash revenue is negligible. Market resources are concentrated in culture and recreation and social services, investment income in social services (because of the importance of their funds invested in short-term bonds) and philanthropic intermediaries (because of the endowment of foundations). Dues are everywhere.

If we focus now on the structure of nonprofit sector revenue with in-kind contributions, we obtain quite a different picture. Recall that we gave an imputed value only to volunteer work and not to other in-kind contributions such as free housing or free use of equipment.

With a money value of 74 billion FF., *volunteer work represents one quarter of total revenue with in-kind resources, and nine times individual giving.* Volunteer work is of the same order as private earnings. Government support remains the first source of revenue for the third sector, but with 44 per cent of the total, instead of 60 per cent of cash revenue. So, when taking account of volunteer work, private resources become more important than public support. However, other in-kind contributions, housing or equipment are provided mainly by local government, and so private and public resources may be balanced.

We can rearrange the data to isolate the specific resources of the third sector, i.e. private contributions, voluntary work and dues and assessments. Those resources are for the nonprofit organizations a guarantee of their independence; they represent less than 36 per cent of total revenue with in-kind contributions, that is less than government support, 44 per cent, but much more than commercial resources, 20 per cent.

4.4.2 Revenue sources by subsectors

Table 4.14 breaks down the revenue sources of the nonprofit sector by ICNPO groups. It shows that the revenue sources are very different according to the subsectors.

For three of the main subsectors, education, health and social services, public financing is largely predominant. Those activities are at the core of the welfare state. Two small subsectors are mainly funded by private contributions: philanthropic intermediaries and international activities; two others balance government support and private earnings: culture and recreation, and civil and advocacy associations. For environment, development and housing, business and professional organizations, private earnings constitute the main resource.

Table 4.14

Revenue sources by subsector, 1990

| Subsector/group | Source of Revenue, percentage | | | |
	Private contributions	Government	Private earnings	Total
Culture, recreation	4.0	40.6	55.4	100
Education, research	9.8	73.1	17.1	100
Health	8.0	84.1	7.8	100
Social services	4.8	60.2	35.0	100
Environment	15.4	32.1	52.5	100
Development and housing	1.8	37.1	61.1	100
Civil & advocacy associations	3.3	47.8	48.9	100
Philanthropic intermediaries	51.4	4.6	44.0	100
International activities	66.4	22.1	11.6	100
Business & professional	7.5	16.5	76.0	100
Other				
TOTAL	7.1	59.5	33.5	100

Inside each group, there are also important differences. In culture and recreation, for instance, culture and arts are mainly supported by public funds, local government first and then the state. Sales and fees are the other major resource. Sports and recreation is mainly commercial, with local government support of one third, and social tourism is merely commercial, with government support of one quarter. In social services, we have a contrast between residential facilities for the handicapped, the elderly and other frail populations, which are financed up to three quarters by public money (primarily social security), and only up to one quarter by the users, and other social services, which rely more on private earnings, dues and fees, and on donative resources, because big charities are inside this subgroup.

As mentioned before, we were not able to present a picture of the changes over time in the size and composition of nonprofit sector revenues. We hope that this first tentative picture of third sector revenue in 1990 may be used for describing further evolution.

In conclusion of this section on the sources of revenue of the nonprofit sector in France, it is important to notice the *very high level of government support*, which in many cases compromises its independence if not guaranteed over time. We will examine this important point in chapter 6. We must also take note of the *very weak financial involvement of users in such sectors as health or education*: this fact will strike a foreign eye but seems quite normal from a French point of view; as we will see in chapter 5, present social movements fight to lower the fees paid by clients in these areas. Finally we want to highlight the *great diversity of the revenue structure according to groups and subgroups* of our classification: there is not a unique pattern of financing nonprofit organizations.

We will end this chapter with a brief presentation and discussion of some output measures collected for selected ICNPO groups.

4.5 Output measures

What do nonprofit organizations do and how do we measure the production of the service activities in which they are engaged? Giving social indicators on the output of nonmarketed services is a great methodological challenge. So we reduce our ambition to the measurement of ten standard indicators. Despite the precision of the definition of target measures, we had great difficulty filling Table 4.15 because of the impossibility of either breaking down overall figures into public/private components or of breaking down the private sector into forprofit/nonprofit subsectors.

In some cases, approximate measures are proposed. The precise methodology and references can be found in Appendix A, with additional data, and we only report here on the ten activities of Table 4.15 and output measures.

For the *health sector*, the number of patient days in hospitals is a very reliable indicator, both in amount and in structure: we see the predominance of the public sector in hospitalization in France (62 per cent), and inside the private sector, the predominance of forprofit clinics and hospitals. However, with 25 million patient days and 16 per cent of the whole hospitalization, the share of the nonprofit sector is not negligible and corresponds to a kind of specialization (see chapter 5).

Table 4.15

Activity and output measures in 1990

Field	Target measure	Nonprofit sector		Forprofit sector		Public sector		Total
		Number	% of total	Number	% of total	Number	% of total	
Health	Number of patient days in inpatient hospitals	25,218,000	15.5	35,958,000	22.2	101,071,000	62.3	162,247,000
	Number of residents in nursing homes for the frail elderly	–	–	–	–	–	–	–
Education	Number of students enrolled in primary and secondary schools	2,095,606	17.1	–	–	10,159,594	82.9	12,255,200
	Number of students enrolled in universities	247,717	15.5	–	–	1,347,039	84.5	1,594,756
Social services	Number of residents in residential care facilities other than nursing homes	440,029	54.9	32,049	4.0	329,449	41.1	801,527
	Number of pre-school children in child-day care facilities	87,300	39.4	–	–	134,100	60.6	221,400
Housing	Number of dwelling units constructed or rehabilitated	–	–	225,250	85.0	39,750	15.0	265,000
	Number of occupants	–	–	597,500	85.0	105,500	15.0	703,000
Culture and arts	Number of attendees of performances by orchestras and operas	–	–	–	–	1,540,000	100.0	1,540,000
recreation	Number of members in sports clubs	8,253,162	37.5	–	–	–	–	22,008,436

Nursing homes could not be isolated from other residential facilities for the elderly. However, the residents of elderly residential care facilities are becoming more and more frail and dependent with the ageing of the French population and the growth of home care services for the elderly. In 1990, there were 482,840 elderly living in residential care facilities, that is 6 per cent of the over-65 population. Sixty per cent of this total were in the public, 6 per cent in the forprofit and 34 per cent in the nonprofit sector. So we still find the predominance of the public sector, but it is declining over time. The forprofit sector is actually low, but rapidly growing in recent years and competing with a steady nonprofit sector.

For *education*, the indicators are also very reliable, but there are no data on the private forprofit sector, very weak in France. We considered it nonexistent.

One pupil out of six, 17 per cent, attends a private nonprofit school, while five out of six attend a public school. This proportion is steady over time; it is higher in secondary (21 per cent) than in primary education (14 per cent). Of nonprofit schools, 95 per cent are Catholic. Between the state and the Church, the control of schools is a long-term challenge, as we have seen in chapter 2, and we will deal with it more precisely in chapter 5.

The next indicator, "number of students enrolled in universities", has been extended to the whole of higher education. Universities, *stricto sensu*, are a quasi-monopoly of the state. Only 2 per cent of students are enrolled in the five Catholic universities and the two universities of theology. But the role of the nonprofit sector is stronger in business schools run by the Chambers of Commerce, other *grandes écoles*, and vocational training for superior technicians. In the case of vocational training for nurses and social workers, the nonprofit sector is in a quasi-monopolistic position.

The first indicator for *social services* is reliable. The number of residents in residential care facilities *includes* elderly homes: of the 800,000 residents, 55 per cent are in the nonprofit sector, 41 per cent in the public sector and only 4 per cent in the forprofit sector. If we exclude all the elderly homes, residential and nursing, we obtain quite a different figure: 320,000 residents, of which 87 per cent are in the nonprofit sector, 12 per cent in the public sector, and only 1 per cent in the forprofit sector. In social services residential facilities, the nonprofit sector is therefore widely preponderant, whatever the indicator.

For day care facilities, the situation of France is very specific because of the early school attendance for children from 2 to 5 years old. This specificity is due to the existence of a very efficient pre-elementary school (*école maternelle*) system in which 2,535,900 children between 2 and 6 were at school in 1990, 88 per cent in public pre-schools, 12 per cent in private nonprofit pre-schools. The indicator in Table 4.15 concerns only children below the age of 2 and not-at-school children above this age, attending crèches, day nurseries or nursery centers. The nonprofit sector may be about 39 per cent, and the public sector 61 per cent of the 200,000 children in such facilities. So child care is more public-oriented than residential services.

For *housing*, the two indicators are of bad quality. The nonprofit sector is active only in rehabilitation, no longer in construction. We have no data on dwelling-rehabilitated people every year. So we provide the number of dwelling units constructed in 1990 by the public sector (15 per cent) and the forprofit sector (85 per cent) and multiply this figure by the average number of occupants in dwellings in the 1990 population census.

The two standard indicators of the last sector, *culture and recreation*, are also not reliable and are rather approximations than indicators. The first one represents the sole audience of operas, as there are no recorded data on attendees of performances of private orchestras. The second indicator is a guesstimate of members in nonprofit sports clubs. There is no longer a public sector in sports clubs, as public school sports clubs had to become 1901 associations, and there are few forprofit sports clubs and these are not recorded. So most people practising sports outside a nonprofit sports-club do it by themselves.

4.6 Membership of nonprofit organizations

We cannot have a complete idea of the role of the nonprofit sector without an overview of membership and involvement of members in the nonprofit sector. As a matter of fact, most nonprofits provide services and therefore they are producers from an economic point of view. But from a sociological point of view, every nonprofit organization creates social ties between individuals and is at the core of a grass-roots sociability, which facilitates social integration of individuals into a community.

So *the membership ratio*, that is the ratio of members of one or more associations to the total population of 18 and over, is well known, thanks to the annual survey of CREDOC on "opinions and living conditions of the French". According to this survey, nearly one French person out of two was a member of at least one association over the 1990–92 period (45.6 per cent). This percentage has been steady over the last fifteen years, contrasting with the "associative boom" of newly created associations: there is some kind of turnover of members across old and new nonprofits.

As 19.1 per cent of the population are members of several associations, the ratio of membership to members is nearly two.[11] Membership of men (52.1 per cent) is more important than membership of women (39.9 per cent). Membership is rather low for young people, but it increases till ages 35–49 which is maximum membership age; then it declines but less than other social practices because of the existence of elderly associations. Membership is highly sensitive to education, from 29.1 per cent at the elementary level to 67 per cent at the university level; according to socioprofessional status, membership is higher among professionals and executives (65.5 per cent), middle management, teachers and social workers (64.8 per cent), farmers (58.5 per cent) and students (53.7 per cent) and lower in low-income groups (workers 39.6 per cent, white-collars 42 per cent, senior citizens 40 per cent).

The CREDOC survey has existed since 1978. So we can observe the evolution of the membership ratio by subgroup as shown in Table 4.16.

The classification of CREDOC is not exactly the same as ICNPO. However, we can notice some trends over the period. Membership in sports and culture/recreation nonprofits is by far the most widespread practice, and it is growing at the beginning of the period for sports and at the end of the period for culture and recreation. Conversely, more militant nonprofit organizations show a decline in membership: unions, youth and student organizations, family or women advocacy or consumer defence.

To conclude, involvement of the French in the nonprofit sector is important and slowly growing. But they behave more and more as consumers of a collective good provided by nonprofit organizations and less and less as militants committing themselves to a cause.

Table 4.16

Membership ratio by subgroup (per cent of population over 18)

Subgroup	1978–1980	1984–1986	1990–1992
Sports	15.3	18.9	19.4
Culture/recreation	12.2	11.6	16.6
Parents-teachers	10.0	8.2	8.1
Professional	6.8	7.1	–
Unions	9.7	6.8	6.8
Charities	5.6	6.6	–
Neighborhood	5.3	6.0	–
Religion	5.1	4.7	5.9
Political parties	2.5	3.1	2.4
Youth and students	4.7	4.5	3.0
Family advocacy	3.1	2.6	–
Consumer defence	2.6	2.4	1.4
Environment	3.4	2.0	3.0
Women advocacy	1.8	1.1	–
Total	44.4	43.8	45.6

Source: CREDOC

To end this chapter, we have to point out that *the output indicators give only salient examples of what nonprofit organizations do, and what the share of the third sector is in selected fields.* A more detailed description and analysis of the major areas of the nonprofit sector is the purpose of the following developments. Similarly in the following chapter we can see that in some subsectors, nonprofit organizations behave as quasi-public agencies and so membership is relatively unimportant; it is the case in health and social establishments, while in other subsectors, such as environment or civic and advocacy organizations, membership involvement and voluntary work is more important.

Notes

1 Our figure includes private Catholic schools, considered in France as a separate entity not included in the associative sector and not recorded in the Padieu or Chéroutre guesstimates.

2 We recall that the third sector is a collection of organizations that are simultaneously filling the five following conditions: formal (institutionalized to some extent), private (institutionally separate from government), nonprofit-distributing, self-governing, voluntary, i.e. involving some degree of voluntary participation.

3 The usual classification of associations in France mixes an activity criterion (health and social services, training, culture, sports) and a recipient criterion (youth and popular education, social tourism). So does Canto (1988). The Deruelle (1984) classification, used in many surveys, relies on the "tutelary" ministries and so relies on a functional classification of government activities.

4 Satellite accounts will be generalized in the 1993 SNA.

5 Simultaneous or more recent surveys (Demoustier, 1993; Kaminski, 1994) on NPOs also give data relatively consistent with V. Tchernonog's survey. But they are less complete and use classifications inconsistent with ICNPO.

6 This figure can be split between 200 bilion for employer nonprofits and 35 billion for nonprofits without paid staff.

7 So total expenditure is less reliable than operating expenditure.

8 This fact explains the discrepancy between SIRENE data and *Ministère de l'Éducation* data on private schools employment. To a lesser extent, the same can be observed for health and social services.

9 Third-party payments can be viewed as sales to social security; they are the exact counterpart of providing services: they are public-commercial revenue.

10 If the organization sells primarily goods and services, it has to choose another legal status than 1901 association or foundation (see chapter 3). In practice, this is not always the case.

11 The French population over 18 is 43 million. Half of this population is a member of two associations on average. So the number of members is 43 million. If they pay 13.9 billion FF. as membership dues, the average due is about 320 FF.

Chapter 5

MAJOR SUBSECTORS:
RECENT TRENDS

In the previous chapter, we analyzed the overall size, scope, composition and output of the third sector in France. It is time now to highlight some subfields in a less parsimonious presentation of the sector. For each subsector, we shall briefly describe the history and legal background, present additional empirical information providing a more detailed view of the internal structure, activity and financing and, finally, we shall show the policy issues and the recent trends. In addition to the five subsectors highlighted by the other countries, we decided to emphasize the "culture and recreation" subfield because of the essential part it takes in the French third sector regarding the number of organizations and the membership especially.

We have seen before that the four first subsectors of our classification, culture and recreation, education, health, and social services, represent about 90 per cent of the third sector. We shall start with these "heavy lorries", regrouping health and social services in a single group because their history, law and policy are very similar. Then we shall focus on two small-sized subsectors because of their social importance, civic associations, and environment. Civic associations, first, are linked to democracy and citizenship, as Tocqueville showed: they apply the fundamental freedoms and they represent the civil society against abuse of administrative authorities. Second, environment nonprofit organizations constitute a new worldwide social movement. Founded on the statement that "there is only one Earth", they are constitutive of a cross-country solidarity and maybe of a joint policy towards sustainable development. Last, we will examine foundations, an underdeveloped subsector in France. To understand the reasons for this backwardness compared to other countries it is necessary to improve the situation and suppress the obvious and the hidden restrictions on foundation expansion.

5.1 Culture and recreation[1]

As mentioned before, the development of the French nonprofit sector is largely due to the emergence of charity and solidarity principles, linked with religious organizations or political protest.

Much more recently, at the end of the nineteenth century, appeared a new form of nonprofit organization taking root in everyday life and aiming at developing popular sociability. Some social clubs, such as those for veterans or alumni, learned societies, musical or literary circles but also gymnastic and shooting societies emerged little by little.

The history of the subsector "culture and recreation" started at the beginning of the twentieth century, and its recent spread proceeds from the great evolution of French industrial society. The economic growth, the reduction in working time and the emergence of a leisure society, allow a change in the way of life, in the mentalities, and induce a growth of cultural and recreational needs and expenditures.

In the 1960s, with the emergence of the "consumer society", this type of nonprofit grew dramatically; it is now *the major component of the French associative movement* regarding the number of organizations and the membership – more than half of all the nonprofit organizations (Tchernonog, 1991), 45 per cent of creations of associations from 1975 to 1984 (Canto, 1988), and a membership of about 31 per cent of the population over 15 years of age (Ministère de la Culture, 1990).

But in France, cultural and recreational activities are not only considered as an individual right but also as a collective concern. As a matter of fact, *the central state has originated and organized this field*, especially since the socialists came into power in 1981. Nowadays, most of the sports and culture facilities in France are owned by the state or by local government.

But in the context of the deepening financial crisis of the state and public agencies, a complementary and sometimes substitutive relationship is emerging between the government and non-profits. Thus nonprofits in this sector are being called to play a larger role than in the recent past. Since the decentralization policy initiated in 1982, many local governments ask them to provide some services and often delegate to them the management of public facilities.

There are four main components of the subsector "culture and recreation" in France: culture and arts, sports, social tourism and recreation (service clubs are almost nonexistent, but there are many social clubs); but it is often hard to draw a real limit between these areas which are very frequently united, especially at a local level.

5.1.1 History

Culture and arts
In the field of culture, France has a *unique place* in Europe and in the rest of the world. Whereas state interventionism in this field is still judged suspicious or even unwarranted in some liberal democracies, it can be said that there is in France a real consensus to consider the state as the main body responsible for cultural heritage. Thus, the extreme political, economic and administrative centralism, typical of French history, also exists in this area. France is one of the few countries where cultural affairs are directly managed by a ministry.

The state role in the defence, diffusion and creation of culture and arts is fundamental, as culture is now a major government concern.[2] Some even pretend that the French system is a "cultural monarchy"; see for instance the very critical essay by M. Fumaroli who, describing the policy of the Ministry of Culture, speaks of France as a "cultural state" (Fumaroli, 1991).

On the other hand, business sponsorship is almost nonexistent in France in contrast to practices in other countries; private businesses just sometimes buy painters' or sculptors' works for museums and support some cultural events.

The French state has always assumed many responsibilities in the field of culture; in the *ancien régime* already, the absolute monarchy was in charge of the preservation and transmission of cultural heritage but also of artistic creation, by ordering architectural or painting works (*Mécénat royal*).

Moreover, one of the French state achievements in this area is to have created many *national cultural institutions*: prestigious ones like the *Comédie Française or the Académie royale de musique* (which became the *Opera de Paris*), or the *Louvre* go back to the seventeenth and eighteenth centuries. Later, many theatres, museums, orchestras, art academies and libraries have been created from the nineteenth century on.

The creation in 1959, at the beginning of the Fifth Republic, of a Ministry of Culture in France, is more an additional stage in the acknowledgement of a centralized political power than a real rupture. André Malraux, first Minister of Culture and famous writer, aimed then to provide the country with many infrastructures in order to extend access to culture.

During the same period, the nonprofits emerged, especially thanks to the *Maisons de la Culture* – multipurpose culture and arts centers – and the *Maisons des Jeunes et de la Culture* – culture and recreation facilities intended for young people – both created by Malraux. Most of them are 1901 Act associations depending on public funding.

From the mid-1970s on, cultural policy has progressively become an important factor of general policy and now influences public life. Thus, the three successive presidents of the Fifth Republic have been personally involved in the cultural life: they have implemented a policy of "great cultural projects" – the arts and culture center created by Georges Pompidou, the *Musée d'Orsay* initiated by Valéry Giscard d'Estaing or the *Grand Louvre* and the *Opéra Bastille* ordered by François Mitterrand.

The growing importance of the nonprofit sector in this area is largely due to the coming of a socialist government in 1981 and to the decentralization policy initiated in the 1980s. On the one hand, this is illustrated by unprecedented public financial support – in 1982, cultural budgetary expenditures doubled and in 1993 they nearly reached the mythic threshold of 1 per cent of the total public budget. This progression is all the more significant since it occurred in a context of deep economic crisis. On the other hand, it is also thanks to the very popular Jack Lang's action. This minister promoted the revalorization of the "minor arts" (gastronomy, circus, comics, fashion, songs, etc.) and organized inventive cultural events often administered by 1901 Act associations (especially festivals which develop in all fields, in the whole country).

At present, it is too early to see the consequences for culture of the recent come-back of the right.

Despite public financing and management of the main collective services and facilities, numerous and diversified cultural and artistic nonprofits dramatically developed in the 1980s. They are now very active in choirs and music ensembles, performing arts, visual arts, monument preservation, historical and genealogical societies. Also, a specific French institution, film-clubs, are 1901 Act associations and spread culture in the cinema. According to Woody Allen, there are as many spectators for his films in Paris as in the whole of America. Furthermore, the authorization of free broadcasting in 1981 which abolished the state monopoly provoked the creation of hundreds of local free broadcasting associations.

Now, since decentralization, nonprofits play an essential part in the provision of services and encourage popular participation, especially at a local level. In the context of budgetary constraints in the public sector, they have been used or even created by local governments to contribute to local development and to provide some services. These special uses of associative status will be emphasized in the legal section on pp. 146–148.

Social tourism

Social tourism is a *movement specific to France*, even though versions of it can be found in other European countries with strong socialist traditions. It consists of low-price vacation facilities to develop tourism among the working class: holiday villages or camps, youth hostels, holiday centers for children.

After World War II, social tourism contributed to regional planning, by creating many infrastructures in deserted areas. Nowadays it actively participates in social policy. It plays also a non-negligible role in the tourist industry (it represents about one third of the total forprofit tourism assets).

Originally, social tourism came from different militant movements: the secular movement (*la ligue de l'enseignement et de l'éducation populaire* which created holiday centers), workers' movement (*Tourisme et travail*, founded in 1944), as well as Catholic (*Fédération Française de Tourisme Populaire*), familial (*Fédération des familles de France*), and youth movements (*Union des Centres Sportifs et de Plein Air*).

142

The first instances of social tourism date back to the latter part of the last century when the first holiday centers for children and the first villages for working-class families emerged (respectively in 1875 and 1890).

But this movement really flourished from 1936 on, when the *Front Populaire*, a socialist government which promulgated the first two weeks a year "vacation with pay" (*congés payés*), came into power. Léo Lagrange, the Secretary of State for Youth and Sports, instigated a network of holiday centers, sports equipment and similar facilities. He played a very large role in the development of social tourism in France and in the access to vacation for working-class families. In his memory the *Fédération nationale Léo Lagrange*, a network of associations promoting cultural and sportive activities, was created in 1951.

Social tourism developed more fully after World War II, owing to the establishment of a comprehensive social security system and to the extension of the "vacation with pay" to four weeks a year; but more significantly in the 1960s by the creation of many new facilities available to the working and middle classes (thanks to a payment according to income and family burden, the *quotient familial*). These constructions are partly financed by central administration and third-party payments (especially those from the French social fund of family allowance (*Caisse d'Allocations Familiales*).

Associative tourism is the main component of social tourism which also includes some cooperatives, mutuals and work councils. It is organized into the umbrella organization UNAT (*Union Nationale des Associations de Tourisme et de Plein Air*, founded in 1920), which embraces thirty-nine associations or federations of tourism and has a total membership of about 8 million people. According to a recent report (UNAT, 1993), the association members of UNAT reported a total turnover of 6.3 billion FF. in 1993 and employed some 32,350 people; 12,500 volunteers also participate in their activities (Bidet, 1993).

Sports
Strongly linked to the republican spirit, the French sports non-profit organizations developed concurrently with social tourism from 1936 on, also thanks to Léo Lagrange's action (promotion of sports, youth and popular education groups). They flourished

after World War II when public administrations built many facilities allowing specialization in sports. Nowadays, a major part of sports activities is managed by nonprofits. Since 1986, voluntary sports activities at school have been undertaken by school sports associations and no longer by the school itself, which has allowed sports associations to develop even more.

The sports nonprofits are nowadays the most important part of the associative movement especially because of the age and longevity of the first sportive societies, which still keep on their activities. The sports movement has been led by the CNOSF (*Comité National Olympique et Sportif Français*) since 1908, a unique committee which regroups all the organizations governing physical and sports activities. This organization gathers all the sports clubs seventy-three sports federations and about 145,000 clubs) and is a member of the international Olympic movement created at the beginning of the century by Pierre de Coubertin. Total membership is about 11 million, of which more than a million are active volunteers. In 1990 there were 6,220,000 French individuals having a sports licence and one can say that more than 22 million French people practice sports (that is to say 48 per cent of the French over 15 years of age) (Ministère de la culture, 1990). Football and tennis are the most popular.

Sports clubs are subjected to a high degree of regulation by the French Ministry of Sports and Youth: they have to receive the "agreement" of the Ministry to be given grants and to organize sporting events. They also have to join a federation (theoretically independent from central government) which defines the rules and delivers the licences.

Recreation

Service clubs are almost nonexistent in France. The only active ones are branches of American clubs – such as Lions clubs or Rotary clubs for example – and they play a very weak role in associative activity. But in this subsector, there are also very small organizations, widely spread in both rural and urban areas such as clubs for the elderly, feast committees, hunting and fishing associations, veterans and specialized or multipurpose recreation clubs. Run by volunteers, their operating expenditures are low, though not negligible. But more importantly, they are, with football and tennis clubs, the very heart of social life in rural areas.

5.1.2 Size, scope and structure

Global economic data

First, it is important to notice the serious lack of data related to this subsector. So, the information we present has to be carefully considered.

In 1988, culture reported an annual revenue of 100 billion FF. and employed some 760,000 people, that is to say 4 per cent of the working population (*Le Monde*, 1988). As for sports, the revenue is estimated at 50 billion FF. (1 per cent of the gross national product), and employment is about 200,000 people (Pratique de l'association, no. 31, 1988). Household expenses for culture and recreation in 1991 reached 198.1 billion FF. (5 per cent of the total national consumption) (INSEE, 1992).

Nonprofit organizations in "culture and recreation" are nowadays, by far, the most numerous component of the French nonprofit sector. This phenomenon is partly due to the emergence of a "leisure civilization" involving a substitution of multipurpose activities for unipurpose ones. They total 47 per cent of the total number of associations and 45 per cent of those created from 1975 to 1984 (Canto, 1988). According to Tchernonog's report, there are about 120,000 organizations in the culture subsector and 140,000 in sports. The social tourism sector reports a turnover of 6 billion FF. per year and delivers services to more than 5 million beneficiaries (UNAT, 1993).

Despite the great number of organizations, *nonprofits in this field play a weak economic role.* They are generally small and only hold about 18 per cent of the total operating expenditures. Moreover, *the number of nonprofit employees is very weak as well*: 11 per cent of total nonprofit employment and 10 per cent of total employment in the "culture and recreation" field. Indeed, many nonprofit organizations in this subsector are run by volunteers and are not employers. The relative amount of wages to total expenditures is therefore lower than average (28 per cent as opposed to 59.8 per cent), above all in sports (23 per cent); the level of wages is very low too. But one has to notice that employment is increasing rapidly especially in cultural and sportive activities – from 1981 to 1991 the growth is recorded at a level of 67.6 per cent, and at 173.9 per cent when social tourism is excluded. That may reveal the entry of these associations into the formal economic sector. Finally, the level of wages is also low: at 26 per cent below the average, it is the lowest among the nonprofit subsectors. Indeed, jobs are more taken by women, more part-time or seasonal (in social tourism), than in any other sector.

Associative participation: membership, giving and volunteering

Membership and volunteer participation is the highest in this subsector: of the 38 per cent of French population belonging to one or more associations, 47 per cent join a sports club and 34 per cent a cultural or artistic association, that is to say 81 per cent of the population who are members (Ministère de la culture, 1990). According to a CREDOC survey, eight and a half million French people of 18 years old (one out of five) join a sports club. Sportive members are principally young men and graduates. As for cultural associations, members are more frequently women, and the average age is higher.

Moreover, the growing success of these associations is also revealed by the *extensive number of volunteers* (Archambault *et al.*, 1991) as they receive 45.4 per cent of French volunteers, which is nearly half the total of volunteer hours.

Individual private giving is very low and only provides 4 per cent of the associations' funding: the number of donors is very low (only 2.3 per cent of the French population contribute to the financing of these activities and 5.4 per cent of the donors) and the amount given is low as well. As for *corporate donations*, they play some part for sports, but are almost nonexistent in the other areas.

5.1.3 Legal position

French nonprofits in the culture and recreation subsector have no distinctive legal treatment, nor any special obligations. They are organized according to the same basic principles as the global nonprofit sector, even though sports and tourism are more regulated by the ministries, depending on public "agreement" to realize their activities.

But they are a *perfect illustration of the looseness of the limits that may exist in France between forprofits, nonprofits and public entities.* In this field, indeed, misuses of the nonprofit legal status are rather frequent. These special uses of the 1901 Act status are perfectly analysed by the Chéroutre report as we will see in chapter 6.

On the one hand, above all in culture and arts, central and local administrations often create associations governed by the 1901 Act, to start a new program, organize some activities or administer some infrastructures. In this case associations are in fact merely quasi-governmental agencies; this legal status allows public agencies to circumvent administrative regulations and public accountability and to take advantage of giving and volunteering. These nonprofits, so-called *para-public or para-administrative organizations*, are the most usual form for culture and arts centers. The *Maisons de la Culture*, for example, are almost totally financed by public subsidies, but their management is trusted to associations directed by civil servants or municipal representatives nominated by the central government. These associations deliver general interest services so, in fact, they are only an *"exteriorization" of the public sector*. In cultural activities, this public use of associative status is growing significantly, especially at a local level.

As far as sports and tourism activities are concerned, the limit between nonprofit organizations and the private sector is sometimes blurred; this encourages the growth of *para-commercialism* that could make associative status controversial.

By its events, its performances and its stars, sport – and especially football – is becoming a real commercial phenomenon. The private sector is more and more interested in sports clubs. Sometimes one can even note an obvious slackening between the actual status of some big football clubs and their commercial requirements. Besides, recent financial scandals and other corruption problems point out the difficulty in managing an associative status in the event of significant nonprofit gains.

A bill voted in 1992 intends to avoid these eventual drifts which may threaten sports practices: the sports clubs whose money revenue and wage bill are higher than 2,500,000 FF. have to take a business status to manage their activities.

Lastly, in the field of tourism, the current necessity of rigor in the context of crisis, and the competition with forprofits, induce some nonprofits to adopt private legal status; conversely, businesses which are run like ordinary societies, especially travel agencies, sometimes use the nonprofit legal status.

Now, in all cases, to preserve an associative legal status, nonprofit organizations in sports and tourism are more often subjected to fiscal controls.

5.1.4 Government policy

Associations in culture, arts, sports and tourism produce both market and nonmarket services which they can sell to their members. In this way, they have access to more diversified resources than other types of nonprofit organizations (such as dues, sales and fees).

According to Table 4.14, culture is among the main fields for which *auto-financing* (donative and non-donative private revenue) *is the highest*: nonprofits receive 55 per cent of their income from fees and services, which is much higher than the amount for the global sector – 40.5 per cent – and is generally very dependent on public funding.

In the field of sports and social tourism, private resources form the most important part of the total revenue, partly thanks to members' subscriptions; in culture, public grants and private revenue are equal.

Although this field is less dependent on public funding than other subsectors, it has had a very intense and favorable relationship with the public agencies for twenty years and especially since the decentralization policy.

Within the government grants system, the level of *central government support is rather limited* because cultural and recreational activities contribute too slightly to national economy to be a state priority. However, central government action towards nonprofits in this field is still very important. On the one hand, it assumes financial and pedagogical control as sports clubs and social tourism organizations have to receive the "agreement" of the respective ministries, a one-sided contract at the discretion of the government; that is to say that they have to commit themselves to respect certain quality and security norms in order to be subsidized and to receive tax support. On the other hand, the state government gives its help to large organizations of state dimension, and to innovative projects with a high degree of professionalism.

But if one cannot consider that the state is disengaging itself from its cultural responsibility (it assumes 22 per cent of public funding to nonprofits in culture), some regret its *relative withdrawal from sports activities* (5 per cent of the public funding) and above all *from social tourism*, in which it had played a very extensive role in the past. As a matter of fact, since 1964, the state had supported the infrastructures built by social tourism organizations, with a system of low-rate loans and grants. But now, public budget constraints have induced the central government to give direct help to working-class families to go on vacation, especially by a system of "vacation vouchers" (*chèques vacances*) combining the household's savings with the public and employers' financial support. Besides, traditional partners of social tourism (social funds like the *caisse d'allocations familiales* and the *caisse de retraite*, and work councils) have sharply reduced their grants (now they provide 19.5 per cent of social tourism public funding) and are powerful enough to create their own facilities or negotiate directly with forprofit tourism. In view of this lack of financing, French social tourism has to practice higher pricing which puts it in competition with the commercial touristic sector. For that reason, social tourism seems to have lost some of its social aims and it is sometimes hard to distinguish its activities from those of private firms. So in the coming years, social tourism will have to find new types of financing and take new orientations, especially with European competition.

But the main particularity of the financing of this subsector is the *predomination of the local grant support* which is one of the most important source of funding for the nonprofits in culture, sports and recreation: local government provides 32 per cent of the money revenue and 80 per cent of the total public funding. Its part in the public support is three times higher than in the nonprofit sector as a whole. This very favorable posture towards nonprofits in this field is largely due to *the fact that the latter are deeply involved in local cultural and social life* and that they are the main source of local sociability.

This complementary relationship is especially developed in sports (financial support of local communities enforces 94 per cent of total public grants) and particularly in little towns where sports is sometimes the only subsidized activity. Therefore, according to Tchernonog's report, sports clubs represent a quarter of the total number of associations and receive 16.4 per cent of the local support; culture and arts associations (20 per cent of the associations) receive 22 per cent of this funding.

This relationship is often reinforced by the creation of "houses of voluntary associations" like the *offices municipaux des sports* or the *offices culturels* gathering most of the associations to negotiate with local agencies; they also profit from the in-kind support of local administrations (free-of-charge use of the facilities, offices, transports, equipment, etc.).

Besides, this partnership has initiated the development of "conventions", general activity contracts with reciprocal commitments which take the place of the classic system of general funding received from year to year. *Associations have to implement specific programs to receive financial support.*

This practice involves an associative *professionalization and specialization.* It also implies strengthened controls by public local agencies, that may increase the risks of dependence on local government. This fear is very strong, especially in the cultural field.

5.2 Education and research

From a monopoly of the church in the field of education till the nineteenth century, to a republican school fighting against the Catholic influence during the first part of the twentieth century, the education sector in France has its roots in a tumultuous history. The "school war" is one of the oldest and most sensitive quarrels which agitates France from time to time, the most recent being the conflict in 1993.

Nowadays in France, most organizations in the educational field, especially schools, are public-owned. Most pre-schools, elementary primary and secondary schools, but also universities, engineering schools and institutes of technology are public entities. However, education is also one of the main nonprofit fields: France has some 11,000 private schools, which enrol 2.3 million pupils. These schools are predominantly Catholic – 95 per cent of the private schools – but also Jewish, Christian Reformed, or even secular. Educational networks, at the periphery of public school, with a private nonprofit legal status, are also very numerous and most of these organizations are managed by associations.

These organizations benefit from *the important official support of the state* and are subjected to its financial control. So the network of relationships they have with the public sector is very specific and intense.

5.2.1 History

The history of educational nonprofit organizations is very specific and is characterized by an *endless conflict of influence between the state and the Catholic Church*. It is at the root of the present situation.

The still existing "school war" has indeed been a constant of the nineteenth and the twentieth centuries in France. Though declining, it contrasts with the pacific relationship between the church and the state which has been predominant since 1901 in every other subsector of the nonprofit sector and especially in health and social welfare activities.

In France, competition between religions is not important in explaining the development of the nonprofit sector because of the quasi-monopoly of Catholic schools and because the French Protestants and the Jews have long ago opted for the Republic and republican public schools. But the "school war" was originated by a strong opposition between the Catholic Church and an active atheism or anticlericalism (see chapter 2).

Till the second part of the nineteenth century, schools were a quasi-monopoly of the Church and especially of some specific congregations. Working-class people and the peasants never went to school or only for a very short time. The end of the nineteenth century was marked by the desire to reduce the Church's monopoly, and introduce compulsory, free, lay public schools.

First, Napoleon I gave public universities the monopoly to grant degrees, as opposed to the Church. Later, the 1850 Falloux Act, which still existed in part (as we will see in the political paragraph), authorized anybody to create primary schools and any qualified person to open a secondary school. But public subsidies to those schools had to stay below one tenth of annual expenses. Catholic schools multiplied after this law.

Finally, J. Ferry (see above, chapter 2) created public, lay, free-of-charge and compulsory education (1882). The principle of laity or secularity means religious neutrality, but as mentioned earlier, public teachers were republican, and as rationalists they fought superstition, which was often assimilated to clerical influence. The Catholic school network was also attacked in the fight against congregations.

The war was on until the 1950s. Indeed, for half a century, the republican public school was the only one to be financed by the government. Private Catholic schools were financed by private money only, that is heavy fees, gifts and some contributions from the Church or of the congregations.

In 1951, the Barangé Act abolished the prohibition on subsidizing private schools. The lay partisans considered this act as a violation of the secularity principle. Then in 1959, the Debré Act proposed the still existing agreement between the state and the associations running private schools (*contrat d'association*): the school follows the same program as in public education, with financial and pedagogical state control; in return, the state pays the teachers and the local government may pay for the equipment and housing beyond one tenth of annual investment expenses, according to the 1850 Falloux Act: in this case, the fees that the pupils' families pay are quite low. A less constraining *contrat simple* takes care only of the payment of the teachers' wage bill. Most Catholic schools – that is most private schools – adopted the *contrat d'association* and the school war calmed down till 1984.

The most important recent revival of the school war was the 1984 conflict. The socialist government tabled a bill which unified public and public-subsidized private education. As most Catholic schools are being financed by public grants and as their teachers are paid by the central government, they saw this bill as a loss of pedagogic and ideological independence. Growing demonstrations, up to 1,000,000 persons, organized by private schools' parent-teacher associations with the support of right-wing political parties, filed into the streets of Paris in the spring of 1984. The government changed and the new one abandoned the bill. We will tackle more precisely these problems in the paragraph concerning government policy as there has been a recent new development of this "school war" with the reform of the Falloux Act in December 1993.

5.2.2 Size, scope and structure

Global economic data
First, we have to notice that, contrary to other subsectors, data in this field are very reliable. We do not have statistical data recorded on private schools without contracts with the state, but they are very few and unimportant.

Associations in education represent about 22 per cent of the total number of nonprofit establishments (Table 4.5). The SIRENE file estimates the number of associations having at least one employee at 9.5 per cent of the associative sector, that is 15,624 establishments. We can note the specially high growth of the number of parents' associations during this period, as they are responsible for about 28 per cent of the creations of educational associations (Canto, 1988).

Organizations in education hold about *25 per cent of the total resources of the nonprofit sector in France*. They total 23 per cent of nonprofit employment and 14 per cent of the employment in this field. Wages take the largest part of total expenditures (77 per cent) and are the highest of the nonprofit sector, at 38 per cent above the average, as the labor force has a higher level of qualification than in other subsectors.

Associative participation: number of pupils, giving and volunteering

The *relatively low number of pupils in private schools* has been steady over the last thirty years or slightly declining (Table 5.1).

Table 5.1

Percentage of pupils in private education, 1989

	1989
Primary schools	14
Secondary schools	20.8
Higher education	15.6

Source: Ministry of National Education – DEP, 1989

One child out of six attends a private primary school, one out of five attends a private secondary school. The others attend public school. However, the proportion is much higher in the western regions of France: nearly one out of three children attends a Catholic school. Nonprofit higher education includes 2 per cent of the students in universities (Catholic universities and universities of theology), nearly all the students in paramedical and social schools, in business schools and in private establishments for higher education (*établissements privés d'enseignement supérieur*), and a proportion of the students in superior technicians' sections (*sections de techniciens supérieurs*) in preparation for *grandes écoles* and in engineering *grandes écoles*.

According to *Le Monde* (13 January 1994), nearly 40 per cent of professionals, 25 per cent of the self-employed, and 30 per cent of farmers choose private schools for their children. But on the other hand, only 17 per cent of the white-collar employees and less than 10 per cent of workers make this choice. Indeed private schools are preferably attended by the middle and upper classes.

The Padieu report shows that, in 1988, 2.3 million pupils attended one of the 11,000 private schools (Padieu, 1990), that is 17 per cent of French pupils. But more than one pupil out of three spends a part of his education in a private school, as private schools are frequently a second opportunity for children rejected by public schools.

The CREDOC, in a survey about associative adhesion, analyzes the parent-teacher organizations. One parent out of five who has children less than 16 years old joins a parent-teacher association. This relatively high number of members – for a militant-type association for which support is generally declining – is largely due to the high importance given by the parents to school results in a period of crisis. Adherents are generally high-income, graduates and involved in a trade union or regular churchgoers (Fourel Volatier, 1993). Parent-teacher organizations exist in public schools and in private schools. The former are gathered in two umbrella organizations: the *Féderation des Conseils de Parents d'Elèves* (FCPE), which is left-wing and linked with teachers' unions, and the mighty network of lay peri-school nonprofits (*Fédération des Oeuvres Laïques, Ligue Française de l'Enseignement*). The other one is PEEP (*Federation de Parents d'Elèves de l'Enseignement Public*), centre-right oriented.

Associations active in education receive 18.4 per cent of the *gifts* to nonprofits but an average contribution lower than average (245 FF.). Moreover, these organizations benefit from 11 per cent of the total *volunteering* but their volunteers only work about 10.5 hours per month which is *63 per cent below the average* (Archambault *et al.*, 1991).

5.2.3 Legal position

Decisions of the French Constitutional Court, especially that of 18 January 1985, have definitely established that the freedom of education is a civil right guaranteed by the French constitution. These dispositions seem to show that a certain consensus about education has been reached in France, even if it is not totally satisfactory either for the supporters of the lay school, or for those of the "free" private school.

The associations active in school education are not subjected to distinctive legal treatment, compared to the general legal model; but there is a *significant seperate body of law* governing the *activities* of this type of nonprofit organizations. Education in school is a highly specialized function which leads to specialized rules, applying only to the activity itself, and not to the inner life of the organization. Moreover, the *contrat d'association* or the *contrat simple* involve *special obligations and privileges* for nonprofits that can be compared to those granted or imposed on "agreed associations" in other fields.

As seen above, the law *adopted on 31 December 1959* allows primary and secondary schools to be associated by contract (*contrat d'association*) to the overall school network, and to receive their share of public funding.

By this *contrat d'association*, the state takes into its responsibility most operational budgets.

For primary schools only, the law permits a lighter type of contract (*contrat simple*) with conditions easier to fulfil but less privileges.

The general set-up of education at large has a much wider field than the sole school network. *Educational associations* (youth organizations, post- or para-school programs) also operate and play a major role. This type of organization was associated from the beginning with the public service of school, as a necessary complement to the teacher's role, especially through youth movements, summer camps, educational associations, etc. For half a century, these associations have had to get the "agreement" of the Ministry of Youth and Sports which opens the doors to public funding and various aids from the state or other public authorities.

5.2.4 Government policy

We explained in the historical section the endless conflict of influence between the state and the Catholic Church on education in general. *The first topic in this school war was the financing and degree of independence of the Catholic private schools over many decades.*

A very important revival of the school war, as we have already mentioned in the historical paragraph, was the 1984 conflict between the Mauroy socialist government and the Catholic hierarchy. The socialist government had tabled a clumsy bill which unified public and public-subsidized private education in a "great public service of education" (the same formula as "public hospital service" which raises no objection). After months of discussion, the government and the Catholic hierarchy were near a consensus, but most of the representatives and managers of the Catholic schools saw the bill as a threat to their ideological independence and to what was left, by their contract with the state, of their pedagogic initiative. With the extremists of both camps adding fuel to the fire, growing demonstrations of up to 1,000,000 persons were organized by the mighty private schools' parent-teacher associations. They were supported by right-wing political parties. Organizations advocating lay public education also took part in these debates. After the most important demonstration in Paris in June 1984, the Mauroy government was changed and the new Fabius government gave up the bill.

Since then, the public financing of private schools seems to be accepted by most French people, as shown by a recent poll revealing that 60 per cent of French people consider the public funding of private education as normal (*Le Monde*, 11 November 1993).

Thus, two recent measures extending public support have been taken by the French government: in 1992, first, it satisfied the Catholic private schools' claims and agreed to finance the continuing education and vocational training of teachers. Moreover, in December 1993, referring to a report which emphasized the bad condition of private schools' infrastructures and the security problems this brings, the government abolished the very ancient Falloux Act which limited public financing by forbidding public support for private schools' investment. According to the new bill, local communities might unrestrictedly support private schools' investment (constructions and repair), in proportion to the number of their pupils. This bill, voted very quickly and without preliminary debates, produced strong opposition from the secular movement. On the one hand, the secular partisans questioned this new legislation as unconstitutional, contrary to the principle of equity with regard to education. On the other hand, this movement was more than a refusal of private schools' public funding; it was an affirmation of public education – the needs of which are enormous – as a state priority. The partisans of public schools launched a great demonstration (up to 600,000 people), in January 1994. At the same time, the French constitutional council declared the abolition of the Falloux Act unconstitutional.

This revival of the "school war" – analyzed as the exact symmetry of the 1984 conflict – shows that consensus about education in France has still not been reached.

But nowadays, *public money is by far the major source of financing*. As we can see in Table 4.14, public financing in this field is the second highest (health is the first with 84 per cent of total resources): nonprofits in education receive 73 per cent of their income from central and local administrations. Public subsidies are by far the major resource of primary and secondary schools (77 per cent of their budget) and "peri-school" associations (82 per cent of their financing), but represent a lower part of research and higher education's financing (respectively 50 per cent and 49 per cent of their income). The financing of these two sectors is more diversified and partly provided by private earnings for research and by businesses' and corporations' donations for higher education.

Within the governments' grants, the level of local government support is very limited and is specially low for "other education" categories and for research; but it plays a more significant part in primary and secondary schools and particularly in higher education (63 per cent of public funding). Schematically, central government pays for the teachers' wage bill, local government pays for the nonteaching labor force and other operating expenses are shared between private and public funders.

Paradoxically – as we have seen above that nonprofits in education are organized according to the same legal principles as other types of organizations, and as they are principally financed by the state – private schools, mainly Catholic schools, have a sense of a very specific identity and do not consider themselves as belonging to any kind of nonprofit sector or *economie sociale*. In particular, they never respond to surveys on associations or the social economy. Reciprocally, the annual *Bilan de la vie associative* and the plentiful literature on associations never refer to private nonprofit schools. How long will this taboo last?

An emerging and growing part of the nonprofit sector is *continuing education*. The Delors 1971 Act encouraged competition between public, nonprofit and business sectors in this field. Employers have to pay at least 1.5 per cent of the wage bill either in continuing education and vocational training programs inside the firm or as a special tax. The product of this tax subsidizes continuing education schemes, run either by forprofit, nonprofit or public entities. The program of these schemes is decided in common by representatives of the employers and of the labor unions.

Many of these new associations were social or educational clubs which have changed their aim with the development of unemployment. In this area the competition between forprofits and nonprofits was severe, and ordinary enterprises saw the financial and tax support to associations as unfair competition. Associations have been active in job training programs, especially for young people. After being convicted by law, many associations created business subsidiaries which are run as ordinary enterprises and preserved the nonprofit legal status for programs oriented towards frail populations: young unskilled workers, the unemployed, women returning to work after a long break. For those populations a public interest mission justifies public support. In 1991, there were about 7,450 associations active in training, with a total turnover estimated at 28,520 million FF. (Chéroutre, 1993a).

Another major change for continuing education is a consequence of decentralization: the training policy was transferred from the national to the local authorities which are the new partners for contracts. This change implies a more regular and higher public financing balanced by more local development oriented programs.

"Peri-school" associations run sports or cultural activities inside or outside school and their number has recently increased. For example, since 1986, voluntary sports activities at school have to be organized by school sports associations and no longer by the school itself. Some of them are subsidiaries of the parent-teacher or education advocacy organizations quoted above; some are self-governing and some are dependent on religious organizations or religion-inspired youth organizations such as the scouts. Many of them have a nationwide structure, and others are only locally based. To give an idea of the importance of the educational network, a word ought to be said about the "peri-school" activity of a very important secular nonprofit umbrella, the French League of Permanent Education (*Ligue Française de l'enseignement et de l'education permanente*), which groups a huge number of associations, mutual societies, cooperatives, etc., and which offers a very large range of activities: school and post-school activities, civic and social education, cultural and sportive activities, for example. This grouping of organizations represents some 50,000 associations, 3,500,000 members, 3,000 full-time employees, and 10,000 part-time (moreover, around 600 civil servants are seconded by different ministries).

Eventually, over the last five years, new associations whose aim is to link schools and enterprises have spread quickly; they work to find work placements and jobs for the pupils and to make the programs closer to business concerns.

5.3 Health and social services

Charity, relief, assistance to poor, disadvantaged and handicapped people, care of sick people, hospitals, help to children, to families and to elderly people represent a traditional field of nonprofit activity. Based on religious and/or humanitarian feelings, this activity has normally been organized for years through individuals, religious congregations, nonprofit organizations, friendly societies or workers' or manufacturers' unions. In the past, it has preceded and given way to public state or local community action, and still remains an important part of the overall health and the main part of social welfare facilities.

These private actions are very often a pattern, a source of innovation and inspiration for the state leadership concerning methods of action and solutions to social and medical problems. More generally, they pose questions about the state's welfare responsibility (the "social question" of the late nineteenth century) –

and also on the issue, the limit and the "crisis of the welfare state" nowadays.

In this subsector, private companies, public entities, associations and mutuals operate together. So there are either complementary or competitive relationships between the different components.

Finally, the field of health and social services is perhaps the one in which *the dialectics between the respective role of centrality and subsidiarity* in the general French set-up appear most acutely.

The relationship between health and social services is obvious and can be illustrated by the fact that the main umbrella organization of the nonprofit sector is the UNIOPSS (*Union Nationale Interfédérale des Oeuvres Privés Sanitaires et Sociales*). This umbrella organization created in 1947 embraces 7,000 associations which employ 300,000 people and provide services to 450,000 users.

One fundamental parameter is the implication of the French social security scheme as the main funder of the sector. Although a partial system of compulsory insurance against illness and accidents at work existed before World War II, a very important and comprehensive system was established just after the war (see chapter 2). Its principle is that *every employee* (and later every professional, every manager, every tradesman), *active or retired, is entitled to receive the necessary health care*; he is reimbursed with part (or all) of his expenses according to the attendance he gets or social security pays for the services provided. Nowadays, 99 per cent of French people are insured by social security. This institution is financed by employers' and employees' subscriptions, and possibly by state funding. Its budget equals or even goes beyond the state budget. Its participation is vital in the creation, maintenance and daily operation of the whole medical and medico-social network of France, and in the way all "health professions" are performed in this country. A complex system of conventions between the French administration, social security and the practitioners of this field establishes the methods and the ways of the overall set-up.

5.3.1 History

As we have already seen in chapter 2, health and social services date back to the origin of the nonprofit sector. Whatever the period, the development of the nonprofit sector has the same basic trend as this subsector.

Originally it was entirely run by the Catholic Church and the congregations, but the hospitals and social services were progressively secularized during the *ancien régime*. Intended for the poor and the underprivileged (orphans, elderly, leprous and other contagious patients), the facilities and services have been extended to the whole population since the eighteenth century.

Health care and social control over marginal populations were mixed in the period between the late Middle Ages and the end of the nineteenth century. Up to the end of the nineteenth century, the subsectors of health and social services merged into one, and social control of marginal populations took the form of social care for underprivileged people. Even nowadays, one single term is commonly used to refer to the whole sector (*secteur sanitaire et social*). However, certain nonprofit organizations specialized in specific kinds of health or social problems; many philanthropists are associated with one kind of organization or another: Vincent de Paul created establishments for orphans or foundlings (*Les Charités* in 1617), l'Abbé de l'Epée for the deaf, Valentin Haüy for the blind (1889), and these organizations still exist.

To put it in a nutshell, the historical evolution of the resource structure in health and social services is as follows: originally, private resources were quasi-exclusive; alms, gifts in kind and in money, legacies, volunteer work were the main resources, and a part of the *dime*, the tax levied by the Church and paid by the peasants and *bourgeois*, was also an important resource, as was the income from the Church and congregation property. Progressively, public financing, at state or local level, has replaced the money coming from individuals or from the Church; the patients' contribution increased and so did money coming from members' subscriptions in mutual organizations till World War II.

After World War II, social security devised more and more schemes to finance health services, whereas the public *aide sociale* partly financed most establishments and social services for the disabled. Contributions from solvent clients or fees are large for family services, nursing homes for the elderly, young workers' hostels and day care.

Because of the diversification of the sector during the twentieth century, and especially after World War II, *we have selected and focused on two examples: the fields of handicap and health.*[3]

In the sector of *handicap*, many associations, the main object of which was advocacy, were created during the interwar period. Disabled people, and especially the victims of the bone tuberculosis epidemic, who claimed the right to work and to earn a living, were the beneficiaries of the first nonprofit organizations which created physiotherapy establishments for the rehabilitation of the disabled. The *Association des Paralysés de France* (APF), which nowadays runs the most important share of the establishments for physically handicapped people, was created in 1933. At that period, the government had taken measures for people injured during the war, but almost nothing existed for the civil handicapped.

After World War II, parents of mentally handicapped children created the first associations centered around mental deficiency. The drift from the land related to the splitting up of the traditional family structure, which means that parents could rely less on other members of the family, and the development of specialized educative programs may explain these parents' concern to ensure their children's future. The *Association des Parents d'Enfants Inadaptés* (APEI) was founded by parents of these children in 1945. In 1960, 670 associations coordinated in a federation: *Union Nationale des Parents d'Enfants Inadaptés*, a mighty lobby, which nowadays runs over 1,500 establishments or services.

Step by step, associations centred around physical handicap as well as mental handicap created facilities and services. They have progressively obtained public financing from social security: private initiative, social movement and public policy on one hand, and advocacy and service on the other hand have been mixed. The APF, the UNAPEI and some other peak associations collaborated with Parliament and the government to promote the 1975 law on the guarantee of resources for handicapped people and on their rights in general. They are regularly consulted by the government.

In the sector of *handicap* most of the associations were created before 1970 (Barral and Paterson, 1991). Since then, the creation of new organizations has not often happened, especially the creation of establishments, provided that the needs are more or less satisfied and that the state is willing to have better control over the expenses.

In the sector of *health*, the hospital public sector is largely predominant. As we have previously mentioned, only a small number of French hospitals are run in the associative sector by big associations such as the Red Cross, which was established in France in 1864. The two main reasons are the early secularization of the sector and government health policy after World War II.

Thus, the democratization of access to health care was one of the governmental priorities after World War II. Step by step, the proportion of the population benefiting from social security increased, and nowadays almost all the French population can claim social security for medical expenses. From the late 1950s to the mid-1980s, the government has largely financed the modernization of the hospital sector. Public *Centres Hospitalo-Universitaires* (CHU) were created in the biggest French towns; the aim was to provide democratic high quality health care and favor the development of medicine on the front line of progress, dealing with high level teaching, research and technology, competitive on the international level.

The aim of the associations of users centred around health problems is quite different from associations dealing with handicaps, provided that most facilities are public. Unlike the associations for disabled people, *health associations were mostly created after 1970 and especially during the last decade* for associations centered around genetic diseases and AIDS.

The most recent scientific discoveries made it possible to provide palliative treatments for diseases which were previously incurable. Therefore the number of people suffering from chronic diseases has increased, and so has the demand for more information and for mutual help between patients and families who share the same bad experience. The self-help and cooperative care associations created on the British model have not developed much in France; most patients suffering from terminal disease pursue their treatment in specialized centres, clinics (which often are forprofit organizations) or in a hospital.

Medical progress also made it possible to get a clear diagnosis for genetic diseases, which were previously unknown, but very often didn't provide any treatment. Apart from the setting up of a support network and the diffusion of specific information, the main claims are centred around the need for scientific research to find therapeutic solutions; a lot of associations, at different levels, give their support to medical research. One of the recent striking associative events was the adoption since 1987 of the North American telethon fundraising campaign led by the French Muscular Dystrophy Association (*Association Française contre les Myopathies*, created in 1958) with the participation of a lot of small associations centered around genetic diseases. This very active association opened the most important research lab of Europe on genetic diseases, the *Généthon*. The success of the telethon has attracted a lot of criticism about the content of the campaign as well as "unfair" competition with other associations and the priority given to scientific research over social problems raised by disability (see chapter 6).

The AIDS epidemic also provoked the creation of many associations (eighty associations were registered in 1991) which can be specialized for the support of particular populations (homosexuals, drug-addicts, children), or on specialized actions (information campaigns for prevention, financial support for research, management of social services like home care, phone assistance, etc.).

Another kind of nonprofit organization, this time created by professionals, has the same historical development: they were set up to organize a specialized field of medicine at a pioneer period, when no regulations existed in their domain. This is the case, for example, with the *Association France Transplant* (created in 1969) which aims at the distribution of organs between the public transplant centers located in the CHU (which are the only hospitals allowed to transplant organs), and of the CECOS (*Centre de Conservation du Sperme*), created for the harvesting and distribution of sperm for insemination. The laws, governmental regulations and ethical debates were promoted with their collaboration and were largely inspired by the regulations and the ethical rules they have previously settled.

Other medical domains, like blood transfusion, are also run by nonprofit organizations, for example *Centre National de Transfusion Sanguine* (CNTS), which collects blood on the principle of non-profit donation, but was at the centre of a scandal after the contamination of patients by the AIDS virus, and provoked a large debate about the respective responsibilities of the government and the administrators of the centre.

We will evoke more precisely these fields of activity, and especially the association *France Transplant*, the CECOS and the CNTS organizations in chapter 6, as they play an essential part in the actual ethical issues related to the French nonprofit sector.

5.3.2 Size, scope and structure

Global economic data

In 1990, expenses for Health in France were about 9.8 per cent of the Gross Domestic Product (OECD – CREDES). Within these expenses, 74.2 per cent are directly assumed by government or social security.

Nonprofit associations in the "health and social services" sector are, by far, the most important component of the French nonprofit sector: they only represent 19 per cent of the establishments recorded in SIRENE but 43 per cent of the total resources and above all 55 per cent of the associative employment. Therefore, *their economic role is fundamental*.

Around 15.5 per cent of the overall hospital network in France is operated by associations. *Nonprofits in health* total 2.4 per cent of the number of associations recorded in SIRENE, but they hold about 14 per cent of the nonprofit revenue, with a budget nearly six times as big as the average revenue.

According to the SIRENE file, associations in health represent about 15 per cent of associative employment (and 11 per cent of the employment in this field). The average number of employees is of course much higher than average (about 37 per association). But these associations have a level of wages slightly below the average. Moreover, employment is decreasing since 1980 (–14 per cent), which reveals a reduction of the relative share of nonprofits in the health sector.

The share of the *associations* in the overall network and operation of *social services* in France is much more important than in the health field, but there is much less information on the exact figure. Indeed, in this sector, the place of the nonprofit sector is preponderant. Associations are estimated to number 100,000 and they provide about 55 per cent of the overall number of residential care facilities at the disposal of the disadvantaged (93 per cent in handicapped adults, 87 per cent in handicapped children, 88 per cent in adults in difficulty) and about 87 per cent without elderly homes which are principally provided by the public sector. Many of them are *reconnues d'utilité publique*.

The associative sector is important as a provider of child day care facilities, nearly 40 per cent of pre-school children attending nonprofit day care facilities such as parent *crèches* or private *mini crèches* or family day nurseries. The situation in France is very specific because of the early school attendance at *école maternelle* for children from 2 to 5 years old. Compulsory primary school begins at 6 but school attendance ratios were as follows in 1989–90:

2 years old :	35.4 per cent
3 " :	98 per cent
4.5 " :	100 per cent

The social services associations represent 16.8 per cent of the total number of nonprofits in SIRENE, and hold about 29 per cent of the associative revenue with an average revenue from 70 per cent above the average.

So this sector is the main component of the nonprofit sector in France, and especially for employment: it totals about 38 per cent of nonprofit employment and *58 per cent of the employment in this field*, with an average number of employees about four times more than average (twelve employees). Moreover, employment is increasing significantly since 1980 (123 per cent) and these activities seem to have developed even more in the last two years. But the level of wages is more or less equal to average as these organizations seem to create above all "artificial" jobs like *contrats d'emploi solidarité* (see chapter 6).

In cooperation with the paid staff, the operation of the associations active in health and social services benefits the main part of the nonprofit giving and an important part of volunteering (Archambault *et al.*, 1991).

Fifty-four per cent of French givers contribute to health association funding and 24 per cent to social services. This high level of participation is largely due to the telethon fundraising and to the in-the-streets campaigns. But the amount given is generally low.

The social sector has the second largest proportion of volunteers, far behind culture, sports and recreation: it totals 17 per cent of French voluntary work. For instance, 100,000 volunteers work for the French Red Cross, 48,000 for the *Secours Populaire*, and

65,000 for the *Secours Catholique* (Padieu, 1990).

Volunteers in health are much less numerous – 8.5 per cent of French voluntary work – and less active – 9.9 hours per month, that is 40 per cent below the average.

5.3.3 Legal position

In regard to the legal aspects of nonprofits in health and social services, there is a need to make the distinction between both, since different legal rules regulate the corresponding actions.

Hospital services
Although the treatment of these associations is not distinct in any way from the general associative model, the way the activities of this type of nonprofit organizations are performed – but not the private inner life of the organization itself – is governed by special acts.

Two fundamental laws of 31 December 1970 and 31 July 1991 are the present legal pillars of the French hospital system. They lay down the principle that hospital is a pluralist public service (*service public hospitalier pluraliste*) carried out under the overall responsibility of the state, and that *there is a total complementarity between the state public hospitals, the hospitals managed by associations or other nonprofit organizations, and the hospitals privately operated by the forprofit concerns.*

Nonprofits' special obligations or special privileges derive from their participation in the execution of the hospital public service; they are subjected to part of the rules regulating the management of the public hospitals, their creation and operation are subject to firm conditions and controls of the state, as well as their finances. But these regulations are closely related to the performance of their service, and not to their legal person, except in special cases (for instance, the way the leadership is designated or elected, the importance of the accounts to be given, etc.).

The private clinics have agreements with social security, so their patients receive reimbursement of their expenses.

Social services
As in hospitals, social and medico-social services follow the basic principles defined by the 1901 Act. These organizations lay down

their own criteria, their own methods of help, rescue and assistance. But also as in hospitals, there are many acts ruling their activities. Regarding their obligations and privileges, they can be compared to the "agreed associations" and the *associations reconnues d'utilité publique.*

Over the past ten years, and even longer, the important legal issues raised by this type of organization pertain to the implementation and interpretation in legal rules, of social action politics, of progress in understanding the social phenomenons, of the contingencies of the economical situation, or of public budget possibilities. So the question is always the same: how to share the responsibilities between the private and the public sectors?

5.3.4 Government policy

During the past ten years, there has been a constant oscillation between the impulse and inspiration given by the organizations to the central public administration and the missions and means granted by the state with the participation of social security to these organizations in the general social service set-up by the nation. The important and original action of the genetic diseases associations to promote medical research, and especially by the French muscular dystrophy association AFM, is the perfect example of the role sometimes played by nonprofits in shaping government policy: in this case, private money goes to public research, reversing the usual process, as AFM is financed by private resources up to 95 per cent. We will go into more detail about the action of this organization in chapter 6.

As a consequence, this field is certainly the one in which appears most acutely the problem of the respective roles of nonprofit providers and of the welfare state in a period of deep financial crisis. More generally, the development of these organizations poses questions for the state on its welfare responsibility.

Nonprofit organizations in health and social services, as they are the oldest part of the nonprofit sector in France, and as they participate in welfare state policy, are by far *the most subsidized,* along with the education and research subsector. Generally speaking, health is financially more dependent on public grants than social services: government provides respectively 84 per cent and 60 per cent of total resources.

On the other hand, within the government grants, the central state plays the most important role in health (58 per cent of public subsidies) while in social services, reimbursement and participation in social security are the main source of public support (72 per cent). Moreover, local communities contribute to the social services budget (19 per cent of public participation) when they are quasi-nonexistent in the financing of current expenditure in health.

But in this matter, the distinction between health and social services is less relevant than the one between *nonprofit establishments and associations providing services*. Indeed, in these two tied activities, the influence of government policy is different according to the distinction between nonprofits running hospitals or residential facilities and therefore having an important economic activity, and nonprofit organizations providing home services, and self-help or pressure groups, which have smaller budgets.

The first ones are sometimes called *para-public organizations*, because of the high level of their public funding. Private hospitals belonging to hospital public service receive 90 per cent of their funding from public grants, especially from the central state. As for the private nonprofit hospitals which do not belong to hospital public service and the establishments for the disabled and underprivileged, public money provides 73 per cent of their financing; but in contrast to hospitals, public money is provided especially by reimbursement of a *per diem* by social security. In both activities, local support is very limited.

On the other hand, the *small-sized health or social services* or the large charities have more diversified resources and therefore they are more independent. Indeed, nursing homes and health services only receive 60 per cent of their resources from public grants. For social services, public support represents less than 38 per cent of the budget and the major part of their revenue comes from private donations (12 per cent) and private earnings (47 per cent).

We can also observe that local support plays a more significant role in the financing of health and social services than in health and social establishments – about 12 per cent for health services and 15 per cent for social services.

The main change in policy in this sector over the last decade is the *shift from third party per diem reimbursement to a global grant* for the main part of private nonprofit hospitals in 1985. This change, also applicable to public hospitals, was intended to reduce the tendency that many hospital managers had to lengthen the patient's hospitalization stay in order to raise the subsidy. This change was a great success. However, the tendency to lengthen hospitalization still exists in the *per diem*-reimbursed establishments.

Over the last decade, we observe a kind of specialization between public, private forprofit and nonprofit hospitals and clinics: private forprofits handle light surgery and ordinary childbirths; public hospitals deal with emergency cases, heavy surgery, investigations and check-ups and all kind of illnesses, even the least common; and private nonprofits specialize in cancer, drug addiction, and all kind of rehabilitation.

Nonprofits run the major part of social residential and work facilities, with a quasi-monopoly for disabled people. For a long time, the *per diem* reimbursement incited the nonprofit managers to fill the establishments, even with irrelevant persons. The policy has changed since the early 1980s, with financial incentives from local governments, turning to home care of the elderly, the disabled, pre-delinquents, the sick, with the help of medical and nursing services at home.

A new system of home care services, which particularly aims at looking after elderly and dependent people, has developed significantly since 1984. It is organized by the main organization SSAD (*Services de Soins A Domicile*). Sixty-nine per cent of services are delivered by the nonprofit sector (SESI, 1992).

The creation of this type of nonprofit organization was also encouraged by social contributions exemptions for employers in January 1992 because these organizations create many unskilled or semi-skilled jobs and therefore they contribute to the employment policy. Particularly, they have created in the last five years a lot of half-time collective utility jobs like *contrats emploi solidarité* (CES).

5.4 Environment

The interest in the relations between man and nature, in the fight against destruction provoked by the intervention of mankind in the natural equilibrium, and in policies aiming to preserve nature against pollution and attacks by industrial civilization, is a *recent but very important phenomenon*. From the mid-1970s on, public environmental policy tends to become a relatively major factor of general policy. Moreover, ecology now plays an important role in public life, partly thanks to the emergence of ecologist parties, which are becoming a real political force.

In France, because of public concern, the most important source of action in this new concern is the nonprofit organization. As in the field of culture, there has been a dramatic development in this type of association since the 1960s and especially since the 1980s. They act for the protection of nature, or protection of landscapes, in the fight against pollution and industrial prejudices. They develop particularly at a local level. But the associative ecomovement is still a *young reality in motion*. It is also a field in which relationships between business, public and associative entities are still in formation.

5.4.1 History

Before 1970, a diffuse associative basis of the ecomovement existed, especially thanks to the French scientists' action, *but the two detonators of the explosion of the ecology associative movement in France were first, the May 1968 revolution, which was soon followed by a second catalyst: the anti-nuclear movement and the Club de Rome report.*

The ideas developed by one of the two main trends of *May 1968* – the other current was based on left-wing political theories like Trotskyism, Maoism, etc. – are at the bottom of the development of ecologism. The mixing of ideas in May 1968 triggered various movements. It praised spontaneity, criticized any kind of dogmatism and rose up against the effect of the development of industrial societies, which neglect the individual and the environment on a global scale as well as on the local scale, in fields as varied as consumption, town planning, economic values, individualism and so on. The will to merge substance and form, criticism and rebellion in the same praxis can also be found there. Thus, after the May 1968, rebellion quite a few activists invested in an ecologist militant movement. They found the way to maintain at different levels the contest spirit joined with concrete action.

Since the late 1960s the dangers of nuclear energy – which were denounced by scientists, stirred up by prospective studies on the resources of the planet and the growing consumption of the industrialized countries – were one of the favorite themes of the ecologists. The voices of the anti-war militants, who were contesting civil and military nuclear power in the context of their opposition to the war in Vietnam and the French nuclear trials in the Pacific, joined the chorus. At the beginning of the 1970s a real wave of opposition appeared: it manifested itself massively on the sites of nuclear plants. The greatest demonstration, gathering over 100,000 people, took place in 1972 on the Plateau du Larzac, in southern France, and fought against the extension of a military camp.

The fight against civil nuclear power encountered the resistance of *Electricité de France* (EDF), the monopolistic producer of electricity in France and a big nationalized company. With the cooperation of the government, EDF have led very active campaigns in favor of nuclear energy, especially on the sites of nuclear plants. These campaigns were a relative success, as polls show that the majority of French public opinion became favorable to civil nuclear energy, unlike in Germany, in the United Kingdom and in other European countries. Nowadays, 75 per cent of the electricity is produced by nuclear plants against 36 per cent in the countries of the EU.

In the 1980s, *ecology as an election stake came forcefully into the French political sphere*. The main traditional parties place the protection of natural and urban environment on their program and ecology appears at the top of the political scene by the creation of two parties, A. Waechter's "Greens" (*Les Verts*) and B. Lalonde's "Ecology Generation" (*Génération Ecologie*), in the early 1990s. The maturing and the political organization of the trend took place from the early 1970s in the associative framework. Ecology did not represent a real electoral force in France until 1977. Its appearance on the political scene was rather late, compared to the phenomenon in Germany.

Nowadays, the environmental associations are active in three major fields: protection of nature and animals, protection of rural and urban environment and associations against nuclear power.

5.4.2 Size, scope and structure

The flourishing of the associative ecomovement is rather new in France. *Thus, the statistics are not effective yet.* Even the most basic data – like the number of establishments – are imprecise. This area only represents 2 per cent of the associative creations from 1975 to 1984 (Canto, 1988), but creations of environmental associations seem to have grown since then.

There are very few large associations representing groups and lobbies in France, but instead there are *many small local entities which mobilize a lot of volunteers.* According to our data, not very reliable for this sector, the number of employees is small, as the level of resources seems to be very weak. But associations in this area are nearly financially independent, as their private revenue is about 68 per cent of their total resources. Government grants only represent 32 per cent of their financing, which is well below the average (59.5 per cent of the money revenue).

According to a CREDOC survey, 3 per cent of French people 18 of years of age join an association active in environment questions. The authors of this survey note that "despite the important part environmental debates take in the French society, the number of members of these organizations does not increase more than the French adult population". They explain this situation by the technical nature of environmental concerns which specially involve the participation of experienced people. As a matter of fact, although in the 1970s the militants in these associations were in most cases young and graduate men (under 39 years old), they are now older (from 40 to 59) (Fourel and Volatier, 1992).

Associations active in environment issues only receive 2 per cent of the *giving* to nonprofit organizations. But they benefit from 9.5 per cent of the total *volunteering* and their members are very active, as they work about twenty-seven hours per month – the average is about sixteen hours (Archambault *et al.*, 1991).

5.4.3 Legal position

Basically, *French associations active in environment concerns follow the same general principles as those governing other types of nonprofits* (the 1901 law). They are not subjected to a separate body of law nor to any special obligations, *but these associations benefit from state recognition and from special privileges.*

Overall, these associations have won this very special and exceptional privilege to have the "interest and right to act" (*intérêt et droit d'agir*), that is to bring an action before a judiciary or administrative court against some private concerns – individual or organization – or against the state. A law of 10 July 1976 and a decree of 7 July 1977 (*Recueil Dalloz*, 1976, 308; *ibid.*, 1977, note 308) authorize associations active in the protection of the environment and "agreed" by the due ministry, to prosecute on matters on which they are entitled to act by legal texts. As shown in chapter 3, this is a particular exception to the general principle of French Law, granted to very few types of nonprofit organizations.

Lastly, more and more, public, forprofit and nonprofit organizations participate in the building of a new section of the French Law (and of European and international laws as well), in which the nonprofit organizations play the role of defender of a public cause, of the collectivities' main cause.

5.4.4 Government policy

In the mid-1970s, as environmental problems represented more and more a real and new preoccupation of the citizens, ecology became a public concern. Then, as usual in France, the state picked up these claims and created a *Ministry of Environment*. Since then, the French central state, as in many other countries, together with the local agencies, have developed a real *policy of environment*. To give an example, in 1992, local communities spent 22 billion FF. on the environment, that is 60 per cent more than in 1989. These contributions are still growing.

Many associations are flourishing in this field. In some cases, they can counterbalance the huge political influences (even if they do not represent in France important groupings and lobbies, in contrast to other countries). More and more, they participate in public action (as public grants provide about 32 per cent).

The political parties in the late 1980s and the 1990s were also more and more concerned by ecology. As seen above, *ecologist parties* (*Les Verts* and *Génération Ecologie*) were created; their leaders came from the associative movement. One of them, Brice Lalonde, was the socialist Minister of Environment from 1990 to

1992. These two parties became a real electoral force of up to 14 per cent in the 1989 European election; at that time, the French situation was compared to the German "Greens" phenomenon. But in the 1993 parliamentary election, the ecologists went down to 8 per cent of the vote.

The heritage of May 1968, teeming with ideas, is closely related to the structuration of these parties which up to now remain scattered and anxious to keep the initiative and the autonomy of their various trends. According to Simonnet's analysis, that was where the strength as well as the weakness of the movement lay during the 1980s: to act from all sides, to bring pressure on centralized institutions on multiple fronts, but being too scattered to play a part in the centralized political game (Simonnet, 1982). The resistance of the main ecologist actors to setting up for themselves a centralized organization, considered nondemocratic and contrary to the freedom of expression, explains why the ecology movement has evolved in successive spurts – and not, as for political parties, in splits. In order to bypass centralization but still make their voice heard, the ecologists have adopted centralized but short-lived structures which were abandoned after the elections, each associative grouping leaving a new organization in place.

Nowadays, ecologist parties seem to pass through a serious crisis, as they are losing part of the trust some people have put in them. On the one hand, their participation is much coveted by political groups, in the majority and in opposition, and they have difficulty in maintaining their unpolitical aim. On the other hand, better integration by private and public entities of environmental concerns wrong-foots the protest movements. Lastly, the two ecologist parties have to face an internal crisis as they have not succeeded in unifying themselves in a single movement.

5.5 Civic organizations

Civic organizations in France stem from the revolution, and were for a long time supposed to frame overall counter-powers, opposition and rebellion groups. Therefore, they were feared or prohibited by the government. History is at the root of the present situation and may explain the relative poverty of French civic organizations.

But for the last half century, there has been a revival of civic organizations linked with immigration flows in France. Such associations have been created in order either to better integrate new immigrants, or on the contrary to try to keep up the specificity of people originating from different regions of the world, or from various parts of the country itself.

Out of this recent development, civic associations follow in France the same basic trends as associative general cases with regard to their legal position and their support by government.

5.5.1 History

Civisme or *civique* are rather recent terms in the French language. Montesquieu (1748), the first to use these terms in French literature, defined civism as a "continual preference for public benefit".

Citizens' organizations during the Middle Ages – fighting both feudal and state powers to obtain civil rights, freedom and tax exemption for their cities – were the ancestors of civil rights and community action organizations.

Later, in the eighteenth century there was a flourishing of learned societies, social clubs (*salons*) or political organizations oriented towards the fight against slavery and the slave trade, and other forms of racism, discretionary punishment and torture and, last but not least, absolute monarchy.

These organizations advocated civil rights, freedom of worship, habeas corpus and constitutional monarchy with the ever-quoted reference to the more liberal British society and political organization. The influence of philosophers – Voltaire, Rousseau, Montesquieu, Diderot – was decisive and characteristic of the everlasting influence of intellectuals in such matters in France. Of course, the involvement of some French people led by Lafayette in the American War of Independence, and in a sense also the French Revolution, are consequences of this mainstream.

During the French Revolution, the political clubs developed themes such as the defence of civil rights, freedom of worship, suppression of discretionary confinement – the symbol of which was the Bastille – the emancipation of the Jews and of the Protestants, etc. But they almost disappear with the general statement of the Le Chapelier Act which is a negation of the existence of intermediary entities. It is quite contrary of course to the "subsidiarity principle", so important in the Catholic and in the

German tradition and which hereafter will become the rule of the European Community.

As a consequence, civic organizations are less developed in France than in Anglo-Saxon countries, but *this particularism is fading out with the recent trend of decentralization and europeanization.*

Indeed, for the last half century, the creation of civil rights or antiracist associations followed the major political events, wars in particular, and the immigration flows. A few examples of the main movements show the correlation between these events and the creation of associations, which in most cases have enlarged their domain of action as new problems appeared.

The fight against racism and antisemitism is a tradition of the French civic organizations since the Dreyfus affair. The still existing *Ligue des Droits de l'Homme* was created during this period (1898); French freemasonry developed the same defence. The *Ligue contre le Racisme et l'Antisémitisme* (LICRA) was created in 1927 for the defence of a Jewish watchmaker in Paris who murdered those responsible for pogroms in the Republic of Ukraine. The CIMADE (ecumenical service of mutual aid) was created in 1939 to help the refugees from Alsace and Lorraine who fled eastern France. It became an organization for resistance against nazism, against petainism and for solidarity with the victims of fascism. The immigration flow of the postwar period, coming from Spain, Portugal and especially from North Africa also stirred up the problem of racism and its consequences for the living conditions of immigrants. So the "Movement against Racism and for Friendship between the Peoples" (MRAP) was created in 1950.

During the 1970s and 1980s, *many associations denouncing dictatorships* were created: the political situations in Chile and in South-East Asia were followed by the creation of associations such as *France Terre d'Asile* (France Land of Asylum in 1971) and some subsidiaries of international civic associations which are still very active in France, such as Amnesty International (the French subsidiary was created in 1971); the arrival of Asiatic refugees (notably Cambodians) had a similar effect, with for example *Enfance et Partage* born in 1977.

The feminist movement, especially in the 1970s, had also incited the creation of nonprofit organizations at this period. The term *feminism* appeared in the French language in 1837 and Fourier and Saint-Simon advocated women's liberation. During the 1848

Revolution women's clubs and newspapers asked for political equality between men and women, especially for the female vote. One century later, in 1944, women voted for the first time in France. In 1949 Simone de Beauvoir published the famous book *Le deuxième sexe*. It was the very beginning of modern feminism in France, and as often in France the debate was launched by the intellectuals. Under the influence of American women's lib, and American writers such as Betty Friedan or Kate Millett, the French *Mouvement de Libération de la Femme* was created; many young women who were active in the 1968 student movement became active feminists. The first nonprofit family planning fought for the freedom of birth control and later, in the early 1970s, for the freedom of abortion, considered as a crime by the law. As abortion was authorized and regulated in 1977, the feminist movement stressed other topical concerns: the defence of professional equality, which is better in France than in many other industrialized countries, the fight against rape and sexual harassment.

As usual in France, the state picked up feminist claims and created a Secretary of State of women's rights in the mid-1970s. The feminist movement is less active nowadays than in the 1970s, following the decrease of the anti-establishment current and as political parties developed the feminist arguments.

But above all, during the 1970s and the 1980s, *many associations were created for the defence of immigrants against racism*, to denounce inequalities in many institutions such as the legal or educational system and the bad working conditions of people removed from their cultural roots and from their families. They were also active in the social field (adult education, aid for administrative problems, teaching of the French language, education and mutual help for women, etc.).

Problems linked to immigration, racism and social problems of young people in the suburbs of big towns incited the creation of "second generation" associations like *S.O.S. Racisme* in 1984, which launched the very popular campaign "*Touche pas à mon pote*" (a small badge representing a hand on which was written "Don't touch my buddy"). Many of these quoted organizations are related to the left-wing trend (even if some of them claim to be apolitical) and are very attached to the idea of a French tradition of defence of the Rights of Man, of political asylum and respect for "differences" and dignity; they are very active in justice proceedings (against racist and antisemitic publications, offences or crimes, against war criminals, against the *révisionistes* – historians who review the nazi period and deny the existence of the Jewish holocaust – and so on); during the 1986 come-back of a right-wing government led by Jacques Chirac, many antiracist organizations feared the calling into question of the measures settled by the left-wing governments since 1981 (for example the familial reunion of immigrants) and participated in 1988 in the campaign for the suppression of the Pasqua law about the entry and the stay of foreigners on French territory. This law was finally voted in 1993, with the second come-back of the right, and provoked a movement of protest by the main civic associations as it is a real limitation of access to French nationality and to the "soil right" (*droit du sol*). Important demonstrations also often gather these associations to protest against the rise of the *Front National*, the extreme-Right political party.

In the meantime, minorities associations flourished, especially Islamic associations (Kepel, 1987), which often aim to build mosques in urban suburbs, as Islam is now the second religion in France.

Some right-wing civic associations, tinged with xenophobia and/or religious fundamentalism, have also been created since the early 1980s: *Légitime Défense* (Self-defence, 1978) which considers that the attitude of justice against criminality is too lax and which fights against the suppression of the death sentence; the "International Federation for the Defence of Fundamental Human Values" which promotes moral behavior and the transmission of moral values to the younger generation (marriage, civic education); committees against abortion, which in some cases have initiated commando actions in clinics and hospitals.

5.5.2 Size, scope and structure

There is nothing particular to emphasize about the size and scope of the associations active in the defence of civic rights. Moreover, few statistics are available and the subsector is tiny.

Civic organizations – which represent about 2.4 per cent of the total number of nonprofit establishments – *are generally small entities* and they only employ some 2 per cent of nonprofit employment. Private resources – mainly membership dues – provide 52.2 per cent of their financing. They also receive central state support.

They receive about 2.2 per cent of nonprofit donations (a contribution of about 30 per cent below the average), and 4 per cent of volunteering to nonprofits. Many reports note the disaffection of people with this type of organization but they seem to retain some keen militants as shown by the level of voluntary hours: volunteer work in these associations is about 23.3 hours per month which is considerably better than average (Archambault *et al.*, 1991).

5.5.3 Legal position

The juridical treatment of civic organizations is not distinct from the general model, apart from perhaps some possible public funding based on the civic performance of such associations. There is no separate body of law governing them. Their only obligation is related to an amendment to the law of 1 July 1901, dated 1935, which forbids the creation of associations which not only have illicit or immoral aims, but also are able to endanger the unity of French territory, or the republican structure of the French government (article 3 of the law).

5.5.4 Government policy

There are no particularities of civic nonprofit organizations with regard to government policy. Overall characteristics of the government's position apply to this industry without any specificity.

5.6 Foundations

In spite of an earlier origin and a recent rapid development, foundations are still widely unknown in France. As a matter of fact, in contrast to other countries where foundations are nowadays a deep-rooted reality, France is, among all the developed countries, the one where foundations are least numerous (less than 800 including the foundations sheltered by *Fondation de France*); moreover, there was no law ruling their existence and operation until very recently.

But since the 1980s, there has been a revival of "patronage" in

France. This patronage is encouraged by public powers, in favor of various sectors of activity, especially in culture and arts. This recent phenomenon has contributed to the development and a better acknowledgement of foundations in France.

5.6.1 History

Foundations are certainly the oldest part of the nonprofit sector, as their legal status dates back to Roman Law.

During the Middle Ages, congregations created foundations to provide health and social services. In the *ancien régime,* there were many poorhouse foundations, where the deprived were given room and board, or foundations supporting poor students and ecclesiastics.

Since they benefited from legacies and donations, some of them became very rich and the centralized power became very suspicious about such an accumulation of wealth and might without any control from the government. The royal power considered bequests to foundations as tax evasion. Therefore Louis XIV and Louis XV restricted the rights of existing foundations and prohibited the creation of new ones (Pomey, 1980). They denounced the economic inefficiency of the mortmain (*mainmorte*) property secluded from the general circulation of goods.

By proclaiming that the state has the monopoly of general interest, of common weal, the Le Chapelier Act (1791) struck at foundations as well as corporations and guilds and any form of voluntary association. The French Revolution suppressed foundations and sold their property as *Biens nationaux* to the rising bourgeoisie. Foundations therefore lost their legal status and disappeared till the end of the nineteenth century. That is why there are very few foundations in France nowadays.

One of the first and most famous foundations created in the late nineteenth century is the *Institut Pasteur* (1887). After the discovery of rabies treatment, Pasteur refused the support of the state and decided to create a private research institute. Although he was a prominent member of the civil service, he feared the inefficiency of public academic research teams and launched a fundraising campaign led by a fundraising committee (Moulin, 1992). Though the research teams have brilliant results – all French Nobel prizewinners for medicine are members – the Pasteur Institute recently met with financial difficulties, and public money, not private gifts, reorganized its finances.

A few foundations were created before World War I and a few more in the interwar period, but, as associations, *they have been flourishing since 1965*, largely under public administration impulse.

But since foundations are mainly financed by endowment, they are vulnerable to inflation. Thus the durable inflation which prevailed in France after World War I is another explanation for the scarcity of foundations in France. The inflationary stop in 1983 was a new incentive to create foundations. Then Sylvie Tsyboula, deputy director of the *Fondation de France*, the most important foundation in France, considers that "a second foundation's renewal is under way, but it is not yet clear how a new political environment, and a deep economic recession will influence their development" (Tsyboula, 1993). Indeed, in the last few years, many large corporations have created company-sponsored foundations in new fields such as environment, education, but above all in arts and culture, partly thanks to the action of Jack Lang, the socialist Minister of Culture who aimed at extending the available resources for arts by the promotion of "patronage".

Most of the foundations in France are operating foundations. They run museums (Vasarely, Arp, Maeght, Institut du Monde Arabe) and health establishments (Fondation Darty, Hôpital Rothschild). Many are active in research (Institut Pasteur, Fondation Nationale des Sciences Politiques, Maison des Sciences de l'Homme, Fondation Royaumont, Fondation Curie), or in the protection of the environment (Cousteau, Ushuaia).

Grant-giving foundations, which are philanthropic intermediaries, are almost nonexistent in Franc: only thirteen (or 3 per cent) were reported in 1992 and they are very small, except for two of them: the *Fondation pour la Recherche Médicale* (1964), which was the first one to launch fundraising campaigns with the participation of the mass media, and mainly the *Fondation de France* (1969), the first and only charitable trust close to the Anglo-Saxon model, a pool of uncommitted money acting as a capital venture. In contrast to the other foundations, the *Fondation de France* is a fundraising *and* a grant-giving foundation. During the last decade, it has created or run foundations within itself (today there are 350 foundations) and has acted as a leader of the whole nonprofit sector.

These two foundations subsidize precise operations, in the sector of medical research for the first one, in any kind of activity for the second.

5.6.2 Size, scope and structure

As mentioned above, probably because of French historic centralism and the too recent implementation of their legal status, *foundations are still very few in France*: only 548 foundations set up in conformity with the law are active (*fondations reconnues d'utilité publique*) and twenty-two corporate foundations. About 350 little foundations sheltered by *Fondation de France* have to be added. The United States, for example, have approximately 32,000 foundations of which almost 96 per cent are grant-making (as compared with 3 per cent of foundations in France). But other European countries of a size comparable to France also have many more foundations than France: 7,000 in Germany, for instance.

In France, *grant-giving foundations are generally quite small*, compared to other countries. Their part in total resources of the nonprofit sector is almost nil though they have a budget more than twenty-four times as big as average, because of their nature (a foundation primarily consists of an endowment). Moreover, they play a very limited economic role with regard to employment and voluntary work.

The structure of their resources is specific: the amount of government subsidies is low, about 5 per cent. Direct individual contributions provide more than half of the foundations' total revenue. The other part of their resources is provided by private earnings, especially investment income: it is the only subsector in which investment income is not negligible.

5.6.3 Legal position

Legal aspects of French foundations are fundamental because juridical texts existing in this field are just starting to be implemented.

This type of organization, although nonprofit, follows a different pattern from the association one. *Before 1987, there was no body of law really governing foundations*: there only was a tradition of giving administrative recognizance to this kind of organization (there were about 400 at that time); they were *reconnues d'utilité publique* by the government, with no legal basis to it. Most of the time, they were mixed up with other types of nonprofit, registered associations for example, without legal personality distinct from that of their creators.

Foundations in France are ruled by two recent laws:

- The law of 23 July 1987 gave for the first time a *legal definition of the French foundation*: it is the legal act by which one or several physical persons or legal entities decide the irrevocable destination of estate, rights or resources to the realization of an action of public benefit, of nonprofit aim. The endowment must be at least 5 million FF.

  This first description of a foundation shows the fundamental difference existing with other nonprofit organizations, especially the association: these are groupings of persons, of partners; in contrast, a foundation is a grouping of goods, of estate earmarked to well-determined nonprofit aims of public benefit. Their action consists chiefly in the distribution of the major part of their income, by grant-making in the fields of philanthropy, education, social services, culture, etc.

- The law of 4 July 1990 *allows corporations to create foundations* under special conditions (a nonprofit aim and an endowment of about a fifth of its planned program, which must amount to 1 million FF.).

The use of the term has been restricted: since 1990, a foundation is either *reconnue d'utilité publique* or a *fondation d'entreprise* (corporate foundation). The period of existence of a foundation *reconnue d'utilité publique* is generally undetermined, for a long term; that of a corporate foundation is for five years, possibly renewable. But many organizations created before 1987 still use the term *foundation* though they depend on the 1901 Act.

The laws of 1987 and 1990 differ from the acts governing other types of nonprofit organizations, in that they are not of the same nature. *They are much more strict, they provide many more controls than the 1901 Act.*

- A foundation *reconnue d'utilité publique*, to exist, has to receive a preliminary public authorization. It derives its legal existence through a decree issued by the state council and from the moment it is published in the *Journal Officiel*. A corporate foundation receives its legal existence either from the authorization given by the administration or from its silence within a period of four months after publication. Alternatively, the association may be simply registered. This means that the title of foundation is protected by the law.

- The foundations *reconnues d'utilité publique* have a *very wide legal capacity*, for instance they may possess as much real estate as they wish; the corporate foundation, on the other hand, has the same restricted capacity as the association.
- Finally, *foundations are subjected to the state's tutelage*: only part of the administrators of the organizations are appointed by the founders; about a third of the board represents public authorities.

Foundations are submitted to state authority for matters such as gifts and legacies (only those *reconnues d'utilité publique* can receive donations according to precise formalities), loans and mortgages.

As they can have a commercial activity, foundations can be subjected to the same taxes as commercial companies. They cannot undertake fundraising or appeals. But they can also benefit from some of the tax privileges enjoyed by associations and have some similar legal provisions. As Tsyboula pointed out, "old fears of mortmain have not disappeared within French administrative culture ... Established within civil law, but submitted to state authority for many matters, foundations are set up at the cross roads of two cultures, which don't always get accorded" (Tsyboula, 1993).

5.6.4 Government policy

The revival of foundations in France is recent and was encouraged by the state government. The first encouragement was the creation of the Fondation de France in 1969 on the initiative of General de Gaulle and André Malraux. The first 16 million FF. endowment was given by the public *Caisse des Depôts et Consignations* (a public agency gathering the funds of savings banks and financing local governments and public social housing) and by seventeen public and private banks. Independent from the government but with many civil servants as board trustees, the *Fondation de France* has two missions: encouraging philanthropy and sheltering individual or corporate foundations. Two types of foundations can be created inside the *Fondation de France*: foundations with an endowment (168 in 1990) and foundations with regular annual funding (158 in 1990). The legal status of foundations sheltered by the *Fondation de France* is less constraining than the ordinary status of public utility foundation, and the endowment can be lower (at least 5 million FF. for a public utility foundation). In 1991, the *Fondation de France* reported an annual revenue of 537.3 million FF. and received gifts and legacies of about 55.4 million FF. (*Fondation de France*, 1992).

More recently the government encouraged companies' patronage, especially on arts. The model of the English-speaking countries, especially, guided the first attempts and steps in this matter. So the development of French foundations has been accelerated thanks to the action of the socialist government and especially the intervention of the Ministry of Culture. Indeed, it initiated the law of 1990 in the general framework of helping and promoting the patronage of organizations or companies to diversify cultural financial resources. Some corporate foundations have been created since 1990 (*MACIF, France Telecom, GAN, Gaz de France, Crédit Coopératif*, etc.) and some associations created by corporations and wrongly called foundations were suppressed or turned into effective corporate foundations. These corporate foundations have to respect specific conditions: a minimal endowment of 200,000 FF. and an annual corporate giving of at least 1 million FF. over five years. But according to the 1987 law on corporate giving, these funds are tax-deductible up to 0.2 per cent of the turnover.

Some public agencies, also, to avoid public accountability and obtain more flexible management, created foundations (half of the total number of corporate foundations). They operate in fields like culture and environment.

Finally, this law encouraged the public utility foundations too because it gave the opportunity to create a foundation by testament. Before this date a bequest could only be addressed to an existing foundation. Despite this encouragement, the progression of public utility foundations is very slow: nine foundations were created in 1991, fifteen in 1992 and thirteen in 1993, for a total number of only 428 foundations in 1993 (Ministère de l'intérieur, 1994).

To conclude, we have to note that the way French foundations are created may explain why they are so few. *Indeed the French pattern of foundations is often resented as constraining* because it is subject to a restrictive legal form and to the quasi-discretionary power of the public authorities. These controls are all the more constraining in that foundations are facing a deep economic crisis. On the other hand, these French status failures may involve in the future some *transfers* to countries where legislation is more favorable to this type of institution. So other steps have to be taken, especially in the field – at the moment not regulated – of a trusteeship system, open to organizations *and* individuals, since the present arrangements are chiefly accessible to organizations, but hardly at all to individuals; there are some attempts in this new direction too: some projects are in discussion in parliament.

Notes

1 This section is written by Judith Boumendil, research assistant.
2 This role is more important from a symbolic than from an economic point of view: the Ministry of Culture percentage in the central state budget is less than 1 per cent, but culture is an important French label.
3 This part (pp. 162–64) is written by Florence Paterson, research assistant.

Chapter 6

POLICY ISSUES

The two last chapters highlighted first of all the importance of the nonprofit sector in the provision of personal services and, secondly, the large preponderance of public financing in third sector revenue sources. These two features, now clearly isolated, are at the root of the two important questions that the *Conseil National de la Vie Associative* (CNVA) periodically asks in its biannual statement. The first one could be: "Isn't the nonprofit sector becoming a standard service industry, a network of quasi-businesses delivering services, contaminated by the aim and behavior of their capitalist environment?" On the other hand, the second question is: "Can the nonprofit sector be independent of its principal founder when more than half of its resources is public money? Some organizations are subsidized by the state, the local government or the social security up to 95 or even 100 per cent. Aren't such organizations quasi-public agencies?"

In its periodical *Bilan de la vie associative*, the CNVA[1] intends to isolate a true nonprofit sector, expressive of civil society and democratically managed, by pointing out the black sheep. But it is a difficult task to find objective criteria for such an elimination (CNVA, 1992).

So the nonprofit sector is on a knife-edge. Despite this ambiguousness – or perhaps because of it – the very liberal legal status of *association déclarée* is more and more used by anybody for any object, as the acceleration of annual creations of declared associations shows. Thus the 1901 Act is questioned: the current discussion of the Chéroutre Report (1993) illustrates this long-standing policy issue.

Conversely some current policy issues are very recent, such as the reduction in government support, the effects of European integration on the legal position of the nonprofit sector, or the ethical issues involved for some nonprofit organizations and beyond for the whole society in the financing of political parties or blood transfusion scandals.

To discover the major issues that the nonprofit sector is facing at the present time, we examined specialized reports and reviews and interviewed some thirty key leaders of the nonprofit sector or policymakers. This chapter summarizes the main concerns.

6.1 Public policy and governance

6.1.1 Overall posture of the government

Overall posture of central government
In general, the overall posture of the French government towards nonprofit organizations has become more and more favorable during the last two decades.

We have seen in chapter 2 the hostile relationship between public authorities and the emerging nonprofit sector which prevailed during the nineteenth century. Neutral or nonexistent relations predominated after the 1901 Act, which provided a legal status to existing and to new nonprofit organizations; and the nonprofit sector grew slowly but surely afterwards. Since 1970 there has been a dramatic nonprofits "baby-boom" as Table 6.1 shows.

When regrouping by subperiods, we have the following annual average growth rates of new associations:

> 1908–60: 1.8%
> 1960–70: 4.0%
> 1970–80: 5.0%
> 1980–93: 5.7%

Of course, it is a very rough indicator as many newly created associations die very quickly. However, it gives an idea of the dynamism of the sector, and as we will see later, the catching up of the size of the nonprofit sector in other industrial countries was encouraged by central and local governments. These figures show that the slower overall economic growth since 1974 created new opportunities for the third sector and that the systematic policy of the socialist government since 1981 promoting the *Économie sociale* was efficient.

Table 6.1

Annual creations of associations reported by Ministry of Interior

Year	Associations	Year	Associations	Year	Associations
1908	5,000*	1976	25,622	1986	50,607
1938	10,000*	1977	33,188	1987	54,130
1960	12,633	1978	35,025	1988	50,650
1965	17,540	1979	31,222	1989	60,630
1970	18,722	1980	30,543	1990	60,190
1971	23,361	1981	33,977	1991	58,840
1972	26,257	1982	40,228	1992	70,403
1973	22,403	1983	46,857	1993	62,736
1974	22,153	1984	48,040		
1975	23,753	1985	47,803		

* Rough estimates, as it is only since 1960 that the Ministry of the Interior has reported an official figure.

This strengthening of the third sector was encouraged by different currents: the first one is composed of reformist senior civil servants who meet in think-tanks such as *Club Jean Moulin* (Bloch-Lainé is the emblematic figure of this current). The Second Left (Rocard, Delors, the CFDT union) is the second current. At the same time, some French sociologists (such as Crozier, Mendras and Touraine) emphasized the role of the "civil society" as counterbalancing the government action in many fields. With this factual and intellectual background, the French government became more and more aware of the complementarity of the public and the nonprofit sectors, as the following quotations show:

> Welfare policy was built on a serrated motion between the legal decisions and the initiatives of groups of citizens coming together to improve either our collective life or the conditions of integration of individuals in our society (General Inspection of Social Services, Report 1984).

The State and public communities have no monopoly on public good. In many cases, private initiative came first to meet people's needs ... According to 1901 Act principles, associations participate to general interest activities and sometimes run a public service (1.27.1975, circular from Prime Minister, quoted in Chéroutre, 1993a).

Compared with the Jacobin tradition, these quotations show a Copernican revolution from etatist to partnership policies. The slowdown of etatism is reinforced by a revival of *"laissez-faire"* ideology and the turning point of the Decentralization Acts (1982–83).

There is really an explicit policy in France towards the whole "social economy" and towards the nonprofit sector, inside the social economy. The overall policy toward the social economy (cooperatives, mutuals, foundations and associations) consists of encouraging the *creation of umbrella organizations* enhancing the visibility of social economy, or federating funds such as:

- the *Comité national de liaison des activités mutualistes coopératives et associatives* (CNLAMCA), created in 1970 (national committee to link cooperative, mutual and nonprofit organizations and to represent them before the public authorities);
- the *Fondation de l'Economie Sociale* (1979). So far, this is an abortive project, but it is possible that a revival will come in the mid-1990s.

More political entities were created after 1981 when the socialists came into power, such as:

- the *Délégation à l'Economie Sociale* (1981), an interministerial agency with great expectations and less money, only 20 million FF., to subsidize nonprofit organizations;
- a short-lived Secretary of State for social economy when Rocard was Prime Minister (1987–91).

This policy also consists of *promoting the concept of social economy* at the European level, and of facilitating the access of social economy organizations to bank financing and to specific securities or bonds. There is also an explicit policy towards the *narrower nonprofit* sector which consists of:

- encouragements to peak nonprofit organizations such as the CNVA (*Conseil National de la Vie Associative*) and representation

of the nonprofit sector (five representatives) in the *Conseil Economique et Social* since 1983;
- fiscal incentives to individual and corporate giving, and tax support to nonprofit organizations;
- heavy financial support to nonprofits running establishments or other facilities according to contracts and lighter and more discretionary financial support to other nonprofits;
- the creation in 1982 of a general fund to promote associative life (*Fonds national pour le développement de la vie associative*) financed by a tax on horse race bets (*pari mutuel urbain*) (only 30 million FF. in 1990);
- encouraging volunteering by favorable regulations.

The philosophy and principles that lie behind the policy encouraging the nonprofit sector is quite well explained in the above-mentioned quotations. We can add that since the Decentralization Acts, nonprofit organizations are seen by the government as important partners for local authorities and as the best private entities to restore social cohesion and prevent the social exclusion of frail or deprived populations in a period of growing unemployment. Nonprofits are closer to people's needs than an impersonal bureaucracy; they are able to detect forthcoming issues and to propose innovative solutions. As they can react quicker than heavy public agencies, they can face emergency issues.

Overall position of local government
As referred to in chapter 2, the Decentralization Acts (1982–83) transferred to local government many activities and simultaneously some taxes. Among these activities, culture and arts, sports, education and training services are important areas, but the social welfare services outside social security (*aide sociale*, intended for the underprivileged) and of course local development became the "game preserve" of local government. Facing these growing responsibilities, local authorities contracted out the provision of many services, sometimes to trade business but more often to nonprofits. What are the advantages of contracting out for local authorities? One is to cut down the costs by evading the severe regulations ruling public sector employment (the impossibility of dismissing workers once hired, higher wages for

unskilled workers than in the private sector); another reason is to escape the heavy rules of public accounting which inhibit innovation. Third, public financing at the local level also implies tighter patronage and even political dependence. Many examples show that nonprofit managers often become local politicians, town council members, mayors, or members of Parliament (for example, Cardo, who defeated Rocard in the March 1993 election to Parliament, is a very active nonprofit manager at the local level).

Tchernonog (1991, 1992) showed that financial support of local communities to nonprofit organizations increased between 1980 and 1989; the average subsidy per association was, in current francs, 9,025 in 1980 and 19,914 in 1989; as the price rise was 81.6 per cent, the volume growth was 21.5 per cent between 1980 and 1989 and during the same period the number of subsidized associations grew dramatically. According to the same author, the bigger the town is, the higher is the average subsidy. Local support to the nonprofit sector does not seem to be linked with the political party position of the town council.

The difference between local and national government support is twofold, in payee nonprofits and in the form of support. Roughly speaking, large organizations benefit from national support and small organizations from local support. National funding goes to education and research, health and social services with residential facilities, as local funding is mainly for culture and arts, sports, other social services, local development and business associations. In some cases, there is a radical specialization; for example, in nonprofit schools, the teachers and a proportion of non-teaching workers are paid by the state, and some capital expenditures and some non-teaching workers are paid by the local community.

The form of support differs too: contractual grants and third-party payments from social security predominate at the national level, while general funding, sometimes symbolic, and in-kind support predominate at the local level. Many local authorities have built during the two last decades "houses of voluntary associations". In those facilities, the local nonprofits can use free of charge offices with the appropriate equipment. Sometimes seconded officials, paid by the local community, can help several nonprofit organizations in management, computing, bookkeeping and so on.

So decentralization afforded a kind of division of labor among state and local governments to support the third sector. 1983 is a turning-point.

6.1.2 Changes in government attitude (1970–90)

Shift in philosophy
During this period government policy toward the nonprofit sector became more and more explicit. It is certainly partly due to the coming to power of a socialist government (1981–93). The rapid come-back of the Right (1986-88) showed a cut in subsidies, and civil servants seconded to nonprofits were asked to reassume their position in public agencies. The 1993 come-back of the Right will not have similar consequences.

What are the main differences in Left and Right philosophies? Roughly speaking, the Rousseauist idea that public interest concerns are a monopoly of the state according to the social contract is still alive in left-wing philosophy; the consequence is that, if some private entities deliver public interest services, the state has to pay for them. The philosophy of the Right is more Smithian: let private interest guide the economic activity on a free market and the invisible hand will afford general interest. So, private non-profits have to rely mainly on private money and government support may not disturb fair competition.

These rough positions have to be shaded. The Second Left (Rocard, *Confédération Démocratique du Travail* – CFDT) supports self-management and decentralization. Edmond Maire (1988), the leader of the CFDT,[2] argued that the socialist government of the early 1980s revealed that the state cannot run a complex society alone and has to demand the help of civil society to face modern social and economic challenges. Partnership has to substitute for contracting out. These arguments could have been signed by the Centre Right Party (CDS), influenced by the social Catholic current, following the tradition of the *Rerum Novarum* encyclical.

Amount and form of support
As we have seen in chapter 4, there is no statistical evidence on the changes in the amount and form of government support. Even on

the present situation of the resource side of the nonprofit sector, figures are tentative.

Our assumption, according to the responses of the nonprofit leaders and government representatives we interviewed, is that the relative amount of government funding increased during the period 1970–90, with a shift from central to local government after the 1983 Decentralization Act, and of course the absolute amount of government financial support increased like other welfare expenditures, but less since the mid-1980s. With a slower rise of grants and sometimes cuts in grants, policymakers and nonprofit managers had to identify their targets more clearly. Nonprofits had to reduce their costs and to find other resources mainly by raising users' contributions to the services provided. Subsidies were granted with increased reporting and accountability requirements, as a standardized accounting classification must, on principle, be observed by subsidized nonprofits. As we saw by experience, only the largest (more than 30 per cent subsidized nonprofits) abided by this regulation.

There is also a shift from relatively discretionary general funding to specific project grants or, more often, to a general activity contract with reciprocal commitments. Facing this evolution, the nonprofit managers enjoy a more regular public funding but unfortunately have to be more dependent on their funders' control.

6.1.3 Encouragements and restrictions introduced by public policies

Encouragements
The government introduced new and significant legislation which encouraged the formation of nonprofit organizations. Figure 6.1, with statistics taken from Table 6.1, shows that such legislation explains some peaks of the curve.

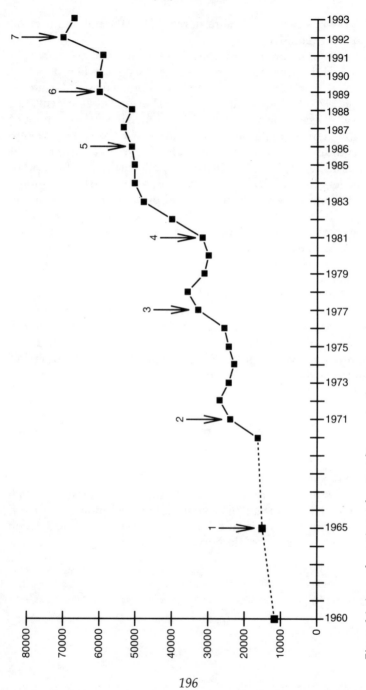

The nonprofit sector in France

Figure 6.1 Annual creations of nonprofit organizations

1 1965: Law on Fishing and Hunting: hunters' and fishers' associations have a monopoly, so that nobody can get a hunting/fishing license without being a member of an association.

2 1971: Law on Adult Continuing Education (initiated by Jacques Delors): many associations, besides business enterprises and public schools, were created to deliver this new service, financed by a compulsory tax of 1.2 per cent of the wage bill paid by enterprises.

3 1977: Encouragements to senior citizens' associations, now existing in every local community (more than 30,000).

4 1981: Free broadcasting is authorized: before this law, the allocation of broadcasting wavelengths was a state monopoly. Mainly nonprofits used this new opportunity.

5 1986: Voluntary sports activities at school have to be delivered by school sports associations and no longer by the school itself. But since then, compulsory school sports activities remain in the school curriculum.

6 1989: Law encouraging "intermediary" associations supplying jobs to frail categories of populations: unskilled young people, potential or former delinquents or drug addicts. In 1989, too, many short-lived organizations were created to celebrate the French Revolution bicentenary.

7 1992: Legislation encouraging (by social contributions cuts) the creation of "neighborhood jobs" by households, such as housekeeping, nursing care for children, the disabled and the elderly. As many households could only afford a part-time job, many nonprofits were created to convert part-time into full-time by multiplying employers. They also provide training and fulfill administrative tasks. At the same time, the policy toward suburban districts encouraged the formation of neighborhood nonprofits.

So the diachronic analysis of the new-born associations according to their declared object is interesting from a twofold point of view: it is an indicator of the new concerns of civil society and, more generally, of social change; it is also a reflection of some precise public policies (Forse, 1984; Canto, 1988).

In order to enhance the visibility of the nonprofit sector, we have seen above that the government encouraged the formation of peak associations and other umbrellas by financing and asking advice on issues which the nonprofit sector is facing.

Tax exemption or privileges are another form of encouragement to nonprofit organizations (see chapter 3). The main recent changes in the tax law are as follows.

In 1977, the taxation authorities fixed the five criteria that a nonprofit has to fulfill to be exempt from corporate tax:

– it must be general interest oriented;
– it must not distribute profit to managers, founders or members;
– the economic activity has to be linked with the general interest aim;
– surpluses must not be aimed at: nonprofits are not businesses;
– surpluses, if existing, must be reinvested in the organization itself.

The five criteria have to be met simultaneously; if not, the tax has to be paid. This *doctrine des oeuvres* is now questioned as being too rigid and too imprecise: what is "general interest" or "social utility"? Who decides that a nonprofit belongs to the exempted category? (Chéroutre, 1993a).

For historical reasons, the French government have not encouraged private contributions to nonprofit organizations as the Anglo-Saxon countries do, because of the fear of congregations' property in mortmain which prevailed in 1901. This posture changed recently, but tax exemption remains less favorable than in other countries:

In 1987, with an appendix to this legislation in 1990, the encouragement of individual and corporate giving by tax incentives is as follows:

• For corporations, contributions to declared associations are deductible up to 0.2 per cent of taxable turnover (and not the tax itself) and to public utility nonprofits (ARUP) up to 0.3 per cent (before 1987 up to 0.1 per cent).
• For individuals, contributions are tax-deductible for 40 per cent of their amount up to 1.25 per cent of taxable income (up to 5 per cent for ARUP, churches, foundations and charities). For free meals for the poor, tax-deductibility is 50 per cent up to 500 FF. ("Coluche amendment" for the "Restaurants of the Heart"). Before 1987 contributions were deductible from taxable income, not from the tax itself.

Restrictions

The growth of the nonprofit sector is too recent to be restricted. The last restriction on nonprofit formation, the prerequisite authorization of foreigners' associations, was waived in 1981 as being against freedom of association, a constitutional right. Fundraising and corporate and individual giving are low in France and have been encouraged more than restricted during the last two decades, and it is the same with tax-exemption. However, restrictions on foundations remained until 1990 and can be seen as a residue of Jacobin fears about wealth accumulation in *ancien régime* congregations (see chapter 5).

Restrictions to business activities do not exist, but if business activities, not directly linked to the social aim of the nonprofit, are significant, the nonprofit organization has to pay the corporate tax to prevent unfair competition with forprofits. And very often the voluntary organization is asked to create a business subsidiary company. For instance, the old Pasteur Foundation, very active in medical research, is now twinned with a corporation, Pasteur Production, processing drugs and vaccines.

6.2 Nonprofit organizations as vehicles of policy

In France, nonprofit organizations are more and more vehicles of policy in introducing, shaping and implementing social, cultural, environment, health, employment and Third World aid policies. They are becoming the partners of government bureaucracy, at national and local levels, as well as the business community and interest groups, when labor unions and political parties are declining actors.

Regular opinion polls show that the French trust first local governments and nonprofit organizations to solve general interest issues, far ahead of national government, political parties or labor unions.

French nonprofit organizations are not very active as *lobbies*, but this is changing. One exception is the role of the disabled associations acting as an interest group till the government promoted the 1975 law on the rights of the disabled and the guarantee of resources for disabled people (see chapter 5).

Another more recent exception is the Besson law on housing for the poor (1990). In the first bill, specialized nonprofits were institutionalized as partners. This fact was criticized during parliamentary discussion, especially in the senate, which proposed amendments banning them from participating. The concerned nonprofits lobbied to restore the bill in its original form and the national assembly voted for the original bill at the second reading. This victory was confirmed by the Constitutional Court.

The irreplaceable role of associations is in *initiative*: detecting new needs of the population and proposing new ways of dealing with them. The fact of being implanted in social and local surroundings implies a real sensitivity to the pluralism of the population, and a proximity to the marginalized marginals. This fact contrasts with the rigidity, the distance, the juridism of the bureaucracy. Finally the nonprofits can be concerned with all the angles of a social case while a public agency has only a functional point of view. The root of "social innovation",[3] the main contribution of nonprofits to social policy, is certainly linked to their capacity to take on a social case in a multipurpose dimension: employment, income, health, social and family position, housing, education and skills, etc.

To illustrate these points we selected three recent case studies in the social services and research sectors: *the policy against poverty and economic vulnerability, the policy of urban suburb rehabilitation and immigrant integration and finally the policy of medical research on genetic diseases.* We also added sketches of two pan-ministerial policies where nonprofits are important actors: *employment policy and European and international policy.*

6.2.1 The policy against poverty and economic vulnerability

According to Claire Ullman[4] (1992, p. 37) "the policy to combat poverty – involved nonprofit organizations more fully than ever before in the process of policy formulation and implementation". First the *Secours catholique* showed evidence on increasing poverty in Paris; during the cold winter of 1983 the government announced an emergency poverty plan, providing special funding to charities supplying emergency services (*Secours catholique, Restaurants du coeur, Aide à toute détresse Quart-Monde*, Salvation Army), distributing food aid, especially EC agricultural surplus, via nonprofit organizations and extending financial assistance to the homeless and other people with housing difficulties.

From 1984 to 1987, the nonprofit organizations involved in the poverty plans met social welfare and local government officials and social housing managers under the auspices of UNIOPSS (the health and social services umbrella organization) to develop a more durable poverty policy under the form of a guaranteed minimum income. The report of Joseph Wresinski, adopted in 1987 by the economic and social council, is the fruit of this brainstorming and the first draft of the 1988 minimum income for insertion (RMI) policy. Father Joseph Wresinski was the very charismatic founder of *ATD – Quart-Monde*,[5] a charity fighting extreme poverty in which the volunteers commit themselves to live several years where and how the poor live.

The Wresinski report (1987) recommended the extension of local experiments on minimum income with the participation of nonprofits to enable the poor to move into the mainstream. It asked for "a tight collaboration between various partners engaged in the fight against poverty".

In the 1988 Act, the nonprofits are empowered to accept applications for RMI and to draw up integration contracts, as local governments or social welfare agencies are. They were in fact very active in the implementation of this social policy. However, they complain of being considered as ranking below public or semi-public partners.

6.2.2 The policy of urban suburb rehabilitation and immigrant integration

The second case is the recent *politique de la ville*, a policy promoting improved urban conditions in deprived suburbs which are becoming more and more immigrant and ethnic minority ghettos. As said in chapter 2, large housing blocks were built by the quasi-public agency HLM (*habitations à loyer modéré*) during the 1950s and 1960s to meet the postwar housing shortage. In the late 1960s and the 1970s immigrants, previously in shanty towns, replaced the working-class families moving to better quality housing.

With the growing unemployment which affects primarily immigrant workers, the suburbs became drug-addiction, drug-dealing and high delinquency areas. The housing became damaged and simultaneously the Communist Party and Catholic volunteer networks weakened. In a sense, the nonprofit network replaced them in the mid-1980s. This nonprofit network at the local level is a mix of old associations such as the multipurpose social centers and new associations such as antiracialist, ethnic and more precisely Muslim associations or neighborhood and local development associations. These associations were involved in the National Council of the Prevention of Delinquency, and in the National Commission for the Social Development of Towns, created in 1983 and combined in 1990 to form an Interministerial Delegation concerning City Issues and Social Urban Development. Subsidized by the national *Fonds d'Action Sociale* and by local governments, the associations in deprived suburbs of big cities are viewed as the way to restore social cohesion and to prevent social exclusion, especially for young people.

In recent years they developed literacy and adult training programs, school help to the children of immigrants, sports clubs and recreation clubs, Muslim activities, education and mutual help for women, legal assistance and aid for administrative problems. Local government encouraged by in-kind and financial support the creation of such nonprofit organizations when they were nonexistent.

A recent book from Bourdieu and his team (1993) shows the omnipresence of associations in the day-to-day life of the underprivileged contrasting with the failure and withdrawal of public agencies in the deprived areas. The presence of the nonprofit network in these areas partially explains why social explosions were more limited than in other countries facing the same urban issues.

6.2.3 The policy of medical research on genetic diseases

Third, we wish to emphasize the important and original action of the *genetic diseases associations* in promoting medical research in the late 1980s and early 1990s. Created during the last decade, these associations challenged the traditional model of handicapped associations running facilities and providing services or the British model of self-help groups of people confronted by chronic diseases. Apart from some more standard activities, the main aim of those new associations is focused on the need for scientific research to find therapeutic solutions to genetic diseases and they give private donative support to private or public medical research. In 1987, the leading association, the French Muscular Dystrophy Association (AFM), launched the first and only telethon fundraising campaign, with great success, rising every year up to 330 million FF. in 1993 (more than 3 per cent of individual giving). Instead of spreading that money over many research projects, the AFM scientific council, to which many famous physicians belong, decided to open the most important research laboratory in Europe on genetic diseases, the Genethon. In 1993, Daniel Cohen and his research team published a complete chart of the whole human genome. This genethon program is a great challenge for public research on genetic diseases which has progressed very recently as well, sometimes with private financing from AFM (*Conference on human genome analysis*, 1992, Barral and Paterson 1991).

In accordance with nonprofit principles, the genethon researchers working in public agencies (INSERM, CNRS, universities) do not want the human genome patented as American researchers do. Even in France, the success story of telethon and genethon raised a lot of criticism; the fundraising campaign is viewed as unfair competition with other nonprofit organizations. The Secretary of State for the disabled, Gillibert, himself seriously disabled, made criticisms in 1991 on the use of the money gathered by telethon, and in 1991 the amount made by the telethon went down.

The health nonprofit organizations and especially AFM are certainly a significant force in shaping government policy on this specific medical research as private money goes to public research teams on competitive bidding, reversing the usual process. The resources of AFM are private up to 95 per cent and public (third-party payments for the facilities intended for the muscular dystrophists) up to 5 per cent, and it is therefore one of the most independent nonprofit large organizations. In France, fundamental research is a quasi-monopoly of public agencies; however, because of its financial independence, AFM could act in orienting research as the American foundations do. Without doubt, it is a breach in the state monopoly.

6.2.4 The employment policy

Finally, we will sketch two pan-ministerial policies which nonprofit organizations participate in. The first one is the *employment policy* and especially the youth employment policy: part-time collective utility jobs (*contrats emploi solidarité* now, and *travaux d'util-*

ité collective before 1991) are proposed to young unemployed people or to the long-term unemployed. These jobs are paid for mainly by the government and symbolically by the recipient organization, a public agency, a local community or a nonprofit organization. The job must not be competitive with a paid job. Training and supervision are ensured by the public or nonprofit organization and the other half of the worker's time is supposed to be devoted to continued education and job search. The number of CES grew dramatically since 1990 and nonprofit organizations are the most active in hiring CES (more than 1,000 in *Secours Populaire*).

According to the SIRENE file, employment in associations increased from 995,000 in December 1991 to 1,295,000 in December 1992. This dramatic growth of 300,000 is due in large part to the CES artificial jobs. But it is also due to the fact that non-profit organizations were very active in the supply of neighborhood or family jobs benefiting social security contribution exemption (see above).

Associations are also firm-creating and hence job-creating: the associative status acts as an incubator for enterprises created by young people eager to be self-employed or by executives who have some capital of their own. The very simple legal status of association is used to test the project; if it proves to be viable the association achieves a business status.

Finally "intermediary associations" are direct agents of employment policies. These associations produce goods or services in the sectors overlooked by businesses and they supply temporary jobs and training to frail populations: unskilled young people, potential or former delinquents or drug addicts. Those nonprofits are run most of the time by former social workers. The time spent to train and follow up the apprentices is compensated by social contributions and tax cuts and by grants. Evaluation studies show that the efficiency of "intermediary associations" is better than any other training program.

6.2.5 The European and international policy

Last, nonprofit organizations can be viewed as agents of the *European or international policy* as many ancient or more recent non-profits have an international dimension: the Red Cross, the Scouts, the Salvation Army, Amnesty International, Caritas, to quote some of them. Many of these organizations initiate a European network, and are lobbying in Brussels, especially on poverty issues.

Third World development assistance is a second dimension where the most active nonprofits are the Catholic Committee Against Hunger (CCFD) and the Protestant CIMADE. They act mainly in developing grass-roots projects and they are very critical about public aid to African governments.

The third less traditional dimension is international emergency assistance. The "French doctors", *Médecins sans frontières and Médecins du Monde,* are the most famous organizations in this field. Bernard Kouchner, the founder of *Médecins sans frontières,* became the first Minister of Humanitarian Affairs. The creation of a Ministry of Humanitarian Affairs is typical of the recovery of a nonprofit concern by the state, as was previously the case for the Secretary of State for Women's Rights or for the Ministry of the Environment. As a politician, Bernard Kouchner advocated "the duty of meddling" at the international level when the Rights of Man are obviously violated in a country. This recommendation was followed in practice in the Somalian civil war and by a beginning of application in ex-Yugoslavia or Rwanda.

At a more local level, many nonprofit organizations are aimed "at friendship between France and another country" and local governments initiated twinning of European towns via ad hoc associations, which are para-public associations. All those nonprofit organizations are active in constituting the European community as a cultural and social entity and not only as a great market for business activities.

To conclude, we recall that the environment nonprofit organizations were incubators for the two ecological political parties, *Génération Écologie* and the Greens (see chapter 5). So nonprofit organizations are more and more involved in economic and social policies; they participate in the three dimensions of government activity according to Musgrave (1959), the function of allocation of public goods, the function of redistribution of income and wealth, and the function of regulation of the whole economy and society.

Table 6.2
Ranking of issues

Issue	Low 1	2	3	4	High 5	N.A.
A-Government policies						
1) Tax treatment of private giving		X				
2) Legal status of nonprofit organizations					X	
3) Reductions in government support					X	
4) Charges in the form of government support					X	
5) Extent of government control					X	
6) Policies on nonprofit/forprofit competition		X				
7) Government social policies					X	
8) Regional integration (e.g. European Community)					X	
B-Other funding						
9) Extent of private giving					X	
10) Extent and character of corporate giving			X			
11) Competition from forprofits				X		
12) Fee income		X				
13) Sales and other business income			X			
14) Other funding problems			X			
15) Volunteer recruitment					X	
C-Management and personnel						
16) Personnel recruitment/management			X			
17) Staff compensation					X	
18) Professionalization				X		
19) Staff training					X	
20) Tension between advocacy & service provision		X				
21) Legal problems (e.g. liability)		X				
22) Accountability within the nonprofit sector			X			
D-Other						
23) Regional, religious and ethnic conflicts	X					
24) Political instability			X			
25) Ideological/political attacks on nonprofits		X				
26) Independence from churches	X					
27) Independence from businesses	X					
28) Extent of service to the poor			X			
29) Ethical issues					X	
30) Research				X		
31) Independence from political parties and labor unions	X					
32) User and client control		X				
33) Volunteer training				X		
34) Maladjusted fiscal system				X		
35) Sensititivity of public opinion to general issues				X		

6.3 Current policy issues

What are the major issues facing the nonprofit sector in France, in the mid-1990s? There is no consensus on ranking the issues confronting the nonprofit sector, as we can observe during the interviews we conducted and according to the filling of the accompanying scoring scale (Table 6.2) by nonprofit leaders. In fact, this absence of consensus on what are the major issues is quite normal, as the situation of the nonprofit organizations is quite different according to their size, sector of activity and structure of resources.

So we propose in Table 6.2 a somewhat subjective ranking of the possible issues, which summarizes at the same time the interviews of the leading experts and policymakers and many recent articles and reports. Policy issues are by far the main topic in French specialized reviews, such as *Lettre de la Fonda, Lettre de l'Économie sociale, Revue des Études coopératives, mutualistes et associatives, Revue de l'Économie Sociale*. We also discussed the issues highlighted by the recent Chéroutre Report (1993) of the *Conseil Économique et Social*.

The main current policy issues include:

- reduction in government support;
- insufficient private giving;
- staff compensation and training;
- obsolescence of the Act of 1901;
- ethical issues;
- European integration.

6.3.1 Foreseeable reduction in government support and changes in forms of government support as a consequence

We have seen that the last decade was marked by a reduction of state government support and increase of local government support. For the next few years, because of the increasing deficits of the state and of social security, cuts in grants and subsidies can be expected from every kind of government, and third-party payments may be less complete. The fact that France has a higher level of government social welfare spending as a share of GDP than other Western European countries (Salamon and Anheier, 1994a) seems to be in the sense of a reduction of this ratio in the future European integration.

This tendency is reinforced by the recent political change of the government from left-wing to right-wing centre (March 1993). Many associations involved in immigrants' integration or suburban issues experimented with dramatic cuts in subsidies. Youth or welfare associations are in the same situation. New forms of contracts such as competitive bidding with forprofit organizations and other nonprofits are emerging and new forms of payments, such as vouchers, are recommended by very recent reports (Cette *et al.*, 1993).

The global reduction of public financing, the main source of income for the whole nonprofit sector, will compel nonprofit organizations to increase private financing. According to the subsector, this increased private financing may be obtained by a rise in fees or payments by the users, by increased dues or private giving.

The fees and payment by the users began to rise in housing and social tourism activities during the last decade and also in day care centers and nursing homes. The rise is before us elsewhere. The increase of members' dues is foreseeable too because they are very low on average in France compared to other countries. Insufficient private giving can be viewed as another important issue linked to the first one.

6.3.2 Insufficient private giving

Individual private giving is low in France compared to the United States. According to Archambault *et al.*, 1991 and Hodgkinson *et al.*, 1992, in 1990 43 per cent of French people 18 years of age and older reported contributing 1,076 FF. (approximately $179). In comparison, 75 per cent of Americans reported an average contribution of $978. So the average household contribution is 1 to 5.46 and the proportion of contributors is 1 to 1.75. Combining the two factors, we can say that the average American gives 9.5 times what the average French person gives. What is at the root of insufficient private giving in France?

We have seen that the present tax treatment encourages private giving more than before. Though progressing in recent years, private individual giving is far below the maximum tax deduction, as the table from the Internal Revenue Service shows (Table 6.3).

To understand this table, it is important to know that before 1983 charitable contributions to general interest nonprofit organizations were deductible from taxable income, with an upper limit of 1 per cent without any verification. So many households deducted imaginary giving!

Table 6.3

Number of households deducting donations to NPOS and amount given (in thousand francs)

Years	Public utility NPOS Number of households	Amount	General interest NPOS Number of households	Amount	NPOS providing meals Number of households	Amount	Total Amount
1981	681,500	370	6,021,700	3,798			4,168
1982	1,841,400	1,253	5,759,680	3,931			5,184
1983	777,600	482	1,873,700	1,314			1,796
1984	1,546,400	847	789,200	418			1,265
1985	1,848,500	1,182	749,200	441			1,622
1986	2,195,300	1,421	841,100	495			1,916
1987	2,593,700	1,900	810,200	587			2,487
1988	2,671,200	2,094	1,007,000	824	44,600	9	2,924
1989	3,064,300	2,521	990,100	783	145,200	39	3,343
1990	3,394,800	2,921	735,200	665	204,700	61	3,647
1991	3,350,700	3,129	691,120	658	244,400	80	3,867

After 1983, tax deductibility necessitates the sending of a receipt by the recipient organization, and then tax evasion disappears, and the total amount of giving reported was divided by 4 between 1982 and 1984. Since 1984, individual giving is growing slowly and the *Mécénat* 1987 Act provoked a shift from general interest to public utility NPOs, which is the main feature of the 1987–91 subperiod.

For our benchmark year, 1990, individual giving according to fiscal authorities, 3,647 million FF., could be compared with what households declared in the 1991 survey: 9,472 million FF. (Archambault *et al.*, 1991). These figures, however, are not incompatible because:

- Half of the households are not subject to income tax, but may nevertheless give.
- Many gifts are too scanty to be declared or are non-deductible, or are not deducted because the receipt has been lost.

So the lack of giving in France is not only a problem of tax-encouragement. It is more a very deep-rooted cultural problem. In France, the state is assumed to be responsible for every public interest concern and once the citizen has paid taxes – sometimes with tax evasion – he or she is exempt from public matters. This mentality still exists though it is decreasing. A more accurate sensitivity of the public opinion to general interest issues is a prerequisite to larger amounts of individual giving in France. We can argue in the same way for corporate giving which is very low in France (with the exception of education and sports), though growing in recent years.

Another cause of insufficient individual private giving in France is the nonexistence of education in philanthropy in public schools in France while this does exist in most of the private Catholic schools. Now five children out of six attend public school. In addition, at public school, the traditional civic education which taught children about public concerns is fading.

Some teachers do the job on their private initiative, but they can be criticized as acting against the secularity principle of public school. In 1992, Bernard Kouchner as the Ministry of Humanitarian Affairs promoted a campaign called "Rice for Somalia". He asked every schoolboy and girl to bring one kilo of rice to school in order to feed the starving Somalians. This campaign was a semi-success because of the difficulty conveying the rice to Somalia and it gave rise to some criticism as well. According to those critics, this campaign was transgressing the secularity of public schools. So it is going to take time to introduce education in philanthropy into French public schools.

6.3.3 Staff compensation and training

Staff compensation is very low in France in the nonprofit sector. With a similar professional qualification, nonprofit organizations pay less than the public sector, itself below the business sector. This is due to the small scale of the organizations, to the lack or weakness of trade unionism in the nonprofit sector and also to the fact that many workers accept over-exploitation because they share the ideals of the NPO. This low compensation is also due to a structural effect, as the labor force in associations is mostly female and more part-time than in any other sector.

The low wages are hereafter an important issue, because non-profit organizations need more professional employees and cannot pay them at the market wage, and above all they afford rather low social benefits. So they have great difficulty in hiring and keeping skilled workers and executives. Staff training is an important issue too, because if the NPO starts an expensive training program, the trainees may move to the business sector.

This staff compensation and training issue is linked with volunteer recruitment and training. During the last two decades many unemployed volunteers became paid employees in the organization they helped to create or to run. These new employees often have more enthusiasm than skills. Many of the experts we interviewed complained of the difficulty of recruiting volunteers[6] and even more of recruiting volunteers conversant with finance, accountability or management. Some volunteers are unreliable, amateurs and have a lack of professionalism. So the training of volunteers is on the agenda, and needs some encouragement. The purpose of the *Fonds National de la Vie Associative* (FNDVA) is to deliver such financial support (Masson and Menard, 1992).

6.3.4 Obsolescence of the Act of 1901?

Is the 1901 Act legal status obsolete? That is the question the Chéroutre Report had to answer. Roughly speaking, the report's answer is no, it is not an obsolete legal status. The 1901 Act is the easiest and the most liberal law of the French legislation and therefore "it opened an unlimited area for freedom and it was able to clear many obstacles" (Chéroutre, 1993b). But the misuses of the law have to be pointed out and suppressed. First of all, too many public agencies created quasi-public associations, without independence, in order to escape public regulations on labor, accountability and so on (see above); and second, too many nonprofit organizations are in fact businesses and the report recommends that business activities be run by subsidiaries with the appropriate legal status while the nonprofit organization itself concentrates on nonprofit activities.

The report also advocates government acknowledgement of general interest associations (see above): "Despite a long cooperation and a tight proximity to government, the nonprofit managers feel the government representatives reluctant on their legitimacy as actors of a social policy ... Public financing seems more dependent on the generosity of public authoritity than on the acknowledgement of a real partnership" (Chéroutre, 1993, p. 18).

We agree with this opinion. However, most of the associations, even those hiring no salaried people, now have significant economic activity. It was one of the important results of our organization survey (Tchernonog, 1992). Therefore the limited legal capacity of 1901 Act-declared associations is certainly an obstacle to fundraising, investing, borrowing, acquiring real estate, in a word to normal economic activity. Most certainly, the new European legal status of association will allow a full capacity, with more accountability requirements and some kind of incorporation as in most European countries. In any case, the historical circumstances which were at the heart of the limited capacity devoted to declared associations in the 1901 Act disappeared; congregations have a special legal status and mortmain property secluded from the general circulation of goods is a risk no longer.

At the present time, nonprofit organizations have great difficulty in borrowing money from ordinary banks because of the lack of security. Since 1984, large associations can issue special bonds called *titres associatifs*. This practice is encouraged by the government but it is not widely spread. Nor are the "ethical investments", a new form of bonds the income of which is shared between the holder and one or many nonprofit organizations. The necessity for declared associations to reinforce their own property is therefore still a major issue.

6.3.5 Ethical issues

This fundamental issue is often concealed by nonprofit sector representatives as susceptible of damaging the good reputation of the sector. As the nonprofit sector is generally regulated and controlled by very few people, any kind of embezzlement can occur as in the business sector, and in fact this does sometimes happen. These facts are emphasized too much by newspapers or sensational books (Beriot, 1987).

This point is more important if the nonprofit organization benefits from important individual giving. So eighteen large associations, umbrella associations or foundations signed a deontological chart in 1989. The signatories agree to observe great integrity in their publicity, to publish their true accounts, to be fair in fundraising and to have a mutual control of these commitments.

The ethical issue is decisive too for nonprofit organizations funded by public money. In principle, controls exist in this case (see above), but recently many scandals dealing with the financing of political parties were pointed out. In many cases, nonprofit organizations, sometimes ad hoc associations, were used to reroute state or local government subsidies to political parties. Those illegal practices came in principle to an end with the recent law on political party financing (1990). At the same time, individual giving to political parties or unions became tax-deductible with the same fiscal privileges as declared associations. However, there is presumptive evidence that some illegal practices of financing political parties via nonprofit organizations are continuing.

But the most important ethical issue in recent years was laid down by the *French blood transfusion network*, and it affected both nonprofit and public health sectors, and left in public opinion a lasting uneasy feeling concerning the whole health system and the hypocrisy of the aims of some main nonprofit leaders.

We evoke two linked ethical issues in the same area; the organization for organ transplants, *France Transplant*, and the associative network for artificial insemination, the CECOS.[7] These two success stories contrast with the scandal of blood transfusion; however, some ethical issues are on the agenda.

The French blood transfusion network

Blood transfusion is interesting for our purpose inasmuch as the associative sector holds an important place in this medical activity, and in the last decade the use of human substances has been stirring up a sharp ethical debate. The recent scandal concerning the CNTS (*National Blood Transfusion Center*) has sharpened the debate even more, especially about the responsibilities of the public powers in the control of collection and distribution policies by local establishments.

Before the scandal, which broke in 1990, the French blood transfusion policy used to be presented by physicians as an efficient ethical model for the therapeutic or research use of human tissues or organs, based on one main principle: the *nonprofit principle*

(1952 Act concerning blood transfusion).

At a centralized level, the public powers supervise the activities of the whole network (the centers as well as their directors are subject to the approval of the Ministry of Health; the prices of blood and its by-products are fixed by the state).[8]

The decentralized organization of blood transfusion is formed by a network gathering all the transfusion centers, in order to assist the public task service in supplying the care units and the patients with blood and blood extracts.

Among the main transfusion centers, the CNTS holds a particular importance: in addition to the manufacturing aspect, it has an applied research department, and fills national tasks, such as the importation of blood for which it holds the monopoly. This monopoly was granted by the Ministry of Health in 1982. The aim was, on one hand, to ease the conflicts with the social security administration (foreign products were less costly than French ones, but they were reimbursed according to the rates of the French products, and this was an incentive for the centers to import blood extracts, sometimes on the borderline of legality); on the other hand, the monopoly enabled the limitation of importations and represented as such an incentive to increase the national production and to reach a national self-sufficient production.

The 180 blood transfusion centers of the network are very heterogeneous, by the nature of their activities and their means (financial and in labor force) and also by their legal status. Since the nonprofit principle rules the entire activity of blood transfusion, the associative sector plays an important part: 50 per cent of the centers have an associative status (1901 Act), while 50 per cent belong to the public hospital sector. This situation has generated tough competition between centers, which had to face problems of budget balance and investment in high technology equipment, in the context of the national rationalization policy of health expenditures. Some of the large centers did not hesitate to propose easy terms to small centers, to recruit them both as "customers" for their own production and as blood suppliers. The competition has favored a hierarchized stratification of the network, without favoring an efficient coordination of the whole.

Although the scandal of the CNTS was revealed by the media in 1990, the facts took place within a few months between 1984 and 1985. The treatment of blood extracts needed a new technological investment, which was to be devoted to the new production unit of the CNTS, created with the financial support of social security and the Ministry of Health. During the period preceding the choice of one of the available blood treatment systems, the CNTS built up a stock of untreated extracts (the new unit had to be productive), the suppression of which would have represented a serious drop in earnings. Under the responsibility of Dr Garetta, the director of CNTS, it was decided to clear the stock, in full knowledge of the fact that hundreds of patients (and their relatives) would be contaminated, and in particular haemophiliacs. Compared to two other centers whose production was equivalent to that of the CNTS (Lille and Strasbourg), the choices were made a few months earlier, and so the accumulation of a stock of untreated extracts was prevented. Dr Garetta was described in the court's report as being both judge and judged. The scope of his fields of intervention was wide: at a centralized level, he held the position of the judge since he was in charge of national services, of the monopoly of importations, but he was also the president of the *National Haemophilia Committee* (CNH) in charge of advising the public powers. At an intermediary level, he held the position of the judged as the director of a blood transfusion center. At a grassroot level, Dr Garetta and Dr Allain (a physician in charge of applied research at CNTS) held the position of judges as the links with the providers of the blood and also the recipients were close: the *French Federation of Volunteer Blood Donors* (FFDSB) and the *French Association of Haemophiliacs* (AFH) were located in the CNTS's buildings. As a representative of the CNTS, Dr Allain benefited from the confidence of the AFH. The information he provided was used by the association to advise patients and stress the claim for the more dangerous but more comfortable treatment (i.e. extracts made from the mix of hundreds of donors' plasma, vs. two other products less convenient by requiring respectively less than five donors and less than ten donors). The confidence in Dr Allain may also explain why the association was apparently not aware of the scandal before 1990. The FFDSB has also been used to ease the conflicts between the CNTS, as the only provider of foreign blood extracts, and the AFH. The FFDSB stressed the qualitative value of blood provided by volunteer donors, vs. paid donors used by foreign industries, arguing that no self-interest would prompt them to give infected blood or to hide risky behavior.

When the fear that even volunteer donors could be contaminated was expressed, the federation was offended by this suspicion: the haemophiliacs should be more grateful for the generous donation of the blood they greatly need, they said. The blood transfusion case has generated the creation of patients' advocacy associations (associations of haemophilic patients and transfused patients infected by the AIDS virus), dissociated from the AFH because of the close links with the CNTS.

Many other industrialized countries have experienced the tragedy of transfused patients infected with the AIDS virus, for the same reasons: a lack of knowledge about this new disease and the underestimation of the risks inherent in the therapeutic use of blood. In France, the scandal is enhanced by the fact that the blood transfusion system is under the state's supervision and that only three physicians, associative and administrative officials have been sentenced by the court. The current debate involves the responsibility of the government, and the necessity to bring former Prime Minister Laurent Fabius, Minister of Health Georgina Dufoix, and Senior Minister Edmond Hervé to the High Court. Finally, this responsibility was rejected.

The management by associations of a great part of the blood transfusion activity is also one of the issues of the debate. The scandal shows that the state has delegated the decisionmaking to public and nonprofit decentralized organizations for the implementation of the transfusion policy, based on the nonprofit principle, but the fact that they do not make a profit does not prevent the centers having to face competition and conflicts of value between ethical issues, the efficiency of their management and the competition with other countries. The recent changes consist of the reinforcement of the government's control (notably by the creation of a public Blood Transfusion Agency supervised by the state and of an advisory commission in which directors of transfusion centers have no responsibility).

The organization for organ transplants: France Transplant

Organ transplantation raises very sensitive ethical issues, inasmuch as, on one hand, it relies for the collection of organs on dead and living donors (raising issues such as respect for dignity and for individuals' beliefs, the prevention of trade and traffic, etc.) and on the other hand, organ scarcity prevents the satisfaction of the needs of all the patients (which raises the issue of social justice in the allocation of the grafts). All the activities linked to organ transplantation are under the Ministry of Health's supervision; this supervision is reinforced by the fact that approval for organ procurement and transplantation are exclusively granted to public hospitals.

Among the different actors involved in the organ transplantation activity (public powers, officials in charge of the management of public health services, patients and their families, but also donors, associations of patients, of donors, transplant physicians and other specialists in the fields of dialysis, emergency care, neurology, etc.), *France Transplant*, the organization for organ distributing, holds a hegemonical part. *France Transplant* is not a public organization, but a 1901 Act association. This central position has been established *de facto*, because, since its creation, the association has been at the heart of the initiatives which allow a balance to be reached between organ supply and demand. The association was founded in 1969 by Professor J. Dausset (Nobel prizewinner) and medical pioneers of organ transplants in France.

Even if organ transplantation is under the supervision of the government, the implementation of the French transplant policy is initiated by *France Transplant*. Government control cannot exist without the collaboration of the association and its members, inasmuch as the association is the only official provider of data concerning organ transplant. As a coherent group of experts, which are concerned with a very specialized activity requiring highly qualified skills, they hardly find their initiatives called into question by the public powers. The fact that most of the ethical positions and the rules elaborated and implemented by *France Transplant* have been taken up in the law project on bioethics is a good example of the intervention and the influence of this medical professional association in the building-up of public health policies.

France Transplant raises the same debate as the transfusion network: is it the role of a private nonprofit organization to manage a public service? Especially concerning medical activities using human tissues and organs which raise ethical issues, do public powers have to delegate a public assignment to associations?

The main difference between transfusion and transplantation is that the latter is exclusively performed in public hospitals, where physicians, members of *France Transplant*, are employed (they are not allowed to have a private practice). The association lives on public resources[9] and does not have to face the difficulties of budget balance that the transfusion centers meet. There are very few exchanges with foreign countries and they are free of charge.

Associative artificial insemination: the CECOS

The CECOS (centers for the study and the preservation of sperm) have followed a rather similar development process. In 1973, the first center was created within the framework of a public hospital, by the pioneers of artificial insemination, with an associative status (i.e. the status of the organization respects the main ethical principle for the use of human substances, the nonprofit principle). By the early 1990s, the centers of the CECOS provided 95 per cent of the sperm used for this medical technique of fertilization. As they were the first to implement and to develop this technique on a large scale, the CECOS have had the initiative of the elaboration of ethical rules concerning both the collection and the allocation of sperm. In comparison to the private centers which also perform artificial insemination, the rules are very strict, the donors are not paid, even a very low compensation, and the CECOS are very restrictive concerning the selection of the donors and the recipients. The donors must comply with strict medical criteria, the donation exclusively occurs between a married couple with children, who donate sperm, and a married couple, who receive it as treatment for a problem of fertilization. It excludes any other type of donor or recipient.

The precedence and the large share held by the CECOS in this medical field, the stress on the nonprofit principle and on the other restrictive ethical principles, have very little influence on the principles implemented by the private centers (the characteristics of the donors as well as the recipients are more diversified).

As the main rules concerning organ transplant, the principal rules of the CECOS were taken up in the law project of bioethics. If the law project is adopted, the private centers will have to change their practice or to disappear.

This means that in both cases, the rules and ethical principles adopted by "experts" of a medical speciality in the frame of an association are approved by public powers and are the guidelines for the elaboration of the legislation.

As the associations are composed of medical professionals, and hardly include representatives of the candidates for the allocation of such scarce human substances, to what degree do the policies reflect the professional norms of ethics or professional interests?

To summarize, public opinion considers the nonprofit aim to be a guarantee of ethical behavior and the nonprofits as specialists on ethical issues; so the managers of NPOs are trustworthy and the services they deliver are expected to have a high quality/price ratio (for a theoretical point of view, see Titmuss, 1971 or Weisbrod, 1988). So that is why the blood scandal is so serious. As Weisbrod said, "the high-quality, public-serving nonprofits can find their reputation, and thus their ability to find support, injured by the actions of the self-serving forprofits in disguise".

6.3.6 European integration

Last, but not least, the European market is a big challenge for the nonprofit sector. French nonprofit leaders begin to be aware of the consequences of European union for their sector but some representatives of the big umbrellas anticipated these consequences earlier. We will now consider the major issues.

- The *necessity to concentrate the nonprofit organizations*, as the average French nonprofit organization is smaller than British or German ones; the creation of mighty European umbrella organizations, able to lobby at Brussels, refers to the same rationale. Similarly corporate or grant-making foundations, quasi-nonexistent in France before, were created within the last two years, but it will be a long way before they catch up the mighty Anglo-Saxon foundations.
- The *eligibility for European funding* such as the European social fund or the regional development European fund. Nowadays this European funding is not important in France and benefits go to education, vocational training and research subsectors and to those NGOS oriented towards the development of Third World countries. Apparently, French nonprofits are poorer at getting European money than British, German or Italian ones.
- The *increase of European competition between nonprofits and forprofits*. The Treaty of Rome's article 58 implies free establishment and free provision of services and prohibits any kind of

discrimination inside Europe. It is questionable if this article 58 applies to nonprofit organizations as it does to forprofit enterprises. The European jurisprudence is that article 58 is relevant if the nonprofit organization has some kind of economic activity. So there is a risk of standardization of nonprofits delivering services in competition with proprietary firms.

Similarly, as article 92 of the Treaty of Rome prohibits subsidies which distort fair competition, the remaining public financial support has to be justified by a contract in which subsidies are regarded as the reward of a general interest service (Chéroutre, 1993).

- The *Europeanization of charitable contributions*. As for other financial flows, charitable giving is now possible without any national discrimination. No doubt it will be an opportunity for the nonprofit organizations which are expert in fundraising. It is not the case for French organizations which are either just beginning to conduct modern fundraising campaigns or are too small.

The French government encourages the Europeanization of the nonprofit sector by promoting at the European level the concept of "*Economie Sociale*": in 1989, the European commission created inside the D.G. 23 a new service which identifies social economy enterprises as different from business enterprises. A conference called "*Les rendez-vous européens de l'Economie Sociale*" was organized first in Paris, in November 1989. The fourth *Rendez-vous européens de l'Economie Sociale* took place in Brussels, in November 1993. National authorities and some key representatives who created a European committee for general interest associations (CEDAG) in 1989 were active to promote uniform legal status, in order to prevent social economy enterprises from becoming standard enterprises under the pressure of competition: they promoted particularly a European legal status of associations. The European legal status of cooperatives will be discussed first.

Roughly speaking, to conform to the European norm, French nonprofit organizations have to be less dependent on public subsidies and therefore have to turn to more private individual or corporate giving and more private earnings (sales, fees and dues and also investment income), as the European status could give in the future a full legal capacity to associations while the 1901 Act gives only a limited legal capacity (Chéroutre, 1993).

In any case, the most important French nonprofits from the economic point of view, the nonprofits active in education and research, and social services subsectors, have much more than 50 per cent of their financial resources from government and are considered as Public Law organizations at the European level. As such, they will be submitted to strict regulations to compete in bidding markets (92/50 Directive). UNIOPSS is very apprehensive about the risk of an assimilation to public agencies (Alix, 1993; Coursin, 1993).

As subsidies would be only the reward of a general interest service, a clear definition of general interest activities and of general interest nonprofit organizations is therefore a major issue for the nonprofit sector in France. This was already a challenge in the early 1980s when the new socialist government proposed a more favorable tax support for general interest registered nonprofits, with a counterpart of increased reporting and accountability requirements. At this time, the representatives of the nonprofit sector rejected the project as being contrary to the freedom of associations. Because of European integration, this issue is once more facing the nonprofit sector at the present time, and will be answered for.

But if nonprofits have to make an effort to be European, the European treatises have to be amended to take account of the nonprofit sector and, more generally, of the whole *Economie Sociale*. Between the public sector and private sector, there is a third sector which was neglected by the Treaty of Rome, signed in a period of high economic growth, low unemployment and East-West competition. Now the circumstances are quite different; European economic integration is a reality but political and social drawbacks appear clearly as the difficulty of voting in the Maastricht Treaty by universal suffrage shows, especially in Denmark and France.

So political and social Europe is backward. As Dominique Wolton says (1993): "to turn from a technocratic Europe, done by 50,000 civil servants, businessmen or politicians to a democratic Europe, as the Maastricht Treaty requires, calls for 350 millions of citizens to be concerned". Is there a better school of citizenship for adult people than the involvement in nonprofit sector "without borders"?

Notes

1. The representatives of the nonprofit sector who constitute the CNVA are appointed by the government and not elected by the organizations; it is a symbolic paradox.
2. On retiring from CFDT, Maire became the head of the main social tourism nonprofit organization, *Villages-Vacances-Famille* (VVF).
3. Since 1992, the *Délégation à l'Economie Sociale* is called *Délégation à l'Innovation Sociale et à l'Economie Sociale*.
4. The information in this paragraph is based very closely on Ullman's quoted article.
5. *Quart-Monde*, Fourth World, is a neologism suggesting that the Third World is inside France too.
6. According to the same sources above, 19 per cent of the French volunteer while 54 per cent of Americans do. In both countries the average is four hours a week.
7. The following pages were written by Florence Paterson.
8. According to the rates reimbursed by social security, they are evaluated to cover only the added value due to the treatment of the blood provided by volunteer donors, i.e. the costs of the collection, the manufacturing and the distribution. Paradoxically the French products are more expensive than the products of foreign firms; one of the explanations is that volunteer donors cannot be mobilized as paid donors according to the needs of the centers, and therefore the exploitation of the equipment is less productive.
9. In 1990, it consisted mainly of subsidies: 37 per cent from social security (CNAM); 39 per cent from the Ministry of Health; 24 per cent from its own resources – laboratory and financial products. Since 1990, 95 per cent of the resources have come from a fixed sum of 3,400 FF. paid by the hospitals for each transplantation, and 2 per cent from financial products (3 per cent come from other benefits).

Chapter 7

CONCLUSION

As a result of recent changes in social and economic conditions and in public attitudes toward the state, increased expectations are now directed to the nonprofit sector and that is why it is important to know what the nonprofit sector does nowadays, and how it is able to expand, to cope with new human needs. We saw in the first chapter of this monograph, and again in chapter 4, how little we tended to know about the third sector and we stated how much more we know as a result of this study: we will first recall the main empirical results that follow from this study in a comparative perspective.

Then, we will look at the theoretical implications of these empirical results. How do existing socio-political and economic theories of the nonprofit sector relate to the French case? What can we learn about the usefulness of such theories based on the evidence presented for France? To what extent does the French case enrich our understanding of the nonprofit sector?

Finally, we will see the major policy implications of a better visibility and public awareness of the nonprofit sector. What is now changing in the relationship between the government and the third sector, at national and local level? And how can this change be related to the move toward European integration?

7.1 The French nonprofit sector in a comparative perspective

7.1.1 An increased visibility thanks to a conceptual clarification

The Johns Hopkins Nonprofit Sector Comparative Project afforded basic information about private nonprofit organizations throughout the world, as it overcame the conceptual confusion prevailing in the field.

A major piece of this conceptual clarification relies on a common definition of the third sector. It includes the organizations that are simultaneously:

- formally constituted;
- separate from government;
- nonprofitsharing;
- self-governing;
- voluntary, to some significant degree.

The two other restrictions introduced in this study – nonreligious and nonpolitical – are not fundamental and can be relaxed in further developments.

The construction of the common ICNPO classification, which fitted the twelve countries involved in the international comparison, is another important methodological output of this project. It is the same for the common approach in developing and assembling the basic information, which is a guarantee to obtain comparable results in the seven countries for which complete empirical data were collected, that is, beside France, the United States, the United Kingdom, Germany, Italy, Japan and Hungary.

7.1.2 The French nonprofit sector: comparable to other countries in size, though different in structure

Size

Much of the French nonprofit sector is of relatively recent origin, because of a long-standing tradition of hostility by the state toward voluntary organizations tracing back to the French Revolution and lasting throughout the whole nineteenth century (see chapter 2). Against this backdrop, the French nonprofit sector is comparable in size to the German or the British third sector.

Table 7.1 shows that over 800,000 salaried people, or 4.2 per cent of the labor force, work in the nonprofit sector, a higher percentage than the seven-country average of 3.4 per cent; with 31 billion ECU in operating expenditures, the French nonprofit sector represents 3.3 per cent of GDP, very near the seven-country average (3.5 per cent); the French nonprofit sector appears as more labor-using than the average, and this is largely due to its composition.

Table 7.1

The French nonprofit sector in a comparative perspective

	France	7-country average
I. Employment (FTE)*		
Number	802,619	
As % of total employment	4.2	3.4
II. Operating expenditures		
Amount (billions)	31.3 ECU	
	39.9 US$	
As % of GDP	3.3	3.5
Distribution by field (%)		
Culture & recreation	17.8	16.5
Education & research	24.8	24.0
Health	14.5	21.6
Social services	28.9	19.6
Environment	0.7	0.8
Development & housing	6.4	5.0
Civic & advocacy	2.9	1.2
Philanthropy	0.0	0.5
International	1.1	1.2
Business, professional**	2.9	9.2
Total	100	100
III. Revenues by major source		
As % of total		
Government	59.5	43.1
Private giving	7.1	9.5
Earned income	33.5	47.4
Total	100	100
* FTE = Full-time equivalent	** includes unions	

Source: Lester M. Salamon and Helmut K. Anheier, *The emerging nonprofit sector; an overview.* Manchester University Press, Manchester 1996.

Composition

Two subsectors, *social services and education,* dominate the French nonprofit sector. Together they account for more than half the sector's operating expenditures and about 60 per cent of employment. While the education percentage is roughly comparable to the seven-country average, the percentage in social services is much higher (28.9 per cent against 19.6 per cent).

In the field of education, this reflects the traditional role of private Catholic schools, especially in the western part of the country; though virtually completely state-funded, private Catholic schools fought to remain independent from the state. This sizable subsector also reflects the growing importance of vocational training and continued education nonprofit organizations since 1971.

In the main subsector, social services, employment is 300,000, and 55 per cent of all residential care residents are in nonprofit homes. It is the result of a kind of specialization between central and local government and nonprofit organizations. Social services directed at the whole population and linked to social security schemes are mainly public while social services oriented toward frail or poor populations, delivering personal care services or coping with new social needs, are mainly nonprofit.

The two other main subsectors, *culture and recreation,* and *health,* are a little over the average for the former and significantly below the average for the latter.

The sizable cultural and recreational component reflects deep-seated public concern over culture. It also reflects the voluntarist policy of the Ministers of Culture Malraux and Lang to develop culture throughout the country. In this field also we observe some specialization: to central government the responsibility of supporting artistic creation and culture for the happy few, and to local governments, which very often contracted out to nonprofit organizations, the decentralization and the democratization of cultural activities. Recreation and social tourism organizations contribute to this popular culture.

The relatively small size of the health nonprofit subsector is due to an early secularization of hospitals and other health facilities during the French Revolution and to the development of a modern public network of state-provided health facilities since 1945, when a comprehensive social security health insurance scheme was created.

For *the six little subsectors,* France stands near the average: a little higher for development and housing which developed recently as a consequence of local policies against unemployment involving local authorities, nonprofits and HLM public agencies; the same for civic and advocacy organizations because of a deep-rooted tradition of defence of the Rights of Man and of a recent concern for immigrants.

Conversely, France is much below the average for business and professional organizations because of the weakness of labor unions and, more generally, of a weak tradition of corporatism tracing back to the 1789 Le Chapelier Act. Similarly, the quasi-nonexistent philanthropy and foundation subsector is due to government restrictive regulations which are a residue of the Jacobin fear about wealth accumulation of *ancien régime* congregations.

Revenue

Table 7.1 shows that two features distinguish the French third sector from its counterparts elsewhere. First, its relatively high level of government support and, by contrast, its low level of private giving and earnings. France ranks second after Germany among the seven countries in the share of public funds in its revenue; six out of ten francs of income represents government grants and contracts or third-party payments, from social security mainly. Only one third, against nearly half for the seven-country average, is earned income from fees and charges. Charitable giving is very limited and represents only 0.2 per cent of household disposable income, and corporation patronage is not common in France, though it has grown in recent years.

This revenue structure has to be related to the strong French tradition of state-provided welfare, health, education and culture services. In recent years, the government strategy was to decentralize public administration and social service delivery. This context developed a partnership between local and central governments and the nonprofit sector, in which government provides the bulk of resources and voluntary organizations deliver human services.

Table 7.2 shows that for the four main subsectors, the government share of nonprofit revenue is much above the average. It is more striking for the culture and education subsectors, in which government does not provide the bulk of nonprofit sector resources in the seven-country average than for two other subsectors, health and social services, in which public funding predominates everywhere. For the six little subsectors, private revenue predominates, as is the case on average.

Table 7.2

Government share of nonprofit revenue in a comparative perspective

	France (%)	7-country average (%)
Culture and recreation	41	22
Education and research	73	42
Health	84	59
Social services	60	51

7.2 Theoretical implications of the results of this study

What conclusions can we draw based on the empirical data presented in this book and summarized above? How can these data confirm or invalidate the existing theories of the nonprofit sector? The theoretical implications of the results of this study could be – and perhaps will be – the subject of another book. However, we will try to outline how the French case enriches our understanding of the nonprofit sector in general through a rapid examination of socio-political and economic theories of the nonprofit sector.

7.2.1 Socio-political theories

Scope of the welfare state
According to a "gap-filling" theory, the greater the scope of the welfare state in a particular country, the smaller should be the third sector (Anheier and Seibel, 1990; Gidron *et al.*, 1992).

With 29 per cent of its GDP devoted to public social welfare expenditures (Eurostat, 1991) France had, by far, the highest level of the seven developed countries in the project. Despite this fact, we observed that France has a sizable nonprofit sector, of the same magnitude as Germany (23 per cent of GDP devoted to public social spending), the United Kingdom (20 per cent) and Japan (12 per cent). So the "gap-filling" theory seems to be invalidated by the evidence.

At a more detailed level, this theory fits the health subsector in France, but it does not fit with the social service field where a complementarity pattern prevails: we can observe in this subsector some kind of division of labor among the state and the third sector to provide human services.

Legal framework

Anheier and Salamon (in Hodgkinson and Schervisch, 1994) argue that common law legal systems seem to provide a more supportive environment for the emergence of nonprofit organizations than do civil law systems. France of course is a country ruled by a civil law system, in the Roman tradition. The apex of this civil law system is the *Code Napoléon* and it corresponds to the more restrictive regulations for nonprofit organizations. Conversely, the 1901 Act which still rules associations in France is very atypical. It is said to be the most liberal, the most flexible law of the French legislation. It is also the least precise one, as a large amount of contractual freedom is given to the founding members of an association, and it seems to be nearer common law than civil law on this point. Of course, the 1901 Act was at the heart of the development of the French nonprofit sector. So the history of French legislation can be read as a confirmation of Anheier and Salamon's argument.

Similarly, a unitary political system with a centralized administrative structure is said to be less favorable to the development of the nonprofit sector than a federal state with a decentralized administrative structure. France is still a unitary state, but recently it experienced decentralization, and we have seen that this change came with a dramatic rise in the rate at which nonprofit organizations are being created (see chapter 6). So this evolution seems to emphasize the legal framework as an important factor in nonprofit sector development, and it is worth a more rigorous confirmation.

Development of an educated middle class

Sociologists insist on the role of an educated middle class to promote a vibrant nonprofit sector. French surveys on membership or volunteering in nonprofit organizations (Heran, 1988; Haeusler,

1988, 1990; Archambault *et al.*, 1991) confirm this link absolutely: professionals, executives, teachers and social workers are predominant in the membership of nonprofit organizations and the percentage of volunteers is growing with the level of education. The founder members and the board members are even more concentrated in the middle class.

We can observe too that the beginning of the so-called "associative boom" is 1965 (see Table 6.1). That year, the new post-World War II generation, more educated than the previous one arrived at adulthood. These "baby-boomers" promoted new public concerns, in the mood of 1968, and originated many nonprofit organizations (see chapter 2).

Competition among religions
Another factor stimulating the development of the third sector would be strong competition among several religions (James, 1989). This argument is verified in Anglo-Saxon countries, and also in developing countries where the competition among Catholic and Protestant missionaries was a strong incentive to create health or education nonprofit organizations.

France confirms *a contrario* this argument. After the 1685 *Edit de Nantes* revocation, French Protestants emigrated to England, Germany, the Netherlands or America. We can observe also that France, unlike Germany, did not develop a tradition of private action and subsidiarity, in spite of the influence of the Catholic Church.

However, the competition between the Catholic Church and an active republican anticlericalism was an essential feature during the second part of the nineteenth century and the beginning of this century; it was a strong incentive to develop Catholic nonprofit schools over the public school network "without God". It is impossible to understand the French "school war" without referring to the competition between these two ideologies.

Competition among religions is a specific example of pluralism in a society, and we will see that the relationship between the growth of the nonprofit sector and the heterogeneity of the population had been emphasized by an economic theory of the nonprofit sector.

7.2.2 Economic theories

Heterogeneity of the provision of collective goods
According to Weisbrod's (1977) and James's (1989) well-known theory, nonprofit organizations frequently deliver collective goods.[1] As private producers of collective goods, they are complementary to the public provision of such goods: government entities tend to provide public goods at the level that satisfies the median voter (Buchanan and Tullock, 1962) to maximize the probability that the government will be reelected. If the society is heterogeneous (in the level of income, but also in religious, ethnic, language or other sociological characteristics), there will exist some residual unsatisfied demand for public goods among the individuals who want a greater provision of these goods or more specific collective goods. Nonprofit organizations meet this residual demand.

In France, Catholic schools, minorities' social or youth clubs, Portuguese or Arab supplementary schools, local environment defence, human rights and civic defence are examples of associations meeting a heterogeneous demand for collective goods. According to the heterogeneity theory, the greater the diversity of the population, the greater should be the size of the nonprofit sector: in France, we can observe that the Jacobin tradition fought all kind of diversities and was a hint toward the development of the third sector. Conversely, decentralized local authorities, a more diverse population due to the successive waves of immigration, and a more permissive society developed associative life during the last two decades.

But it is important to note that most of them deliver *impure* collective goods, that is private goods with some kind of externalities:[2] for instance education or day care services are consumed only by one person but the quality of the service is dependent on the number and the characteristics of the co-consumers. Regulated proprietary enterprises can compete with nonprofit organizations and public agencies in delivering impure collective goods.

Whatever the degree of purity of collective goods, the producer has to solve the *free-rider* problem: if nobody can be excluded from the consumption – or from a part of the consumption – of a collective good, nobody can have an interest in revealing their willingness to pay for such a good. So taxation is the normal way of financing collective goods, whatever the producer.

We can observe that in ICNPO, the amount of government funding is very high in education and health, and a little less in social services. In all these subsectors, we are dealing with impure collective goods, more collective than in other categories. Conversely, there are other resource structures in the countries involved in the project, which means that there are many ways to cope with free-riding.

Free-riding is also assumed to be more probable in large than in small organizations, as in small organizations everybody can identify the free-rider and enforce on him a moral or social constraint to pay; it is not the case in anonymous organizations, or in a nation. In confirmation of this assumption, we can observe that the percentage of public resources grows with the size of the organization in France, while earned income decreases with this size.

Asymmetrical information and transaction costs

The contract failure theory of the nonprofit sector (Hansmann, 1987; Ben-Ner, 1986) emphasizes the importance of asymmetrical information in the industries where the nonprofit organizations are relatively the more frequent. Indeed it is not easy for the user to judge the quality of the services provided in such industries as health, education, social services for frail populations or international aid. These services are not standardized or highly technical; in some cases, the user and the purchaser (or donor) are not the same individual, or the recipient of the aid is very far away. Information and transaction costs to cope with this asymmetry of information between the producer and the consumer are very high. So in proprietary enterprises there is a strong incentive to lower the costs and the quality of the service delivered to maximize the profit.

To solve this agency problem (Williamson, 1979), the nondistribution constraint in nonprofit organizations acts as a guarantee for the consumer that the managers of the organization cannot benefit personally in providing low-quality services. *Trust* in this specific form of organization is a response to the contract failure. The consumer control of nongovernmental organizations delivering private goods is another type of response to contract failure: it is the case in social and recreation clubs or in professional associations.

The fact that in our comparative study, ICNPO fits with all the countries involved in the project, and that, in France, we had no use of the "not elsewhere classified" category, shows that the nonprofit legal status is chosen in human services industries everywhere. Nonprofit organizations are more in competition with the public than the forprofit sector. The nondistribution constraint is indeed a label of trust and quality.

Conclusion
Some other theories, of course, could have been part of this brief outline. Not one of the theories referred to can be said to be predominant, and in France as elsewhere, the importance of historical traditions cannot be ignored. Contradictory currents cross the contemporary nonprofit sector which take root in remote history, and all the historical periods have laid strata which shape the French nonprofit sector to-day.

7.3 Policy implications

This study brings the French nonprofit sector into better focus in a reliable and comparatively empirical way. We observed that the third sector is larger than expected and comparable to other European countries. This better visibility has policy implications that we will now develop.

7.3.1 The end of the state's monopoly on public good
The acknowledgement that nonprofit organizations participate in general interest activities is a consequence of the efforts of successive recent governments to promote a network of peak organizations and more generally to promote associative life. It is also a consequence of the rise of a civil society eager to initiate the provision of new forms of human services and the defence of new concerns.

The end of the monopoly of the state and the public agencies on public interest throws out the strong Jacobin tradition; but facts go before mental representations. Only one French person out of five volunteers and the relationship between central and local government and the nonprofit organizations has to change: too often nonprofit organizations are considered as simple executive agents and not as partners by the state or the local communities.

This change means for the government that it has to be less suspicious of nonprofit organizations; in particular, a full legal capacity is necessary for declared associations to have a normal economic activity and to expand. Similarly, the old prejudice against the endowments of foundations is obsolete and French foundations have also to catch up with the European level. Partnership also means that central and local governments must not create "quangos" to escape public law regulations, or, worse, to reroute public money toward political parties. Finally, a thorough partnership implies that nonprofit organizations' leaders have to be consulted on the definition and the ways and means of new social, cultural, health or environment policies, as international nongovernmental organizations have to be involved in Third World aid policies.

The move toward partnership also means a strong effort for the nonprofit sector: more professionalism, a greater transparency in accounting and managing, no divergence from the use at associations' general meetings: of the democratic rule "one man, one vote", no transgression of the nondistribution constraint by wages over the average for the executives or by excessive fringe benefits. Long-term contracts with government also imply more reporting requirements. Finally, nonprofit organizations have also to meet greater competition in the next few years in relation to European integration: competition among nonprofit organizations, and competition between nonprofit organizations, businesses and public agencies.

7.3.2 The shift from public to private resources

As a result of more active competition, the atypical resource structure of the French nonprofit sector will have a tendency to draw nearer to the European pattern. Cuts in grants can already be observed which force nonprofit organizations to identify their main targets, to reduce their costs by better management, to earn more money by raising fees for solvent users and/or to get more from individual or corporate contributions. More tax-deductibility may encourage private contributions. Clearer tax-exemption rules, in place of the obsolete *doctrine des oeuvres* (see chapter 3), are also a prerequisite to the shift from public to private resources in the French nonprofit sector which is also a guarantee of its independence.

7.3.3 Toward a European citizenship through the nonprofit sector

The nonprofit sector is a way to citizenship and a way to everyday democracy. It was the main reason for François Bloch-Lainé to incite the state to promote the third sector in France during the 1960s.

Mutatis mutandis, the same reason may predominate today in the process of European integration. Debates about the ratification of the Maastricht Treaty showed in every country where the debate was open that the main objections to the Treaty were the lack of democracy, the statism of Brussels Eurocrats, the risk of losing national identities and of reducing high-level social rights as economically inefficient in a competitive Great Market.

Of course, all the answers to these objections do not rely on the third sector, and political institutions are first. However, the nonprofit sector could be a way toward European citizenship. It could be an antidote to Brussels Eurocratism as it was an antidote to Jacobinism recently in France, by promoting social innovation and by developing "do it yourself" instead of dependency. The long-standing German tradition of subsidiarity in the nonprofit sector is also a pedagogy of European subsidiarity, one of the main principles of European working.

European citizenship is fundamental to counterbalance a market-based economic union. Procedural and institutional mechanisms to balance self-interest are not enough and some level of public spirit is needed; it is perhaps the most important role of the nonprofit sector to promote civism and responsibility among its members, and to teach them the sense of multiple loyalties. With a common legal status and European umbrellas, nonprofit organizations will help to shape a cultural and social Europe balancing the business-oriented common market and sustaining a common ethic.

Notes

1 A collective good is enjoyed by several persons at the same time; it costs no more to provide it for many than for one (nonrivalry between consumers) and once the good has been produced, nobody can be excluded from its consumption (nonexclusion). Examples are: TV broadcasts, air pollution control, national defence, fundamental research, etc.

2 An externality is an interdependence between the consumption of two individuals, the production of two enterprises, or the production and the consumption of two economic agents; for instance, a vaccination program will benefit those inoculated and their neighborhood.

Appendix A

METHODOLOGY

General notes on the tables

These tables are tentative. In a general way, the expenditure tables are more reliable than the resource tables. But many gaps had to be filled by assumptions, the main ones of which are reported in the following pages.

1 When two or more data sources gave inconsistent data for the same cell on a table, we have used the lower result to prevent overestimation. It is therefore plausible that, in order to avoid inflated and too optimistic reports, our data are underestimated.

2 The data on employment are the most reliable ones. They are provided by the SIRENE file, out of which we have selected the data given at the most detailed level. We were not able to reallocate all the residual subsectors (9723 not elsewhere classified).

Full-time equivalent is not commonly used for employment in France, except for employment in health and welfare establishments. The rule of equivalence in this category is the following: full-time employment = (full-time + part-time) x 0.8

In some other fields, we have also made extrapolations when no other data were available.

3 Data on operating expenditures are more reliable than those on total expenditures. Then, on the expenditures side, column 4 (table 4.2) consists in

$$\frac{\text{Wage bill}}{\text{Operating expenditures}}$$

column 7 consists in (3×4) and column 5 is $(7 - 6)$.

Capital expenditures are reported for education, health and a proportion of social services subsectors. For the other sectors, considering that the nonprofit sector has a weak capital intensity, the cells have been filled on the basis of the assumption that the capital expenditures represent 4 per cent of the operating expenditures.

4 There are very few data on the *average annual wage* in the nonprofit sector. Therefore we rely on general data concerning the wages in 1990 (source: DADS updated by INSEE):

- The average net wage for full-time wage-earners in the private and semi-public sectors is 109,300 FF. per year (*Déclaration annuelle de données sociales*).
- The average net wage in the public sector is 114,400 FF. per year.

When adding the social security contributions (i.e. the total contributions paid by both the employee and his employer) the average wage bill is as follows:

– in the private sector: $109,300 \times 1.2 \times 1.37 = 179,700$ *FF. per year*;
– in the public sector: $114,400 \times 1.2 \times 1.37 = 188,000$ *FF. per year*.

When using the national accounts, we found that the total compensation of the employers in 1990 is 3,382 FF. $\times 10^9$ and that the salaried labor force (without FTE) is 18,979,000. Therefore the average wage bill is *178,200 FF.* $(3,382 \times 10^9: 18,979,000)$.

As regards occupational qualification, the nonprofit sector is closer to the private sector than to the public sector, which shows a higher level of qualification. But considering that on one hand, the labor force is made up of more female workers and less-qualified workers, and on the other hand that many employees accept low wages because they adhere to the purpose of the organization, we assume that in a general way, the average annual wage in the nonprofit sector is 10 per cent to 20 per cent lower than in the whole private sector.

5 The data on *volunteer working hours and individual giving* were provided by our Population Survey (ISL, Fondation de France, Laboratoire d'Economie Sociale, May 1991). Individual giving is reported from the year 1990. Data on volunteer working hours consist in the reported monthly hours multiplied by 10 (volunteers are assumed to work less than 12 months). The imputed value per hour consists in the annual average wage for each sector divided by the maximum duration of work per year, i.e. 52 weeks × 39 h = 2028 h. The annual average wage includes social security contributions and other fringe benefits. It is questionable whether those contributions have to be included in the imputed value per hour. The use of a maximum duration of work per year corrects this effect and prevents overestimation.

6 For the resource side of the working matrix, we had very few reliable data, except for the sectors of education and international activities. Therefore we mainly used the survey data to obtain the percentage of resources of each kind and we assume that the global current resources equals the global operating expenditures for every sector. This assumption means that at the global level there is neither surplus nor deficit, and also that the capital expenditures are financed by borrowing.

7 The extrapolation from the resource structure provided by the survey to the whole field, and also the extrapolation from the ratio of the wage bill to the operating expenditures to the whole sector presuppose the reliability and the relevance of Viviane Tchernonog's survey. In order to obtain relevant data from this survey, Viviane Tchernonog and ourselves have built the questionnaire with respect to the subsectors given by the Johns Hopkins Project. As the questionnaires have been submitted to the associations by the local councils which list them, the response rate has been very good (about 25 per cent); therefore this bias led us to enlarge the estimation of the subsidies provided by local governments. According to the different subsectors, the resource percentages rely on data collected from between several tens and sometimes several hundreds of nonprofit organizations.

8 In France, the distinction between grants, contracts and statutory transfers is unusual. Third party payments are provided by

social security or other social funds. We used the two first columns to make a useful distinction between subsidies (grants, contracts, and so on), provided by the central government or by local governments (at the regional, departmental or local community level). Dues are isolated, but sales and fees merge into the same category. Federated fundraising campaigns are few in France and cannot be isolated (except for the unique telethon campaign).

Table 4.3 The third sector in relation to total employment and Gross Domestic Product, 1990

The GDP is not the sum of all the expenditures, but only the sum of the *final expenditures,* or the sum of the *added value.* Our operating expenditures in the third sector include the intermediate consumption (as regards the services, the intermediate consumption is about 25–27 per cent of the total operating expenditures).

Consequently, the ratio $\dfrac{\text{operating expenditures}}{\text{GDP}}$ *overestimates* the importance of the nonprofit sector (the appropriate correction consists in dividing the ratio by 1.25).

1 SIRENE 12/31/91: 992,500
Annual employment growth in the NPS: 5 per cent
Employment in the associative sector: 992,500: 1.05 = *945.250*

2 Total labor force according to the National Accounts (p. 70)

3 Working matrix

4 Total labor force in 1990: 22,140 (National Accounts, p. 70)

For the full-time annual work time calculation, we used the evaluation quoted by Michel Husson ("Le volume du travail et son partage. Étude comparative de sept grands pays". *La revue de l'IRES,* winter 1993, no. 11).

$$\text{FTE} = \frac{22{,}140 \times 1{,}539 \text{ h}}{1{,}784 \text{ h}} = 19{,}099$$

1,539 h = average annual work time (part-time included) – (National Accounts, 1990).
39 h is the full time duration of work/week
45.74 is the duration of the full total work year in weeks (5 weeks of vacation and 8 legal holidays)
1,784 h = 39 h × 45.74 weeks.

Table 4.4 Nonprofit employment in relation to total employment by subsector, 1990

numerator: annual actual work time (National Accounts)
denominator: full-time annual work time (1784)
(1990 census: NAP level = 100)

1 *Education, research*
$$[(NAP82 + NAP83) \times \frac{1512}{1784}] + [(NAP92 + NAP93) \times \frac{1390}{1784}]$$
$$= (114,816 \times 0.848) + (1,570,040 \times 0.779) = 1,320,425$$

2 *Health*
$$(NAP84 \times \frac{1512}{1784}) + (NAP94 \times \frac{1390}{1784})$$
$$= (1,425,773 \times 0.848) + (5,092 \times 0.779) = 1,213,022$$

3 *Social services*
$$(NAP85 \times 0.848) + (NAP95 \times 0.779)$$
$$= (434,648 \times 0.825) + (208,632 \times 0.758) = 531,106$$

4 *Culture, recreation*
$$(NAP86 \times 0.848) + (NAP96 \times 0.779) + (67 \times \frac{1587}{1784})$$
$$= (188,852 \times 0.848) + (105,516 \times 0.779) + (740,229 \times 0.890)$$
$$= 901,147$$

5 *Civil & advocacy associations & business*
$$(NAP77 \times 0.848) = 1,065,516 \times 0.848 = 903,558$$
(counselling, legal services activities, and so on)

Business and professional associations, and unions are assumed to be 100 per cent nonprofits.

6 *International activities*
Diplomatic activities, international organizations
(NAP99 × 0.779) = 21,124 x 0.779 = 16,455
16,455 + 8,644 = *25,099*

7 *Environment – development and housing*
No NAP category available for Total Economy.

Table 4.5 **The third sector, by subsector, 1990**

1 * number of establishments in SIRENE file 24/12/91 (i.e.:
organizations which employ at least one employee or which
pay taxes). We made the same assumptions as in working
matrix (expenditures).

** guesstimate (for environment quoted in Padieu, 1990).

Table 4.10 **Change in the third sector, 1981-1991 (without FTE)**

There are no data to compile the 1980 expenditures. Data on
employment in 1981, given by the SIRENE file, are a poor substitute for the operating expenditures, as the SIRENE file for the year
1981 is not very reliable. We can assume that the change in FTE
employment are equivalent to the change in total employment.

Third sector employment growth contrasts with a stagnant
labor force during the decade (+2.2 per cent). As the third sector
benefits from the employment policy, many of the new employment creations in the third sector are assisted jobs (i.e. with an
exemption from the social security contributions, such as jobs in
the domain of home help to the elderly or to the handicapped) or
state-paid jobs.

Table 4.11 **Change in third sector employment, by subsector, 1981–1991**

We make the same assumptions as for Table 4.10.

1 P. Kaminski. *Note INSEE 320/447*, April 1982.

2 The growth of every item reflects an actual employment growth in addition to a decrease of the NEC category, which is due to a better accuracy of the SIRENE file about the associations' principal activity.

Specific notes on the working matrix tables

For each sector, there is a general judgement on the reliability of the tables and on the specific characteristics of the sector. In a general way, the expenditure tables are more reliable than the resources tables. General assumptions are those presented in the general notes above.

Culture and recreation

The data on this sector are not reliable. It is a quick-growing sector, consisting of little and recent nonprofit organizations, mainly run by volunteers. The main part of volunteer work turns to this sector. Wages are very low and part-time work is more important than elsewhere. The subsectors in the tables do not fit French statistics. So we isolated the following subsectors:

- culture and socio-cultural organizations;
- sports, hunting and fishing;
- social tourism
- service clubs and those not elsewhere classified.

Expenditure 1990

A. FULL-TIME EMPLOYMENT

1 *Culture and socio-cultural organizations*
– in SIRENE File 1991:
(8601 to 8608) + (9611 to 9616) + (9621 to 9623) = 80,356 wage-earners
1990 figure = 80,356: 1.05 = 76,530
Assuming that, according to experts of the field, only 20 per cent work full-time and 80 per cent half-time, we have a lesser multiplier than elsewhere:

(0.8 x 0.5) + 0.2 = 0.6
76,530 × 0.6 = *46,000 FTE*

2 *Sports, hunting and fishing*
– according to Padieu Report, employment in this subsector is 100,000.
– according to Viviane Tchernonog's survey, sports is 96,000 salaried and hunting and fishing 3,200.
– according to the SIRENE File (8609, 8610, 8611 + 9617, 9618 + 9624, 9625) = 39,603 wage-earners (1990 = 37,717).
As volunteer work is widely spread in this area, we assumed that these wage-earners are qualified coaches and managers and retained *35,000 FTE*.

3 *Social tourism*
– according to National Social Tourism Federation (UNAT): 100,000 wage-earners (of which 75 per cent is seasonal work).
– according to Padieu Report, 10,000 full-time and 20,000 seasonal work.
– according to the SIRENE File (6712 + 6713: holiday centers, camping, youth hostels,...) = 20,550.
We assumed SIRENE figures × 0.5 = *10,300 FTE* (the multiplier is low as seasonal work is short-lived).

4 *Service clubs and those not elsewhere classified*
This subsector is inside the "not elsewhere classified" section of the SIRENE File (9723 = 125,000 salaried). It includes recreation clubs, mainly elderly clubs, in every local community, some country clubs, not well known in France, and service clubs. We assumed *4,000 FTE*, without any source. It may be higher.

B. AVERAGE WAGE

The average wage for each subsector is very low. For culture and sports, the figure comes from the Tchernonog survey, approximately 6,000 FF. per month average net wage, plus social security contributions. The average wage of social tourism is computed (see below) and extrapolated to service clubs; this wage is near the average wage in the whole nonprofit sector.

C. WAGE BILL AND OPERATING EXPENDITURES

Column 3, wage bill is (1×2). The ratio of wage bill to operating expenditures is computed on the Tchernonog survey's results, on each subsector except social tourism. The ratio is rather low because of the importance of volunteer work in the whole sector. For social tourism, UNAT published a turnover of 6 billion FF. in 1990 which is reported as operating expenditures.

D. CAPITAL EXPENDITURES AND TOTAL EXPENDITURES

Capital expenditures is assumed to be 4 per cent of operating expenditures.

E. VOLUNTEER WORK IMPUTED VALUE

a) $52.74 \times 10 = 527.10^6$ hours
b) 119.2×103 FF.: $2,028 = $ FF. 58.8 per hour
c) $527.4 \times 10^3 \times 58.8 = $ *FF. 31,000.10⁶*

As the procedure is the same for all sectors, we will not describe volunteer work imputed value hereafter.

Revenue 1990
Assuming as elsewhere that total cash = operating expenditures, we used the Tchernonog survey's data to obtain the percentage of resources of each kind and applied these ratios to the goal. We used this procedure for the whole sector and for the subsectors culture and sports. The remaining subsectors, social tourism and service clubs, are obtained by subtraction. For non-donative resources, when applying the ratios at the detailed level, we obtained some inconsistencies, so these data are given only at the sector level.

At the sector level, the ratios are the following:

	Global	**Culture**	**Sports**
Government revenue	0.406	0.505	0.326
– state	0.064	0.113	0.017

– local government	0.324	0.387	0.306
– 3rd party	0.018	0.005	0.002
Private donative	0.040	0.019	0.101
Private non-donative	0.594	0.476	0.572
– members' dues	0.114	0.071	0.228
– fees and sales	0.437	0.399	0.340
– investment income	0.003	0.006	0.004

Education and research

The reliability is very high for education because we have a very comprehensive and consistent data source which is the *satellite account for education*, published by the Ministry of Education, *Direction de l'Evaluation et de la Prospective*. From this source, we can obtain directly the operating expenditures, total expenditures and resources by financing sources. It is more tentative for research, but private nonprofit research is not very important in France, with the exception of *Institut Pasteur*.

For employment, virtually the only source is *Repères et références statistiques sur les enseignants et la formation*, Ministry of Education, D.E.P., 1991.

Expenditure 1990

A. OPERATING EXPENDITURES

We reported from *Compte de l'éducation*, p. 134 (cf. Appendix B) the following items:
– expenditures of private establishments financed by public resources: they are private nonprofit organizations which signed a contract with the state and they stand for the nonprofit sector in the field of education.
– the establishments run by *organismes consulaires* (*Chambres de Commerce* mainly), which are mainly management higher education.
– training nonprofits (*formation interne des administrations privées*).

We obtained (unit: FF. 10^6):

Primary and secondary education	38,138
– primary	12,044
– secondary	26,094
Higher education	5,777
– private higher	1,797
– management	3,980
Other education	6,729
– continuing education	5,675
– special (disabled)	376
– continuing education in NPOs	678

Total expenditures are obtained by applying the overall ratio of capital expenditures to total expenditures, 6.8 per cent. As the data are missing for capital expenditures for most private schools, we assume that they invest like public schools.

B. WAGE BILL

Education activity is highly labor intensive. The ratio of wage bill to operating expenditures is observed in *Compte de l'éducation* and the wage bill is computed. The wage bill is compared to full-time employment to compute an average wage for each subsector.

C. FULL-TIME EMPLOYMENT

Data on employment come from *Repères* 1991 quoted above for teachers and from *Le Monde* 14/5/92 for non-teaching employment in private education. The percentage of part-time employment is given. We computed FTE assuming that part-time is half-time:

	employment	per cent part-time	FTE
primary teachers	42,195	12.6 per cent	39,536
secondary teachers	82,423	29.8 per cent	70,060
non-teachers	40,000	30.0 per cent	34,000

We deduced average wages higher than elsewhere in the nonprofit sector because of the high degree of qualification in education.

For higher education, there are no data in *Repères*, so we added SIRENE (8203, 9215) = (10,625 + 4,869): 1.05 = 14,413.

With few part-time in higher education we assumed *FTE* = 12,700.

D. THE SPECIFIC CASE OF RESEARCH

Here the data are less reliable and we had to apply the general procedure.

Employment according to a survey by the Ministry of Research in 1991 on 1,206 private nonprofit research units = *7,336 FTE*.
Employment according to SIRENE (8301, 9311, 9321): 8,702: 1.05 = 8,287.

We retained the first figure, consistent with the second one. We assumed an average wage of FF. 260,000 and a ratio of wage bill to operating expenditures of 60 per cent (less than in education, to take account of a greater intermediate consumption).

Revenue 1990

The revenue side is very reliable for the first three subsectors, as we reported the figures from *Compte de l'éducation 1990*. As no donative revenue is given in this data source, we put revenue coming from business and corporation (often via a specific tax) in this column. And we retained the figure given by our population survey *Giving and Volunteering in France*, 1827, and deducted the amount from the resources coming from households to obtain sales and fees.

So in sales and fees, we have (unit = FF. 10^6):

Primary and secondary education	7,725
Higher education	1,038
Other	686
Research	1,590
Total 1	*11,039*
less individual giving	− 1,827
Total 2	*9,212*

For research, we have no information on the revenue side. The Ministry of Research survey shows that the same proportion of research nonprofits claim to have private resources and public resources. So we assumed 50 per cent government resources and 50 per cent sales and fees.

Health

For this sector, we have good data for all establishments (public and private) on employment, from the SESI (statistical unit of the Ministry of Health and Social Affairs). SESI conducts annual statistical surveys on public and private hospitals, which are the main data source. Operating and total expenditures can be read in *Compte satellite de la santé*.

When only global data are available, they are split according to the ratio of *beds in each subsector to the total number of beds in hospitals.* These ratios are:

Public	65%	
Private	35%	100%
– nonprofit participating in public hospital service	11%	31%
– nonprofit non-participating in public hospital service	5%	14%
– total private nonprofit	16%	45%
– forprofit	19%	55%

Public hospitals and private nonprofit participating in public hospitals service are funded by a global grant from social security. Other nonprofits and forprofits get a "per diem" which is a third-party payment from social security.

Expenditure 1990

A. EMPLOYMENT AND WAGE BILL

In private hospitals, non-medical employment is 232,674 (214,142 full-time and 18,532 part-time, assumed to be 80 per cent). The FTE is 228,968.

The proportion of nonprofit private employment is: 228,968 × 0.45 = *103,035 FTE.*

A direct estimation on Hospitals Survey 1990 gives 28,792 FTE + 75,490 FTE = 103,182 for non-medical employment (SESI, *Documents statistiques n°152*, August 1992).

For doctors, in private hospitals there are 13,510 full-time + (0.25 × 32,240) = 21,500 and the proportion in nonprofit hospitals is 21,500 × 0.45 = 9,075 FTE. This full-time employment is multiplied by an average wage of FF. 140,000 for non-medical employment and FF. 280,000 for medical labor force.

$$103,035 \times 140,000 = FF.\ 14,425.10^6$$
$$9,075 \times 280,000 = FF.\ \ 2,541.10^6$$

$$TOTAL = FF.\ 16,966.10^6$$

B. OPERATING EXPENDITURES AND TOTAL EXPENDITURES

These are directly reported from *Compte de la santé* (p. 22): private hospital care cost is FF. 59,230 × 10⁶.

Applying the ratio 0.45, nonprofit hospital care is: 59,230 × 0.45 = FF. 26,654.10⁶

The derived ratio of wage bill to operating expenditures is 64 per cent, very near the ratio for public hospitals (67 per cent). Knowing that in 1990 private nonprofit hospitals deliver 27,742,000 days of hospitalization, that means about FF. 1,000 per day.

Capital expenditures = 7 per cent of operating expenditure is the ratio observed in public hospitals (*Compte de la santé*).

C. NURSING HOMES

There is no exact French equivalent of this term: what is computed here are the data for medical homes for the elderly. Residential homes for the elderly or the handicapped are recorded in the sub-sector "social establishments".

We followed the general procedure: 8,073 FTE is the proportion of employment in medicalized elderly establishments, FF. 140,000 is assumed to be the average wage and the ratio of wage bill to operating expenditures is assumed to be the same as in hospitals.

D. OTHER HEALTH NONPROFIT ORGANIZATIONS

This subsector does not focus on mental health (including hospitals), but embraces self-help organizations, crisis intervention, prevention and health services organizations including home hospitalization and blood transfusion.

Employment is SIRENE (8401):	10,079
(8406):	19,865
(9411 and 9421):	1,331
Total	*31,275*

Part-time employment is widely spread in this area so FTE is 31,275 x 0.5 = *15,640*.

Average wage is the same as in hospitals – FF. 150,000 – and these activities are supposed to be more labor intensive than hospitals (ratio 0.8).

Revenue 1990
For the biggest part of the sector, hospitals, the *Compte de la santé* gives the ratio of resources:

Social security	87.6%
State and local government	1.9%
Households	8.6%
Mutuals	1.9%

Giving and volunteering in France adds up to FF. 2,519.10 individual giving for health, subtracted from sales and fees.

For hospitals, the proportion of social security has been split between grants and third party payments according to the ratio participating/non-participating in public hospital service (see below):
grants: $0.63 \times (0.876 \times 26,654.10)$ = FF. $14,710.10^6$
third party: $0.37 \times (0.876 \times 26,654)$ = FF. $8,639.10^6$
government resources: $0.019 \times 26,654 = $ FF. 506.10^6 was split between 2/3 state and 1/3 local government.

For other subsectors, the assumptions are the following:

nursing homes   60% government (mainly social security, third party)
40% payment by households

other   50% government
50% private (half donative, half non-donative)

Social services

This is the most important sector of the French nonprofit sector, owing to the great number of establishments for the handicapped, the elderly and other facilities for people with specific needs.

Social services, child day care and what is called *action sociale* are very innovative too and the whole sector is growing very fast. So we have very reliable data on employment and output measures coming from annual or biannual surveys by SESI, where the nonprofit sector is isolated; expenditures too can be computed with a small margin of error.

For the revenue side, we used the ratios observed in the Tchernonog survey.

The subsectors in the table do not fit French statistics so we adopted the following subsectors:
  - social establishments (residential homes) for specific populations
  - social services and charities (including income support, emergency, youth organizations ...)
  - child day care (0–3 years).

Appendix A

Expenditure 1990

A. FULL-TIME EMPLOYMENT (establishments)

We have consistent data coming from SIRENE (85 and 95) = 376,633 salaried in 1991 in the whole sector and from SESI, *Documents statistiques n° 134* (handicapped) and *n°159* (elderly). We gave priority to the SESI data because the FTE equivalent is calculated at a relatively fine level:

	FTE (all estblishments)	% of NPO	FTE in NPO
establishments for handicapped children	75,263	0.91	68,489
establishments for handicapped adults	51,436	0.92	47,321
establishments for protection of children	49,832	0.72	35,882
Other establishments	8,191	0.92	7,535
Total	*184,722*		*159,227*

The elderly homes employ 146,288 FTE:
　　59 per cent in the public sector
　　12 per cent in the private business sector
　　29 per cent in the private nonprofit sector.

So the FTE employment in establishments for the elderly is $(146,288 \times 0.29) = 42,434 - 8,073$ (employed in medicalized sections and considered as employment in nursing homes in the health sector) = 34,351.

Total FTE employment is *193,578*.

Average wage is given by SESI for 1989 (and rounded) for establishments; the wage bill is:
$159,227 \times 160 = FF. 25,476.10^6$
$22,640 \times 140 = FF. 3,170.10^6$

　　Total = FF. $28,646.10^6$

B. OPERATING AND TOTAL EXPENDITURES (establishments)

These are given in SESI, *Documents statistiques n°44* (unit FF. 106):

establishments for children (handicapped or in need of protection)	18,867
establishments for handicapped adults	6,578
establishments for adult rehabilitation	1,785
elderly homes *	12,560
Total	39,790

* excluding nursing homes, we have 33,500,000 days in 1990: 33,500,00 × FF. 375 = 12,560

The deduced ratio of wage bill to operating expenditures is 0.754, which is exactly the ratio of wage bill to operating expenditures reported by SESI in 1989 for establishments for children. We assumed the same ratio.

C. SOCIAL SERVICES AND CHARITIES

This subsector is more heterogeneous, with a mix of highly labor intensive activities (such as home hospitalization or housekeeping help for the elderly or the handicapped) and income or in-kind transfers to poor households or individuals.

We adopted the general procedure with the following SIRENE data for 1991:

9521 (charities)	110,322
9522 (income support-emergency)	23,856
9511 (multipurpose social services) *	(19,718)
1/3 × 19,718	6,708
	140,886

* of this category 2/3 are assumed to work in *bureaux d'aide sociale*, that is quasi-public agencies and 1/3 in *centres sociaux* which are nonprofit organizations.

1990 FTE is: (140,886/1.05) × 0.8 = *107,342*

We assumed a very low wage of FF. 120,000 as, in this subsector, many salaried workers are militant too. The ratio of wage bill to expenditures (0.6) is lower than in establishments to take into account income maintenance activities.

Capital expenditures, as for day care centers, are 4 per cent of operating expenditures.

D. CHILD DAY CARE CENTERS

We adopted general procedure with SIRENE employment × 0.8 = FTE, the same low average wage as in social services, and a high ratio of wage bill to expenditures as day care is highly labor intensive.

E. VOLUNTEER WORK

We followed the general procedure for volunteer work, which is important in this sector (ranked second after culture and recreation). We added volunteer work coming from religious orders, especially nuns.

The SESI records 3,962 volunteer nuns. Assuming a FTE = 3,962 × 0.8 = 3,170 and the average wage FF. 140,000, the imputed value of religious volunteer work is FF. 444.10^6.

Revenue 1990
As data on revenue are lacking, we used the same procedure as for the culture sector, by extrapolation to the whole field of Tchernonog's survey ratios for establishments and social services. The ratios are the following (for day care, figures are given by an expert, F. Leprince):

	establishments	soc services	day care
Government revenue	0.73	0.372	0.63
– state	0.037	0.102	
– local	0.091	0.140	0.41
– 3rd party	0.602	0.131	0.22

Private donative		0.128	
– foundations		0.022	
– corporations	0.006	0.061	
– individuals		0.045	
Private non-donative	0.026	0.500	0.37
– members' dues	0.0218	0.286	
– fees and sales	0.249	0.180	0.37
– investment income	0.002	0.034	

Other sectors

With the exception of international activities, the six last sectors of ICNPO present very few statistical data. Most of them are impossible to isolate in the SIRENE file and are recorded in the 9723 (n.e.c. services not elsewhere classified for the collectivity, political parties, work councils). Happily, those sectors are not so important as the first ones, so the unreliability of their figures doesn't sully the reliability of the overall figures.

For most sectors, our guesstimates are for the whole sector, without any breakdown by subsectors. If an assumption can be made on employment, we have divided all the columns of the tables between the subsectors, proportional to employment. For the revenue side, we adopted the Tchernonog survey ratios.

A. ENVIRONMENT

Expenditure 1990
There are *no data at all in this sector*. According to the Ministry of the Environment, there are maybe 5,000 people employed in the sector, assumed to be FTE. Without any information, we assumed a "mean average wage" of FF. 150,000, a ratio of wage bill to operating expenditures of 0.5 and a capital/operating expenditures ratio of 0.04. The imputed value of volunteer work in this sector is more than five times operating expenditures.

Revenue 1990
The ratios rely on very few data: only six environment associations in 1990 when the ratios of other sectors rely on fifty to 500

responses! Assuming that they are representative of the sector, the ratios are:

Government revenue	0.321 (mainly state and EEC)
Private donative revenue	0.154
Private non-donative	0.525
– members' dues	0.293
– fees and sales	0.223
– investment income	0.008

B. DEVELOPMENT AND HOUSING

Expenditure 1990

Local development is a growing sector because of decentralization and employment policies. So, nonprofits in this sector are recent and not recorded in a specific category of the SIRENE file. The following figures are very tentative and maybe underestimated.

On employment and training, C. Alphandery (*Structures d'insertion par l'économique*, La Documentation Française, September 1990) reported 5,500 FTE in *entreprises intermédiaires* in 1988. This subsector is quickly growing.

The SIRENE file reports 21,121 wage earners (in 6701 to 6711), that is young workers' housing, students' campus housing, canteens and other housing facilities.

Tourism-promoting associations and entrepreneurship-promoting associations (9712) employ nearly 5,000 people according to SIRENE.

We can assume too that many associations belonging to the development and housing sector are recorded in the "not elsewhere classified" category in SIRENE (9723). So, our guesstimate is 37,500 FTE with a "mean average wage" of FF. 150,000, a ratio of wage bill to operating expenditures, as observed in the Tchernonog survey, of 0.41, and the usual 4 per cent of capital expenditures.

We observe that volunteer work is very low in this sector.

Appendix A

Revenue 1990

As usual, here are the ratios of the Tchernonog survey, showing the prevalence of local subsidies:

Government revenue	0.371
– state	0.021
– local	0.324
– 3rd party	0.026
Private donative	0.018
Private non-donative	0.611
– members' dues	0.053
– sales and fees	0.556

C. CIVIL AND ADVOCACY ORGANIZATIONS

Expenditure 1990

All data are lacking, so we lean on SIRENE file category 77, that is advising, consulting, helping activities with the exception of 7715 (professional associations): (77) – (7715) = 30,483.

Because of the importance in category 77 of disguised business enterprises (to escape taxes) or of business on trial, we assumed that only the half of the figure is 1990 FTE employment in an advocating organization. The supposed average wage, FF. 180,000, is high, as qualification is higher as elsewhere in the non-profit sector. The ratio of wage bill to operating expenditures is observed in the Tchernonog survey: 0.42.

Revenue 1990

The revenue side is obtained by applying the Tchernonog survey's ratios to only seventeen associations of the field. So the reliability is low.

Government revenue	0.478
– state	0.374
– local	0.104

Private donative 0.033

Private non-donative (sales) 0.489

D. PHILANTHROPIC INTERMEDIARIES AND VOLUNTARISM PROMOTION

Voluntarism promotion is not common in France. The *Centre National du Volontariat* employs 1.5 FTE! *The Fondation Claude Pompidou* promotes voluntarism but is also an operating foundation. Grant-making foundations are very rare too and the sole important one is *Fondation de France*. So we have adopted the following minimal solution: *Fondation de France* accounts for 1990 were increased by 10 per cent.

Legacies and current giving are the main resources, and investment income secondary. In this sector, the FTE employment is deduced from the wage bill, with a "mean average wage".

E. INTERNATIONAL ACTIVITIES

For this subsector, resources are very reliable and expenditures are more tentative. The basic data for the sector is a summation of the results from the 560 first non-governmental organizations in the sector by the Ministry of Cooperation.

The 1989 data were increased by 17 per cent, the observed growth of expenditures 1988/89. International activities is the sole sector where private donative resources are prevalent.

For expenditures, the functional classification in the quoted data source does not fit our purpose. So we assumed a low average wage (because of a percentage of voluntarism) and a 0.5 ratio of wage bill to operating expenditures and a deduced FTE employment.

The figures in this sector are maybe underestimated because international cultural exchanges (such as twinning of towns) or educative-exchange nonprofit organizations (such as linguistic exchanges for children) were overlooked, first because of a lack of data, second because of a risk of duplication with culture or education sectors and third because many such organizations are quangos.

F. BUSINESS AND PROFESSIONAL ASSOCIATIONS, UNIONS

Expenditure 1990

We also had to use the general procedure for this subsector. Reliability is very low.

SIRENE file employment data are: (7715) + (9711) = 13,607. That is some professional associations and only employment in umbrella organization of chambers of commerce, agriculture and crafts.

People employed in trade unions, business associations, trade associations and employers' federations are in another category of the SIRENE file, the data from which we could not yet obtain.

So we assumed that FTE employment was about *15,600.* The average wage is high as manpower is qualified. The ratio of wage bill to operating expenditures is supposed to be 0.5 and capital/operating expenditures ratio to be 0.04.

Revenue 1990

We used the survey's ratio which showed a prevalence of private non-donative resources:

Government revenue	0.165
– state	0.050
– local	0.115
Private donative	0.075
Private non-donative	0.760
– members' dues	0.220
– sales	0.518
– investment income	0.022

Appendix B

GLOSSARY

Average wage is the average full-time equivalent remuneration per year.

Capital expenditures are expenditures that are incurred for acquisition of land, construction of buildings, and purchase of major equipment and vehicles with a useful life of more than one year.

Direct individual contributions are monetary donations to nonprofit organizations by private individuals.

Direct private foundation contributions are grants and other contributions by grant-making, operating and community foundations to the organization (contribution by corporate foundations are not included).

Direct private corporate contributions are grants, donations and other contributions by corporations and other private businesses, and corporate foundations to the organization.

Dues and assessments are income generated through charges which are paid as a condition of membership in an organization.

Endowments are stocks, bonds, property and funds given permanently to a foundation, or hospital or school so that it may produce its own income for grant-making purposes.

Fees for service are income generated through service charges which are paid directly by clients in exchange for some kind of service, e.g. fees for day care or health care.

Full-time equivalent employment indicates total amount of employment in terms of full-time jobs. Part-time employment is converted into full-time jobs, and added to the number of full-time jobs to equal full-time equivalent employment. In France, a full-time work week is 39 h x 45.74 = 1784 h where 39 h is the full time duration of work per week and 45.74 is the duration of the full total work year in weeks (five weeks of vacation and eight legal holidays).

Government refers to all the branches of the government, including the executive and judicial, and includes administrative and regulatory activities of central and local political entities. It also includes social security and other social funds. The terms *government* and *public sector* are used synonymously.

Grants and contracts refer to direct contributions by the government to the organization. Grants are non-specific and general public funding to nonprofits' activities, as contracts are agreements in support of specific activities and programs with reciprocal commitments. However, the distinction between the two categories is not always clear.

Gross domestic product is the common measure of the standard of living of a country. There are three approaches to measuring GDP: totalling the added values of all domestic industries (production less productive consumption equals added value) is one way. Aggregating the different incomes of the domestic economy is another way. Adding the final expenditures in the domestic economy is the last way.

Imputed value for volunteers is calculated by converting the total volunteer hours into full-time equivalent employment, multiplied by the average wage for the subsector.

International classification of nonprofit organizations (ICNPO): see Appendix C.

In-kind revenues refer to non-cash inflows of goods and services that can be used by the organization, e.g. free housing, materials, food, use of facilities, office or transport equipment.

Investment income includes interest on savings and temporary cash investments, dividends and interest on securities, net rental income and capital gains.

Local government refers to the three administrative levels of public local agencies: the regions (twenty-two in total) which were labelled by the 1982 Decentralization Act, the departments (ninety-five in total) and the communes, the number of which exceeds 36,000.

NAP (Nomenclature d'Activités et de Produits) is the French nomenclature of goods and services. It is the French version of the European NACE classification. In force since 1973, it includes 3,000 elementary groups of activities and products which are regrouped in 600 categories (level 600) and aggregated in ninety classes (level 100). This classification is used in all the public statistics. The NAP system suffers from limitations so far as the nonprofit sector is concerned. Although education and health and social services activities are separately identified in the classificatiòn system, the rest of what we have defined as the nonprofit sector is lumped into the catch-all category called "other collective nonmarket services".

Non-agricultural labour force equates to employment and self-employment in non-agricultural establishments.

Number of organizations indicates the number of establishments. An establishment is essentially the place of operation of an organization. The establishment is a smaller unit than an organization. The establishment is the unit of analysis used. In tables, *number of organizations* refers to the establishments included in the SIRENE file.

Operating expenditures refers to the costs of the general operations of the organization, including wage and salaries disbursements, purchases of goods (other than capital equipment), material and services, fees and charges paid.

Population between 15 and 65 refers to the population between the ages of 15 and 65 years, and stands for the total pool of the economically active population.

Revenues are inflows of spendable resources received by the organization during the year.

Sales refer to the income from the sale of goods and services. The distinction between sales and fees is not clear in NPO accounts.

SIRENE file (Système Informatique de Répertoire des Entreprises et des Etablissements) is a national administrative file which compiles a permanent inventory of all businesses, organizations and establishments with wage earners in France. The SIRENE file provides information about their localization, number of employees and activity. Theoretically, it includes all nonprofits having at least one employee, paying value added tax or receiving a public grant. In practice, this last condition is not fulfilled.

Third-party payments are indirect government payments for reimbursement to the organizations for services rendered to individuals. The payments can be made directly to the organization or through an individual. In France, these payments are made by social security and other social funds as *aide sociale*.

Total expenditures are spendable resources dispersed in acquiring goods and/or services during the year, regardless of whether they are consumed in carrying out operating activities during the year. Total expenditures are the sum of operating and capital expenditures.

Volunteer hours are the average number of hours volunteered by the population per year. The number is estimated from the "Giving and Volunteering" survey and the like by multiplying by 10 the average number of hours volunteered in a month (volunteers have longer vacation than paid staff).

Wage bill refers to the total sum of wage and salary disbursements, including fringe benefits, employers' and employees' social security contributions and other compulsory contributions.

Appendix C

THE INTERNATIONAL CLASSIFICATION OF NONPROFIT ORGANIZATIONS: FRANCE

Group 1: Culture and recreation (*culture et loisirs*)

Organizations and activities in general and specialized fields of culture and recreation.

1 100 Culture (*culture*)

- *media and communications*
  production and dissemination of information and communication; includes radio and TV stations, publishing of books, journals, newspapers, and newsletters; film production and film clubs; libraries.

- *visual arts, architecture, ceramic art*
  production, dissemination and display of visual arts and architecture; includes sculpture, photographic societies, painting, drawing, design centers and architectural associations.

- *performing arts*
  performing arts centers, companies and associations; includes theatres, dance, ballet, opera, orchestras, chorals and music ensembles.

- *historical, literary and humanistic societies*
  promotion and appreciation of the humanities, preservation of historical and cultural artefacts, commemoration of historical events; includes historical societies, poetry and literary societies, language associations, reading promotion, war memorials, commemorative funds and associations.

- *museums*
  general and specialized museums covering art, history, sciences, technology, culture.

- *zoos and aquariums*

1 200 Recreation (*loisirs*)

- *sports*
  provision of amateur sports training (collective or individual), physical fitness, and sports competition services and events. Also includes hunting and fishing associations.

- *recreation*
  provision of recreational facilities and services to individuals and communities; includes elderly clubs, youth clubs, country clubs, *amicales*, specialized or multipurpose recreation clubs, socio-educative and popular education associations, feast committees.

- *social tourism*
  provision of vacation facilities and services with a social purpose; includes holiday villages or camps, youth hostels, holiday centers for children.

1 300 Service clubs (*clubs*)

membership organizations providing services to members and local communities, for example Lions, Rotary.

Group 2: Education and research
(*education et recherche*)

Organizations and activities administering, providing, promoting, conducting, supporting and servicing education and research.

2 100 Primary and secondary education
(*enseignement préélémentaire, primaire et secondaire*)

- *pre-elementary, elementary, primary and secondary education*
  education at pre-elementary, elementary, primary and secondary levels; includes pre-school organizations other than day care.

2 200 Higher education (*enseignement supérieur*)

- *higher education (university level)*
  higher learning, providing academic degrees; includes universities, business management schools, law schools, medical schools, superior technicians schools, *grandes écoles*.

2 300 Other education
(*autres enseignements et formation continue*)

- *vocational/technical schools*
  technical and vocational training specifically geared towards gaining employment; includes trade schools, paralegal training, secretarial schools.

- *adult/continuing education*
  institutions engaged in providing education and training in addition to the formal educational system; includes schools of continuing studies, correspondence schools, night schools, literacy and reading programs. It also includes programs to improve skills of staff manpower of enterprises run by associations.

- *peri-school associations*
  includes parent-teacher associations, alumni clubs, in-school sports or cultural activities, school cooperatives, social clubs for students.

2 400 Research (*recherche*)

- *medical research*
  research in the medical field, includes research on specific diseases, disorders, or medical disciplines.

- *science and technology*
  research in the physical and life sciences, engineering and technology.

- *social sciences, policy studies*
  research and analysis in the social sciences and policy area.

Group 3: Health (*santé*)

Organizations that engage in health-related activities, providing health care, both general and specialized services, administration of health care services, and health support services.

3 100 Hospitals and rehabilitation
(*hôpitaux et établissements de rééducation*)

- *hospitals* primarily in patient medical care and treatment.

- *rehabilitation*
  inpatient health care and rehabilitative therapy to individuals suffering from physical impairments due to injury, genetic defect or disease and requiring extensive physiotherapy or similar forms of care.

3 200 Nursing homes
(*maisons de convalescence et maisons de retraite médicalisées*)

- *nursing homes* (there is no exact French equivalent of this term) inpatient convalescent care, residential care as well as primary health care services; includes medicalized elderly establishments.

3 300 Other health services (*autres services de santé*)

˙ental health
˙ychiatric hospitals; includes inpatient care and treatment for mentally ill.
˙al health treatment; includes outpatient treatment for lly ill patients; includes community mental health cen-
d halfway homes.

- *crisis intervention*
  outpatient services and counsel in acute mental health situations; includes suicide prevention and support to victims of assault and abuse.

- *sanitary education*
  organizations promoting health education; includes sanitation screening for potential health hazards, first aid training and services and family planning services.

- *emergency medical services*
  services to persons in need of immediate care; includes ambulatory services and paramedical emergency care, shock/ trauma programs and lifeline programs; ambulance services.

- *self-help organizations*
  includes organizations for home hospitalization and blood transfusion.

Group 4: Social services (*services sociaux*)

Organizations and institutions providing human and social services to a community or target population. The subsectors in the table do not fit French statistics so we adopted the following subsectors:

4 100 Residential homes (*établissements sociaux*)

- *establishments for handicapped children*

- *establishments for handicapped adults*

- *establishments for elderly people*

- *establishments for children in social difficulty*

- *establishments for adult rehabilitation*

- *establishments for persons or families in social difficulty*

4 200 Social services and charities
(*services sociaux et associations caritatives*)

- *income support and maintenance*
  organizations providing cash assistance and other forms of direct services to persons unable to maintain a livelihood.

- *material assistance*
  organizations providing in-kind transfers to poor households or individuals; for example food, clothing, transport and other forms of assistance; includes food banks and clothing distribution centers.

- *youth services and youth welfare*
  services to youth; includes delinquency prevention services, teen pregnancy prevention, drop-out prevention, youth centers and clubs; includes Boy Scouts, Girl Scouts.

- *child welfare, child services, day care*
  services to children, adoption services, child development centers, foster care; includes infant care centers, creches and nurseries.

- *services for the handicapped, the elderly, families (not including nursing homes) and other specialized services*
  includes housekeeping help for the elderly or the handicapped; includes homemaker services, transport facilities, meal programs

- *emergency and relief*
  organizations that work to prevent, predict, control, and alleviate the effects of disasters, to educate or otherwise prepare individuals to cope with the effects of disasters, or provide relief to disaster victims, includes volunteer fire protection, life boat services, etc.

  organizations providing temporary shelters to the homeless; includes travellers' aid, and temporary housing.

  organizations providing food, clothing, shelter and services to refugees and immigrants.

Group 5: Environment
(*protection de l'environnement*)

Organizations promoting and providing services in environmental conservation, pollution control and prevention, environmental education and health, and animal protection. There is no subgroup in the French classification.

- *natural resources conservation and protection*
  conservation and preservation of natural resources, including land, water, energy and plant resources for the general use and enjoyment of the public.

  organizations that promote clean air, clean water, reducing and preventing noise pollution, radiation control, hazardous wastes and toxic substances, solid waste management, recycling programs, and global warming.

  botanical gardens, arboreta, horticultural programs and landscape services; includes organizations promoting anti-litter campaigns, programs to preserve parks, green spaces and open spaces in urban or rural areas and city and highway beautification programs.

- *animal protection and welfare*
  animal protection and welfare services; includes animal shelters and humane societies, veterinary services.

  animal hospitals and services providing care for farm and household animals and pets.

Group 6: Development and housing
(*développement et logement*)

Organizations promoting programs and providing services to help improve communities and the economic and social well-being of society.

6 100 Economic social and community development
(*développement économique et social local*)

- *community and neighborhood organizations*
  organizations working towards improving the quality of life within communities or neighborhoods; includes local development organizations, landlord and tenant associations, poor people's cooperatives.

- *economic development*
  programs and services to improve economic infrastructure and capacity; includes entrepreneurial programs, and technical or management consulting assistance, rural development organizations.

- *social development*
  organizations working towards improving institutional infrastructure and capacity to alleviate social problems and to improve general public well-being.

6 200 Housing (*logement*)

- *housing association*
  development, construction, management, leasing, financing and rehabilitation of housing; includes young workers' housing, student campus housing, canteens.

- *housing assistance*
  organizations providing housing search, legal services and related assistance.

6 300 Employment and training
(*aide à l'emploi et formation professionnelle*)

- *job training programs*
  organizations providing and supporting apprenticeship programs, internships, on-the-job training, and other training programs for youth, women or the long-term unemployed.

- *vocational counseling and guidance*
  vocational training and guidance, career counseling, testing, and related services; includes "intermediary associations"*and*

enterprises d'insertion (associations producing goods and services and supplying temporary jobs to frail people).

Group 7: Law, advocacy and politics
(*associations civiques et de défense des droit de l'homme*)

Organizations and groups that work to protect and promote civil and other rights, or advocate social and political interests, offer legal services and promote public safety. There is no subgroup in the French classification.

7 100 Civic and advocacy organizations
(*associations civiques et de défense des droits*)

- *advocacy organizations*
  organizations that protect the rights and promote the interests of specific groups of people – e.g., the physically handicapped, the elderly, children, and women.

- *civil rights associations*
  organizations that work to protect or preserve individual civil liberties and human rights.

- *ethnic associations*
  organizations that promote the interests of, or provide services to, members belonging to a specific ethnic heritage.

- *civic associations*
  programs and services to encourage and spread civic mindedness.

7 200 Law and legal services
(*services juridiques*)

- *legal services*
  legal services, advice and assistance in dispute resolution and court-related matters and in relationships between individuals and public agencies.

- *crime prevention and public safety*
  either social work or cultural and educative activities towards the pre-delinquent population in deprived areas.

- *victim support services*
  counsel and advice to victims of crime.

- *consumer protection associations*
  protection of consumer rights, and the improvement of product control and quality.

- *political parties and organizations* (partis politiques, organisations politiques)
  activities and services to support the placing of particular candidates in political office; includes dissemination of information, public relations and political fundraising. This subgroup is *empty* (see chapter 1).

Group 8: Philanthropic intermediaries and voluntarism promotion
(*intermédiaires philanthropiques et promotion du bénévolat*)

Philanthropic organizations and organizations promoting charity and charitable activities.

8 100 Philanthropic intermediaries and voluntarism promotion (not widespread in France)

- *grantmaking foundations*
  private foundations; including corporate foundations and public utility foundations.

- *voluntarism promotion and support*
  organizations that recruit, train, and place volunteers, and promote volunteering.

Group 9: International activities
(*activités internationales*)

Organizations promoting greater intercultural understanding between peoples of different countries and historical backgrounds and also those providing relief during emergencies and promoting development and welfare abroad.

9 100 International activities (*activités internationales*)

- *exchange/friendship/cultural programs*
  programs and services designed to encourage mutual respect and friendship internationally.

- *development assistance associations*
  programs and projects that promote social and economic development abroad.

- *international disaster and relief organizations*
  organizations that collect, channel and provide aid to other countries during times of disaster or emergency.

- *international human rights and peace organizations*
  organizations which promote and monitor human rights and peace internationally.

Group 10: Religion (*cultes et congrégations*)

Empty (see chapter 1)

Group 11: Business, professional associations and unions (*associations professionnelles et syndicats*)

Organizations promoting, regulating and safeguarding business, professional and labor interests.

11 100 Business, professional associations and unions

- *business associations*
  organizations that work to promote, regulate and safeguard the interests of special branches of business – e.g., manufacturers' associations, farmers' associations, bankers' associations. Includes chambers of commerce, agriculture and crafts.

- *professional associations*
  organizations promoting, regulating, and protecting professional interests – e.g., bar associations, medical associations.

- *labor unions*
  organizations that promote, protect and regulate the rights and interests of employees.

- *work councils*
  borderline social economy organizations, specific to France. They are operating in every enterprise with more than fifty employees. Administered by salaried employees, they manage canteens, day care and holiday centers, cultural activities and other personal or family social services.

Group 12: [Not elsewhere classified] (*non dénommé ailleurs*)

Appendix D

TRANSLATION IN FRENCH OF ICNPO

Groupe 1: Culture et loisirs

1 100 – Culture et beaux-arts

1 101 – Média et communications
1 102 – Arts plastiques, architecture, céramique
1 103 – Spectacles (orchestre, théâtre, opéra, etc.)
1 104 – Sociétés savantes (historiques, littéraires, etc.)
1 105 – Musées et conservation du patrimoine
1 106 – Zoos et aquariums
1 107 – Centres culturels et artistiques à objet multiple
1 108 – Assistance et conseil, aide à la mise en place et à la gestion des associations culturelles
1 109 – Autres organisations culturelles et artistiques (ou organisations culturelles et artistiques non dénommées ailleurs)

1 200 – Sports et loisirs

1 201 – Clubs et associations sportives (y compris associations de chasse et de pêche)
1 202 – Associations de loisirs et amicales diverses
1 203 – Organisations de loisirs à objectif multiple
1 204 – Assistance et conseil, etc.
1 205 – Autres organisations de loisirs (dont tourisme social)

1 300 – Clubs de service

Groupe 2: Education et recherche

2 100 – Enseignement élémentaire, primaire et secondaire

2 200 – Enseignement supérieur (au delà du baccalauréat)

2 300 – Autres enseignements et formation continue

2 301 – Ecoles professionnelles ou techniques
2 302 – Formation continue et éducation permanente
2 303 – Organisations éducatives à objet multiple

2 400 – Recherche

2 401 – Recherche médicale
2 402 – Recherche scientifique et technique
2 403 – Recherche en sciences sociales et politiques
2 404 – Organisation de recherche à vocation multiple
2 405 – 2 406

Groupe 3: Santé

3 100 – Hôpitaux et établissements de rééducation

3 101 – Hôpitaux généraux
3 102 – Etablissements de reeducation

3 200 – Cliniques, maisons de convalescence et maisons de retraite medicalisées

3 300 – Santé mentale

3 301 – Hôpitaux psychiatriques
3 302 – Soins ambulatoires en santé mentale
3 303 – Prévention du suicide, centres de désintoxication
3 304 – 3 305 – 3 306

3 400 – Autres services de santé

3 401 – Prévention et éducation sanitaire
3 402 – Hospitalisation et autres soins à domicile
3 403 – Services de rééducation
3 404 – Services médicaux d'urgence
3 405 – 3 406 – 3 407

Groupe 4: Services sociaux

4 100 – Services sociaux

4 101 – Établissements et services sociaux pour enfants, aide
sociale à l'enfance, crèches
4 102 – Établissements et services sociaux pour adolescents en
difficulté (y compris mouvements de jeunesse)
4 103 – Services sociaux pour les familles
4 104 – Établissements et services pour personnes âgées (sauf
medicalisés)
4 106 – Services d'entraide et autres services sociaux
4 107 – 4 108 – 4 109

4 200 – Secours d'urgence et aide aux migrants

4 201 – Services de sécurité et de secours d'urgence
4 202 – Hébergement temporaire
4 203 – Aide aux réfugiés et aux immigrés
4 204 – Organisations de secours d'urgence et d'aides aux
migrants à objectifs multiples
4 205 – 4 206

4 300 – Associations caritatives

4 301 – Secours financiers et autres services aux personnes en
difficulté
4 302 – Secours en nature, distribution de nourriture et de
vêtements
4 303 – Associations caritatives à buts multiples
4 304 – 4 305

Groupe 5: Protection de l'environnement

5 100 – Environnement

5 101 – Contrôle et réduction de la pollution
5 102 – Conservation et protection des ressources naturelles
5 103 – Embellissement des espaces naturels
5 104 – 5 105 – 5 106

5 200 – Animaux

5 201 – Protection des animaux
5 202 – Protection et préservation de la faune sauvage
5 203 – Services vétérinaires
5 204 – 5 205 – 5 206

Groupe 6: Dévelopment et logement

6 100 – Développement économique et social local

6 101 – Associations de voisinage, régies de quartier
6 102 – Développement économique, pépinières, entreprises à objectifs multiples
6 103 – Développement social local
6 104 – 6 105 – 6 106

6 200 – Logement

6 201 – Construction et réhabilitation de logements
6 202 – Aide au logement
6 203 – 6 204 – 6 205

6 300 Emploi et formation

6 301 – Stages d'insertion et de formation professionnelle
6 302 – Orientation professionnelle
6 303 – Réinsertion professionnelle et ateliers protégés: entreprises d'insertion et associations intermédiares
6 304 – 6 305 – 6 306

Groupe 7: Associations civiques et de défense des droits de l'homme

7 100 – Associations civique et de défense

7 101 – Associations civiques
7102 – Organisation de défense des minorités et des groupes
    spécifiques
7 103 – Défense des libertés publiques et des droits de l'homme
7 104 – Associations d'étrangers ou d'immigrés
7 105 – 7106 – 7107

7 200 – Services juridiques

7 201 – Assistance juridique, boutiques de droit
7 202 – Prévention de la délinquance et sécurité publique
7 203 – Réinsertion des délinquants
7 204 – Aide aux victimes
7205 – Organisations de protection des consommateurs
7 206 – Services juridiques à objectifs multiples
7 207 – 7 208

Groupe 8: Intermédiares philanthropiques et promotion du bénévolat (not widespread in France)

8 100 – Intermédiaires philanthropiques

8 101 – Fondations recueillant et distribuant des fonds
8 102 – Promotion et aide au bénévolat
8 103 – Organisations spécialisées dans la collecte de fonds
8 104 – 8 105 – 8 106

Groupe 9: Activités internationales

9 100 – Activités internationales

9 101 – Relations et échanges culturels internationaux
9 102 – Associations d'aide au développement
9 103 – Secours d'urgence international

9 104 – Défense des droits de l'homme et de la paix dans le monde
9 105 – 9 106 – 9 107

Groupe 10: Cultes et congrégations

Groupe 11: Associations professionnelles et syndicats

11 100 – Associations professionnelles: chambres de commerce,
  d'agriculture, des metiers
11 102 – Ordres et associations de professions libérales
11 103 – Syndicats

Groupe 12: Organisations non dénommées ailleurs

BIBLIOGRAPHY

Alix, Nicole and Sami Castro. *L'entreprise associative: aspects juridiques de l'intervention économique des associations*. UNIOPSS. Paris: Economica, 1990.

Relying on its own features like a facility of constitution or great adaptability, associative structure appears as a particularly efficient form of organization to solve some specific social needs and to manage many collective activities. For this reason the association can be considered now as an important economic agent. The purpose of this law book is to study the status of association from an economic and legal point of view (the subtitle of the book is "Legal aspects of an economic intervention from associations").

Archambault, Edith. "Les associations en chiffres." *Revue des études coopératives* n°12, 1984, pp. 10–46.

This article is a summary and a critical examination of the statistical evidence on associations existing in 1984. It deals first with the number of organizations; there are reliable figures on the formation of associations and tentative figures on living organizations; second, the surveys on membership are compared and the socio-demographic characteristics of members are highlighted; third, the treatment of associations in national accounting is described and shows that the associative sector is split up and overlooked. Finally some methodological propositions are made to improve the data on volunteering and to give a money value to volunteer work. The article also emphasizes the necessity of building a unique standard classification of nonprofit organizations.

Archambault, Edith. "L'économie sociale est-elle associée aux grandes fonctions économiques des pouvoirs publics?" *Revue des études coopératives, mutualistes et associatives* n°18, 1986, pp. 3–35.

The relationship between the Jacobin state and the social economy in France has moved from mutual hostility during the nineteenth century to a recent partnership during the last two decades and especially since the decentralization acts (1982–1983). This article shows that mutuals and associations participate in the three economic activities of modern government according to Musgrave's distinction: the allocation of public goods, the redistribution of income and the regulation of economic growth and employment. This complementary relationship between government and social economy organizations works through contractualization and public financing. The advantages and the limits of the partner relationship are examined as the strength and the weakness of the social economy.

Baumlin, Laurence and Maryvonne Lemaire. "Place de l'économie sociale dans la protection sociale: contour et représentation." *Revue des études coopératives, mutualistes et associatives* n°28, 3ème trim., 1989.

This study, presented at the sixth ADDES symposium (1989) and published in *Revue des études coopératives, mutualistes et associatives,* proposes a definition of social welfare and an analysis of the place occupied by social economy in social welfare. In its concern to use the most appropriate statistical instruments (the satellite account for social welfare), this analysis shows that many actors in the third sector are involved in social welfare, not only as a real social welfare system themselves (mutual benefit companies) but also as producers of social services (especially the associations).

Bilans du CNVA, 1982–1991.

Created in 1983 and dependent on the French Prime Minister, the CNVA (National Council of Associative Life) realizes every year an "annual assessment of associative life". The documents published until now present several aspects of associations drawn up by specialists. For example:

- the world of associations in the 1970s and at the beginning of the 1980s (1982);
- associations and public authorities (1983–84 and 1990–91);
- associations and decentralization (1983–84);
- demography of associations (1983–84);
- associations and communication (1986–87);
- financing of associations (1986–87);
- associations and international action (1986–87);
- patronage: juridical aspects (1988–89);
- voluntary work (1988–89);

Bloch-Laine, François and Jean-Marc Garrigou-Lagrange. *Associations et développement local*. Paris: Librairie Générale de droit et de jurisprudence, 1988.

The main purpose of this law book is to show the connection between the development of associations in France and the expansion of activities run by local communities after administrative decentralization. In this perspective, it proposes an examination of the trends and the real conditions of the growing role played by associations in local life: legal capacities and financial means of associations, legality of their actions, etc.

Boulte, Patrick. *Le diagnostic des organisations appliqué aux associations*. Paris: PUF, 1991.

This book presents the conditions in which the concept of organization analysis developed in France by sociologists like Michel Crozier, Erhard Friedberg and Renaud Sainsaulieu can be transposed to associations. Noting that associations are often very close to the main current problems of society, its author, a senior consultant in a business consultancy, shows that their management is very complex, involving several different logics (administrative, cultural, social, and economic). For this reason, what he calls the "pluridisciplinary diagnosis" appears particularly appropriate to realizing an evaluation of such an organization as the association.

Canto, Jean-François. *Localisation et caractéristiques principales par secteurs d'activité des 336220 déclarations d'associations de la décennie 1975–1984.* F.N.D.V.A., 1988.

This report, concerning more than 300,000 creations, is the most important study of French associative demography for ten years, from declarations supplied by the Interior Ministry to the *Journal Officiel*. The author establishes a file according to the main activity and makes a list of fifty-seven groups of associations incorporated in nine sections. This study describes the phenomenon of the birth of an association and sheds very interesting light especially on:

- evolution of associations' birth by year and month and distribution of these creations according to the main activity;
- evolution of the localization of creations according to the region, the department and the nature of the municipality of setting up (rural or urban); the author introduces in this way a high differentiation between associations typical of the rural areas and urban associations;
- type of head office according to the nature of the activity and the geographic localization.

Chadeau, Ann and Jean-Claude Willard. "Les Formes et la mesure de l'emploi dans l'économie sociale." *Revue des études coopératives, mutualistes et associatives* n°15, 3ème trim., 1985, pp. 65–89.

Nowadays, employment is certainly one of the most crucial problems for national economies. Because they are conducted according to a kind of equity and "spirit" of solidarity. The organisms of social economy can be considered as an exception to the market rules. For this reason, do they have a specific capacity to create work? This is the main point that this study tries to answer. In this perspective a knowledge of employment in the third sector is necessary, in quantitative (counting of jobs) and qualitative (permanence of work, mechanisms of creation) terms.

Chéroutre, Marie Thérèse. *L'essor et l'avenir du bénévolat, facteur d'amélioration de la qualité de la vie.* Paris: Conseil Economique et Social, 1989.

Presented to the CES, this report deals with voluntary work and more specifically its capacity to improve quality of life. After a global presentation of social and economic aspects of voluntary work (voluntary work as a very significant social practice creating a special relation between people), this study analyzes it more precisely in the associative sphere, which is an opportunity to remind the reader of generalities concerning associations (juridical aspects, attitude of authorities, situation in other countries, etc.). How to develop voluntary work in associations? This question constitutes the last part of this report and gives rise to several propositions in that respect, concerning training and its financing, professional risks, patronage, etc.

Chéroutre, Marie Thérèse. *Exercice et développement de la vie associative dans le cadre de la loi du 1er juillet 1901.* Avis et rapport du Conseil Economique et social. Conseil Economique et Social, Avril 1993.

Nowadays, the association is an undeniable economic and social reality: 70,000 associations are created every year in France out of a total of 700 or 800 thousand; 43 per cent of French people join one or more associations. Associative life developed rapidly, owing to the founding law of 1901, virtually unchanged since then. This report takes stock of the use of the 1901 law, notes several misuses that appeared recently, and suggests clarifications and initiatives to make easier the exercise and the development of associative activities. It points out the two characteristics of the evolution of the use of the law:

– on one hand, the "meeting" between associations and administrations: the report warns against an unreasonable use of the status for parapublic associations. It advises clarification of the relationship and the systemizing contractual relations, and recommends accelerating the reform of the administrative procedures;
– on the other hand, the entry of the associative world into the economic and competitive sphere that also causes some misuses (some associations are only a means to evade the commercial fiscal system and its constraints). The CES suggests a clarification of the fiscal system regarding associations.

Lastly, the author stressed the necessity of supporting and

acknowledging associations of public interest that mitigate the inadequacies of government action in this situation of crisis.

CNVA. *Les associations et l'Europe*. Paris: La Documentation Française, 1989.

It's the will of the European Parliament to acknowledge the economic, social and cultural sectors of associations within the Community that motivates these reflections of the study group "Associations et Europe" set up by the CNVA. This report presents an examination of the obstacles that now impede the transnational activities of associations: legal and fiscal disparities, inequalities between financial capacities, differentiations as regards access to European administrations. The proposals set up aim at creating a favorable environment for European associations and at giving them instruments to act at a European level: legal recognition, legislative harmonization by the creation of an European status for associations, construction of a permanent structure for concertation and cooperation.

Courtois, Josette. *Les associations, un monde méconnu. Enquête nationale: poids économique et social des associations employant des salariés. Paris*: Crédit Coopératif, 1991.

The Crédit Coopératif is the main financial partner for the third sector in France. As such, it has been conducting many researches on associations for many years. In its concern to contribute to a best statistical knowledge of associations, this document presents the results of several years investigation in each region of France. These results, particularly rich and various, concern the employers' associations: their number (more than 80,000), demography of their creations (5,000 per year in the 1950s, 10,000 in the 1960s, 50,000 today), their financing and budget, their audience, their employees, their geographical distribution, their activities, etc.

Davezac, Georges. *Les entreprises de l'économie sociale*. Paris: Conseil Economique et Social, 1986.

This report, intended for representatives of socio-professional organizations, presents a global view and an assessment of organizations of social economy. Several propositions are expressed in this document: among them, the most interesting are certainly the points concerning encouragement to voluntary work and explanation of fiscal adjustments related to donations. Some of the figures presented here are particularly significant to the importance of the third sector in France: more than 100,000 firms and one million salaried employees are concerned.

Debbasch, Charles (dir.). *Les fondations: un mécène pour notre temps?* Paris: Economica, 1987.

The sponsoring revival created an interest in foundations in France. A round-table conference, convened in Aix-en-Provence on June 1987, allowed the collection of these studies about the legal and fiscal status of foundations and their relations with sponsorship. The French pattern of foundations is judged constraining by the authors because it is subject to a restrictive legal form and to the quasi-discretionary power of the authorities. Then the French situation is compared to a few foreign cases.

"Le monde associatif". *Economie et statistique* n°208, March 1988, pp. 17–44.

This document draws up a panorama of associative life in France, from the survey "contacts" made by INSEE in collaboration with INED from May 1982 to May 1983. First, it notes the important regression of associations of "militant" type (political, syndical, consumer or religious associations), that mobilize a minority of members, in contrast to associations that give access to leisure or various services, especially in sectors of sport and culture, that rapidly develop. This document also defines the profile of associative members according to:

age: associative participation is to a maximum age of about 40 years;
- sex: at every age, the membership of men is much higher than that of women;
- social position: the membership is closely connected with the

academic standard; professors come foremost.

Finally, the phenomenon of multi-membership is analysed: in 1983, 1.5 million people joined at least four associations; they only correspond to 7 per cent of the members but concentrate 21 per cent of the membership. This concerns essentially men, with an over-representation of graduates.

Fouquet, Annie, Nicole Tabard and Michel Villac. *La vie associative et son financement.* Fonjep-Credoc. La documentation Française, 1990.

In association with INSEE and CREDOC, the FONJEP (cooperation founded for youth and popular education) conducted this survey among its members (associations) with two main concerns:

– to have a better knowledge of which fields of activity these associations have in charge;
– to estimate the origin and amount of financial resources of associations;

The results inform the reader in a very interesting way on the financing of associations (who are the financial backers, which are their priorities and particularities) and on the various fields in the charge of FONJEP members (youth, popular education, rural development, environment, social economy, international cooperation, professional training, etc.).

Forse, Michel. "Les créations d'associations: un indicateur de changement social." *Observations et Diagnostics Economiques* n°6, January 1984, pp. 125–45.

Based on an analysis of creations of associations since the beginning of the century (between 1977 and 1982, creations of associations increased by 20 per cent), this document notes that it constitutes a good indication of social change. As a matter of fact, many changes of society appear in the sphere of associations: for instance, development at local level or decline of ecology (this last trend having been reversed for a few years). A typology of associations is proposed including twenty categories: sport, religion, politics, research, production, social, environment, etc.

Gueslin, André. *L'invention de l'économie sociale, le 19ème siècle Français*. Paris: Economica, 1987.

The French model of social economy is the result of a long historic evolution. This very comprehensive book explores the history of emergence of the different movements and the great doctrines that gave rise to this third sector in the nineteenth century:

- the associationist socialism with Owen, the pioneers of Rochdale, Saint Simon, Fourier, Cabet, Beluze, and Proudhon;
- the contribution of Catholicism and its part in social action;
- the construction of mutuality and the development of social welfare policies;
- the birth of cooperation and its blossoming in the urban and rural areas.

Gueslin, André and Pierre Guillaume (eds). *De la charité médiévale à la sécurité sociale*. Paris: Les Éditions Ouvrières, 1992.

This very comprehensive book is the result of a conference between a group of economists, sociologists, historians and practitioners of social welfare which took place in Paris, January 1991. It presents an analysis of the history of social welfare in France, its evolution, its ideological issues and its economical constraints from the Middle Ages on. Among various themes it explains the emergence of public and private charity and the development of organizations such as charities, brotherhoods and guilds in various regions and different fields of activity. Finally, from a multi-disciplinary point of view, it sheds light on the development and the recent issues of the French social security system.

Gontcharoff, Georges. *Guide du partenariat des associations et des pouvoirs publics locaux*. Paris: L'Harmattan, 1988.

The process of administrative decentralization begun in France since 1982 encourages the development of relations between associations and local communities. Since then, far more than before, the associative sector has run many public local services in the sectors of culture, sport, health and social services especially. This guide sets out a pragmatic analysis, stage by stage, of the construction and realization of a partnership between associations and local authorities: preliminary study of the objects, type of legal relation, different stages of the negotiation, comparison of the logics, conflicts, etc. It also offers a few suggestions to attain a balance between these two legitimacies and to avoid associations involving themselves in relations of subordination with local authorities: plain contractual relations, precision of the objectives and the means used, estimate of the results, etc.

Haeusler, Laurence. "Evolution du monde associatif de 1978 à 1986." *Les rapports du CREDOC* n°51, December 1988.

Since 1978, the CREDOC survey on "conditions of life and aspirations of the French", owing to a range of questions related to the frequentation of associations of various types, has analyzed the membership of associations and identified its main characteristics. This report presents the main evolutions of the associative world from 1978 to 1986: high rate of creation (50,000 a year), development of the sporting movement, loss of influence of the trade unions and the disappearance of a certain militancy. The typical member is an employed man, a graduate, living usually in the provinces; executives are the most involved. Lastly this document analyzes the membership characteristic of each type of association.

Horaist, Jacques. *Rôle économique des associations*. Paris: PUF, 1983.

More and more, social and economic analysis considers the "associative phenomenon" as more efficient than traditional economic solutions, particularly in fields such as health, culture, social or leisure activities. This study especially appreciates the capacity of associations to create jobs, their ability to drain off voluntary work, arguing about the specificities of interaction between these two kinds of working.

Kaminski, Philippe. "Des chiffres pour l'économie sociale: où en est-on en 1987?" *Revue des études coopératives, mutualistes et associa-*

tives n°37. 1er trim., 1991, pp. 27–34.

At the beginning of the 1980s, P. Kaminski was the first to realize a statistical analysis of social economy producing the first figures on the place and role of the third sector in France. Achieved by a very simple but original method in social economy (observation of the administrative files of firms), these figures have been very successful despite their inaccuracy (admitted by the author) due to the nature of the source.

Marchal, Emmanuelle. *Du désintéressement au marché: les différentes formes d'entreprises associatives.* Dossier du Centre d'études de l'emploi n°33, September 1990.

The "associative firm" realizes the juxtaposition of two separate worlds: the world of the firm and the world of the association. By clearly separating the resources of each of these two worlds, it is possible to discern opposing (for example, the object of the association and activity of the firm) and complementary resources (for example, the different forms of working). About forty associations have been studied here leading to a definition of three different types of associative firms according to the features of their managers (they can be voluntary founders, salaried founders or salaried nonfounders). The author shows that each of these three forms has its own capacities and limits. Associative firms managed by voluntary founders are particularly suited to proximity services, whereas management by salaried founders is more flexible and therefore more suitable to market rules. Finally, management by salaried nonfounders appears more efficient for public services.

Marranche, Victor. *Communication sur les associations.* Comité Economique et Social Ile de France, November 1986.

Presented to the Economic and Social Committee of the Paris area, this communication deals with the managing associations (a quarter of all the associations in this area). Many proposals are set up concerning information, communication, relations with communities, financing of training, etc. This report is also on statistical inadequacy for the third sector: it appears really urgent to build a "satellite account" for social economy including regional and national levels.

Padieu, Claudine. *Statistiques de l'économie sociale, constat et propositions*. Rapport présenté à T. Dreyfus, secrétaire d'état à l'économie sociale, février 1990.

At the government's request, this report presents existing statistical sources concerning the social economy. After an examination of the general characteristics of the organisms of social economy (principles of functioning and structure) and of some statistic data about them, C. Padieu proposes an identification and an evaluation of the surveys and national statistic files (SIRENE file, declarations to the prefectures, statistics kept by each ministry, investigations carried out by organizations of the third sector themselves, etc.). Finally, some proposals to improve the French statistic system are put forward: elaboration of a reliable typology, improvement of the understanding of the organizations in SIRENE, launching of national investigations, etc.

Pomey, M. *Traité des fondations d'utilité publique*. Paris: PUF, 1980.

In spite of an earlier start and a considerable and rapid development, public service foundations are yet widely unknown in France. Such a gap the author intends to fill by means of this treatise, from a legal point of view but also presenting several historical and economical outlines. Through many examples, this work considers successively the form of the foundations, the scope of their activities, their objectives and means of action, their financing, their fiscal system, their organization, etc. Then it compares the French model to the American, British and German ones.

Tchernonog, Viviane. *Gestion des politiques sociales locales – Analyse du recours communal aux associations*. Commissariat Général du plan-Laboratoire d'Economie sociale, 1991.

To what extent do the municipalities use the associative structure to realize some of their missions in the field of social policy? Answering this is the main purpose of this study, carried out at the request of the Commissariat Général du Plan. Collecting information in different ways (interviews and a systematic mailed inquiry by the largest French communes), this report aims at evaluating four aspects of the question: importance and evolution, forms and functions. The quantitative results are particularly indicative of the range of the phenomenon:

- more than 500,000 associations get subsidies from municipalities;
- municipalities dedicates on average 5 per cent of their budget to associations (1 per cent for little rural towns, 8 per cent for larger districts);
- the intervention of communities is very concentrated: 4 per cent of associations get 70 per cent of subsidies;
- health and social associations are the most supported, followed by culture and sport.

On a qualitative level, the observations are also very interesting, showing that, more than just a simple confrontation between two rising actors (associations and local communities), the studied phenomenon is the result of two elements: a real collective wish to develop local democracy and the necessity of finding solutions to inefficiency of municipal management.

Théry, Henry. *La place et le rôle du secteur associatif dans le développement de la politique d'action éducative, sanitaire et sociale.* Conseil Economique et Social, 1986.

Backed up by figures, this report deals with the role and the activities of associations in the sectors of social services, health and education. This precise study shows, if necessary, that this sphere of associations is really significant in France: in 1985 it concerned more than 200,000 unities of which about 170,000 still exist. Finally, several suggestions are set out, especially:

- to develop the knowledge of associations thanks particularly to the "satellite-account" of social economy;
- to make simpler the fiscal systems applied to legacies and donations;
- to base the relations between associations and Civil Service on agreements;
- to encourage the gathering of associations;

- to develop voluntary work;
- to assure clearness of resources allocation;
- to suit social and fiscal costs to specificities of employment in associations.

Vienney, Claude and Jean Louis Weber. *La délimitation et l'organisation du champ statistique de l'économie sociale*. Colloque de l'AD-DES du 8 Juin 1983.

The necessity of having statistical knowledge of social economy to act efficiently for its development and its recognition motivates this reflection on the problems facing the construction of a system of economic information on this sector. C. Vienney, on one hand, proposes the concepts and defines the fields of activity of the social economy to build a systematic description. J. L. Weber, on the other hand, draws up a draft of a satellite account.

Vienney, Claude. *L'économie sociale*. Paris: Repères-La découverte, 1994.

The purpose of this very comprehensive book is to summarize all the available data on the organizations of the so-called "social economy" (associations but also mutuals, cooperatives and credit institutions). It gives very important findings on the number, size, scope and composition of these organizations. But it also proposes an examination of the trends and real conditions of their development, the means of their evolution and organization.

REFERENCES

AFTA. *Transparence et associations*. Paris: Nouvelles éditions fiduciaires, 1990.

Agulhon, Maurice. *1848 ou l'apprentissage de la République*. Paris: Seuil, 1973.

Agulhon, Maurice. "Le cercle dans la France bourgeoise: 1810–1848, étude d'une mutation de la sociabilité". *Cahier des annales*, 36, Paris: A. Colin, 1977.

Aguhlon, Maurice. "Vers une histoire des associations". *Esprit*, 6, 1978.

Alfandari, Elie. *L'action et l'aide sociale*. Paris: Dalloz, 1987.

Alfandari, Elie and Amaury Nardone. *Les associations et les fondations en Europe: régime juridique et fiscal*. Brussels: Librairie Européenne-Juris-Service, 2nd ed., 1994.

Alix, Nicole· and Bertrand Tisserant (with the participation of Sami Castro). *Associations et activités économiques*. Paris: UNIOPSS, 1986.

Alix, Nicole and Sami Castro. *L'entreprise associative: aspects juridiques de l'intervention économique des associations*. Paris: Economica, 1990.

Alix, Nicole. "Associations sanitaires et sociales et pouvoirs publics". *Revue des études coopératives mutualistes et associatives*, 47, 3rd trim., 1993, pp. 92–9.

Alphandery, Claude. *Les structures d'insertion par l'économique*. Paris: La Documentation Française, 1990.

Anheier, Helmut K., and Wolfgang Seibel, eds. *The Third Sector: Comparative Studies of Nonprofit Organizations*. Berlin and New York: Walter de Gruyter, 1990.

Anheier, Helmut K., Martin Knapp and Lester M. Salamon. "Pas de chiffres, pas de politique. Eurostat peut-il mesurer le non lucratif?" *Revue des études coopératives, mutualistes et associatives*, 46, 2nd trim., 1993, pp. 87–96.

Archambault, Edith. "Les associations en chiffres". IIème colloque de

References

l'ADDES. *Revue des études coopératives*, 12, October–December 1984, pp. 11–46.

Archambault, Edith. "L'économie sociale est-elle associée aux grandes fonctions économiques des pouvoirs publics?" *Revue des études coopératives, mutualistes et associatives*, 18, 2nd trim., 1986, pp. 3–35.

Archambault, Edith. "Public authorities and the nonprofit sector in France", in *The Third Sector, Comparative Studies of Nonprofit Organizations*. Edited by Helmut K. Anheier and Wolfgang Seibel. New York and Berlin: Walter de Gruyter, 1990.

Archambault, Edith. "Secteur nonprofit et secteur philanthropique aux États-Unis". *Revue des études coopératives, mutualistes et associatives*, 38, 2nd trim., 1991, pp. 33–50.

Archambault, Édith. "Defining the nonprofit sector: France". *Working Papers of The Johns Hopkins Comparative Nonprofit Sector Project*, 7, 1993.

Archambault, Edith. "L'opinion se mobilise". *Projet*, 237, spring 1994, pp. 16–24.

Archambault, Edith and Xavier Greffe. *Les économies non-officielles*. Paris: La Découverte, 1984.

Archambault, Edith and Viviane Tchernonog. "Le poids économique du secteur associatif". Xème Colloque de l'ADDES. *Revue des études coopératives mutualistes et associatives*, 253–54, 3rd trim., 1994, pp. 118–46.

Archambault, Edith, Christine Bon and Marc Le Vaillant. *Les dons et le bénévolat en France*. Paris: ISL-LES – Fondation de France, 1991 (mimeographed).

Arnaud, Gilles, Frédérique Leprince and Xavier Greffe. *Nouvelles demandes, nouveaux services*. Paris: La Documentation Française, 1990.

Balme, Richard. "La participation aux associations et le pouvoir municipal". *Revue Française de sociologie*, 28, 4, 1987.

Bardout, Jean-Claude. *Les libertés d'association: histoire étonnante de la loi 1901*. Lyon: Juris-Service, 1991.

Barral, Caroline. *Naissance et développement du mouvement de lutte contre les maladies neuromusculaires en France*. AFM-CTNERHI, 1991, mimeographed.

Barral, Caroline and Florence Paterson. *Impact du téléthon sur les associations du secteur sanitaire et social*. AFM-CTNERHI, 1991, mimeographed.

Barthe, Marie-Annick. "Pauvretés et État-Providence. L'approche du Comité de Mendicité", *Revue Française des Affaires Sociales*, 3, July–September 1991.

Barthelemy, Martine. *Les associations dans la société française*. 2 vols. Paris: Les cahiers du CEVIPOF-CNRS, 1994.

References

Baumlin, Laurence and Maryvonne Lemaire. "Place de l'économie sociale dans la protection sociale: contour et représentation". *Revue des etudes coopératives, mutualistes et associatives*, 28, 3rd trim., 1989, pp. 28–42.

Ben-Ner, Avner. "Nonprofit organizations: why do they exist in market economies?", in *The Economics of Nonprofit Institutions; Studies in Structure and policy*. Edited by Susan Rose-Ackerman. Oxford: Oxford University Press, 1986.

Beriot, Louis. *Le bazar de la solidarité*. Paris: J.C. Lattès, 1985.

Bidet, Eric. "Le tourisme associatif a-t-il encore une utilité sociale?" *Revue des études coopératives, mutualistes et associatives*, 47, 3rd trim., 1993.

Blaise, Henri. "Une transaction sans concessions". *Droit social*, 5, 1988, pp. 432–38.

Blanchet, Jean. *Gestion du bénévolat*. Paris: Economica, 1990.

Bloch-Lainé, François. "Entre l'administration et le marché: les associations". *Revue d'économie politique*, 27, 4, 1977.

Bloch-Lainé, François and Jean-Marc Garrigou-Lagrange. *Associations et développement local*. Paris: Librairie Générale de Droit et Jurisprudence, 1988.

Blonde, Marie-Hélène and Jean-Charles Willard. "Économie sociale et financement public: les flux et leur enregistrement comptable". *Revue des études coopératives, mutualistes et associatives*, 18, 4th trim., 1986, pp. 45–58.

Boulte, Patrick. *Le diagnostic des organisations appliqué aux associations*. Paris: PUF, 1991.

Boumendil, Judith. *Analyse économique des politiques culturelles locales*. Mémoire de diplôme d'études approfondies. Université Paris I, 1992, mimeographed.

Bourdieu, Pierre (ed.). *La misère du monde*. Paris: Seuil, 1993.

Bouyer, Christine. "Tourisme associatif, un système en crise?" *Revue des études coopératives, mutualistes et associatives*, 251, 1st trim., 1994, pp. 24–38.

Braudel, Fernand. *Civilisation matérielle, Economie et Capitalisme – XVe – XVIIIe siècle*. Paris: Armand Colin, 1979.

Braudel, Fernand. *L'identité de la France*. Vol. I, Les hommes et les choses. Paris: Arthaud, 1986.

Brichet, Robert. *Associations et syndicats*. Paris: Litec, 1992.

Buchanan, James and Gordon Tullock. *The Calculus of Consent*. Ann Arbor, University of Michigan Press, 1962.

Bürgenmeier, Beat. *Plaidoyer pour une économie sociale*. Paris: Economica, 1990.

Caire, Guy. "Syndicalisme, sécurité sociale et mutualité". *Revue de l'é-*

conomie sociale, 1, 2, 1984, pp. 56–67.

Canto, Jean-François. *Localisation et caractéristiques principales par secteurs d'activité des 336220 déclarations d'associations de la décennie 1975–1984*. Fonds National de Développement de la Vie Associative, 1988.

Casteret, Anne-Marie. *L'affaire du sang*. Paris: La Découverte, 1992.

Castro, Sami. *Les associations exerçant une activité économique, contribution à la théorie de l'entreprise*. Thesis, Université de Paris I, 1987.

Cette, Gilbert, Philippe Cuneo, Didier Eyssartier, Jérôme Combier and Laurent Pourquet. "Nouveaux emplois de services". *Futuribles*, March 1993.

Chadeau, Ann and Jean-Charles Willard. "Les formes et la mesure de l'emploi dans l'économie sociale". *Revue des études coopératives* 15, 3rd trim., 1985, pp. 65–89.

Chapron, Jean-Etienne and Jean-Charles Willard. "Travail et emploi dans les associations: réalisations et projets". Xème colloque de l'AD-DES. *Revue des études coopératives mutualistes et associatives*, 255, 1st trim., 1995, pp. 31–9.

Chéroutre, Marie-Thérèse. *L'essor et l'avenir du bénévolat facteur d'amélioration de la qualité de la vie*. Paris: Conseil économique et social, 1989.

Chéroutre, Marie-Thérèse. *Exercice et développement de la vie associative dans le cadre de la loi du 1er juillet 1901. Avis et rapport du conseil économique et social*. Paris: Journal Officiel, 1993.

Chéroutre, Marie-Thérèse. Interview in *La Croix*, 26 February 1993.

Clapham, J. H. *The Economic Development of France and Germany*. Cambridge: Cambridge University Press, 1961.

Clavagnier, Brigitte. "Les associations en forme de convention". *Juris associations*, 73, February 1993, pp. 29–34.

Collard, David. *Altruism and Economy: A Study in Non-selfish Economics*. Oxford: Martin Robertson, 1978.

Comité Européen des Associations d'intérêt général (CEDAG). *Les associations et l'Europe*. Paris: CEDAG, 1990.

Commissariat Général du Plan. *Cohésion sociale et prévention de l'exclusion*. Rapport de la commission no. 4 du XIe Plan. Paris: La Documentation Française, 1993.

Commission des Communautés Européennes. *Le droit des associations. Volume 1: Belgique, France, Italie, Luxembourg, Pays Bas. Statut de l'association Européenne*. Paris: Lamy, 1992.

Conference on human genome analysis. Paris, December 1992, mimeographed.

Conférence internationale sur l'Économie de la culture. *Économie et culture*. Avignon, 12–14 May 1986. Paris: La Documentation Française, 1990.

References

Conseil de l'Europe. *La politique culturelle de la France*. Paris: La Documentation Française, 1988.

Conseil National de la Vie Associative. *Bilans de la vie associative*. Various issues, 1982–92. Paris: La Documentation Française.

Conseil National de la Vie Associative. *Les associations et l'Europe*. Paris: La Documentation Française, 1989.

Conseil National de la Vie Associative. *Les regroupements associatifs par secteurs d'activité*. Paris: CNVA, 1989.

Coursin, François. "La politique européenne de concurrence et les entreprises de l'économie sociale". *Revue des études coopératives, mutualistes et associatives*, 47, 3rd trim., 1993, pp. 58–72.

Courtois, Guy and André de Montalembert. "Droit et fiscalité des associations et fondations". *Nouvelles fiscales*, December 1989, 80pp.

Courtois, Josette. *Les associations, un monde méconnu. Enquête nationale: poids économique et social des associations employant des salariés*. Paris: Crédit Coopératif, 1991.

Crédit Cooperatif. *Associations de santé et établissements privés à but non lucratif*. Nanterre: Crédit coopératif, 1992a.

Crédit Cooperatif. *Associations: personnes âgées, aide à domicile et hébergement*. Nanterre: Crédit coopératif, 1992b.

C.R.E.D.O.C. *Participation des Français à la vie associative. Tableaux des données détaillées*. June 1993.

Culture et liberté-Délégation générale à l'innovation et à l'économie sociale. *Associations d'utilité sociale: des financements en évolution*. Actes du colloque. Paris: 24 February 1992.

Davezac, Georges. *Les entreprises de l'économie sociale*. Avis et rapport au Conseil Économique et Social. Paris: Journal Officiel, 1986.

Debbasch, Charles (ed.). *Les fondations: un mécène pour notre temps?* Paris: Economica, 1987.

Defourny, Jacques. *Vers une politique économique des associations*. Congrès européen de Barcelone, May 1993.

Délégation générale à l'innovation sociale et à l'économie sociale. *L'Europe et l'innovation sociale*. Actes du colloque. Paris: 22–23 October 1992.

Délégation générale à l'innovation sociale et à l'économie sociale. *L'Europe et l'économie sociale*. Actes du colloque. Paris: October 1992.

Delsol, Xavier. *Mécénat et parrainage: guide juridique et fiscal*. Lyon: SA2-Juris-Service, 1991.

Demoustier, Danièle and François Saparelli. "Les organismes privés sans but lucratif au service des ménages". *Revue des etudes coopératives, mutualistes et associatives*, 49, 1st trim., 1994, pp. 39–48.

Deruelle, Dominique. "La construction d'une nomenclature fonctionnelle des associations: un travail expérimental". *Revue des études coopératives*, 12, 4th trim., 1984, pp. 51–67.

Descours, Bernard. *Guide annuaire des fondations et des associations*. Lyon: SA2-Juris-Service, 1991.

Desir, Harlem. *Situation et devenir des associations à but humanitaire*. Avis et rapport du Conseil Économique et Social. Paris: Journal Officiel, 1994.

Desjonqueres, Pascale and Anne Grivotet-Robert. *Guide de l'association employeur: les collaborateurs occasionnels et permanents*. Paris: Juris-Services, 1990.

Desroche, Henri. *Pour un traité d'Economie sociale*. Paris: CIEM, 1983.

Desroche, Henri. *Histoires d'économies sociales. D'un tiers État au tiers secteur: 1791–1991*. Paris: Syros/Alternatives, 1991.

Dewarrat, G. "La mesure d'efficience des organisations non profit". *Direction et Gestion des Entreprises*, 4, July 1984, pp. 7–20.

Direction des études et de la prospective – Ministère de l'éducation nationale. *Repères et références statistiques*, 1991.

Djlder, Zohor and Maryse Marpsal. "La vie religieuse: chiffres et enquêtes". *INSEE, Données sociales*, 1990, pp. 376–84.

Donnat, Olivier. *Les français face à la culture; de l'exclusion à l'éclectisme*. Paris: La Découverte, 1994.

Donnat, Olivier and Denis Cogneau. *Les pratiques culturelles des français (1973–1989)*. Paris: La Découverte/ La Documentation Française, 1990.

Donzelot, Daniel. *L'invention du social*. Paris: Fayard, 1984.

Douglas, James. "Political theories of the nonprofit organizations", in *The Nonprofit Sector – A Research Hand Book*. Edited by Walter W. Powell. New Haven and London: Yale University Press, 1987.

Dumont, Jean. "Le tourisme social". *Dossier du CRES*, 160, September 1989.

Dumont, Jérôme. "Comprendre les associations du secteur sanitaire et social". *Juris-Associations*, 86, October/November 1993.

Dupuy, René-Jean. "Le droit des fondations en France et à l'étranger". *Notes et Etudes Documentaires*, 4879. Paris: La Documentation Française, 1985.

Durkheim, Émile. *De la division du travail social*, 1893. Paris: PUF, 1983.

Duroy, Jean-Pierre. *Le compagnonnage aux sources de l'Economie Sociale*. Paris: Mutualité Française, 1991.

Elster, Jon and Nicolas Herpin, eds. *Ethique des choix médicaux*. Arles:Actes Sud, 1992.

Enjolras, Bernard. "Vers une théorie socio-économique de l'association: l'apport de la théorie des conventions". *Revue des études coopératives, mutualistes et associatives*, 48, 4th trim., 1993, pp. 79–92.

Ewald, François. *L'État Providence*. Paris: Grasset, 1986.

References

Femeau, A. and Gérard Martin. "Le financement des associations du secteur sanitaire et social". *Cahiers du CEPES*, 60, 1989.

Fenet, Francine. *L'aide sociale à l'enfance: exemple de régulation d'un système économique non-marchand*. Thesis, Université de Paris I, 1988.

Ferrand Bechmann, Dan. *Bénévolat et solidarité*. Paris: Syros Alternative, 1992.

Ferrand-Nagel, Sabine. *Les centres de santé*. Thesis, University of Paris I, 1990.

Fondation de France. *La vie associative en France*. 3èmes journées d'études internationales sur les associations. Lille: 22–26 June 1991.

Fondation de France. *Meeting People's Needs in France*. Fondation de France-Europhil association, 1991.

Fondation de France. *Activité et comptes de la fondation de France*, 72, October 1992.

Fondation de France. *Les associations, l'éthique et la transparence: pratique associative et systèmes de contrôle*, 1992.

Fondation de France. *Repères à travers le monde des fondations*, 1992.

Fondation de France. *Fondations, Donations et Legs*, 1992.

Fondation pour la vie associative (FONDA). *Rapport d'activités*, 1989.

Fondation pour l'économie sociale (FONDES). *Entreprises de l'économie sociale et lois de décentralisation*. Paris: La Documentation Française, 1985.

Forsé, Michel. "Les créations d'associations: un indicateur de changement social". *Observations et Diagnostics Economiques*, 6, January 1984, pp. 125–45.

Foucault, Michel. *Surveiller et punir, Naissance de la prison*. Paris: Gallimard, 1975.

Foucault, Michel. *Histoire de la folie à l'âge classique*. Paris: Gallimard, 1978.

Fouquet, Annie, Nicole Tabard and Michel Villac. *La vie associative et son financement*. FONJEP-CREDOC. Paris: La Documentation Française, 1990.

Fourel, Christophe and Jean-Luc Volatier. "Associations, l'âge de raison". *C.R.E.D.O.C. Consommation et modes de vie*, 78, June–July 1993, 4pp.

Fourquin, François. "La chrétienté des clochers et des champs vers 1300". In *Histoire économique et sociale du monde*, Vol. 1. Edited by Pierre Leon. Paris: Armand Colin, 1977.

Fumaroli, Marc. *L'État culturel*. Paris: De Fallois, 1991.

Furet, François and Mona Ozouf, eds. *Dictionnaire critique de la Révolution Française*. Paris: Flammarion, 1988.

Garrigou-Lagrange, Jean Marc. *Recherches sur les rapports des associations avec les pouvoirs publics*. Paris: LGDJ, 1970.

References

Gateau, Gilles. "De l'emploi au travail associatif: réflexions sur la notion d'emploi dans les associations". *Revue des études coopératives,* 15, 3rd trim., 1985, pp. 94–112.

Gaudin, Jean. *Initiatives locales et création d'emplois.* Paris: La Documentation Française, 1982.

Gazier, Bernard. "L'économie sociale dans l'économie mixte aujourd'hui". *Revue des études coopératives, mutualistes et associatives,* 44–45, 1st trim., 1993, pp. 174–82.

Gershuny, J. "L'innovation sociale: nouveaux modes de prestation de services". *Futuribles,* February 1986.

Gibaud, B. *De la mutualité à la sécurité sociale.* Paris: Éditions sociales, 1986.

Gidron, Ben, Ralph Kramer and Lester M. Salamon. *Government and the Nonprofit Sector: Emerging Relationship in Welfare States.* San Francisco: Jossey Bass, 1992.

Godbout, J. *L'esprit du don.* Paris: La Découverte, 1992.

Gontcharoff, Georges. *Guide du partenariat des associations et des pouvoirs publics.* Paris: L'Harmattan, 1988.

Gros, Françoise and Laurence Hauesler. *Evolution du monde associatif de 1978 à 1986.* Paris: CREDOC, 1988.

Guerrand, R. H. and Rupp, M. A. *Brève histoire du service social en France.* Paris: Editions Ouvrières, 1969.

Gueslin, André. *L'invention de l'économie sociale, le 19ème siècle Français.* Paris: Economica, 1987.

Gueslin, André and Pierre Guillaume, eds. *De la charité médiévale à la sécurité sociale.* Paris: Les Éditions Ouvrières, 1992.

Gui, Benedetto. "Fondement Économique du tiers secteur". *Revue des études coopératives, mutualistes et associatives,* 44–45, 1st trim., 1993, pp. 160–74.

Haeusler, Laurence. "Evolution du monde associatif de 1978 à 1986". *Les rapports du CREDOC,* 51, December 1988.

Haeusler, Laurence. "Le monde associatif de 1978 à 1986". *INSEE Données sociales,* 1990, pp. 369–75.

Hammack, David C. and Dennis R. Young, eds. *Nonprofit Organizations in a Market Economy: Understanding New Roles, Issues and Trends.* San Francisco: Jossey Bass, 1993.

Hansmann, Henry. "Economic theories of nonprofit organization", in *The Nonprofit Sector – A Research Hand Book.* Edited by Walter W. Powell. New Haven and London: Yale University Press, 1987.

Hatzfeld, Henri. *Du paupérisme à la sécurité sociale.* Paris: A. Colin, 1971.

Henry, André. *Pionniers et fondateurs: histoire de la longue marche des associations, des coopératives et des syndicats.* Paris: Editions de l'Instant/FEN, 1987.

References

Heran, François. "Un monde sélectif: les associations". *Economie et statistique*, 208, March 1988, pp. 17–32.

Heran, François. "Au coeur du réseau associatif: les multi-adhérents". *Economie et statistique*, 208, March 1988, pp. 33–44.

Hodgkinson, Virginia A., Richard W. Lyman and Associates. *The Future of the Nonprofit Sector – Challenges, Change and Policy Considerations*. San Francisco and London: Independent Sector/Jossey Bass, 1989.

Hodgkinson, Virginia A., Murray S. Veitzman, Christopher M. Toppe and Stephen M. Noga. *Nonprofit Almanac 1992–1993, Dimensions of the Independent Sector*. San Francisco: Jossey Bass, 1992.

Hodgkinson, Virginia A. and Paul Schervisch, eds. *The Future of Caring and Service to the Community*. San Francisco: Jossey Bass, 1994.

Holzer, Bernard and Frédéric Lenoir. *Les risques de la solidarité*. Paris: Fayard, 1989.

Horaist, Jacques. *Rôle économique des associations*. Paris: Direction de la prévision, 1983.

I.C.O.S.I. *Information Material on Social Economy in the Twelve Countries of the European Community*. Conférence CIRIEC. Bruxelles: 19 October 1989.

Imbert, Jean. *Hôpitaux en France*. Paris: PUF, 1981.

INSEE. "Evolution de l'emploi salarié dans les associations 1971–1980". *Note INSEE*, 320/169, May 1983.

INSEE. "La consommation des ménages en 1991". *INSEE Résultats*, Série consommation-modes de vie, 39–40, May 1992.

Inspection Générale des Affaires Sociales. *La politique sociale et les associations: rapport 1982–1984*. Paris: La Documentation Française, 1984.

Institut National de la Jeunesse. *Associations et emploi*, 1989.

James, Estelle. *The Nonprofit Sector in Comparative Perspective*, in *The Nonprofit Sector – A Research Hand Book*. Edited by Walter W. Powell. New Haven and London: Yale University Press, 1987.

James, Estelle, ed. *The Nonprofit Sector in International Perspective – Studies in Comparative Culture and Policy*. New York and Oxford: Oxford University Press, 1989.

Journal Officiel de la République Française. *Fondations: tutelle, contrôle des subventions, fiscalité*, 1988.

Journal Officiel de la République Française. *Associations syndicales, associations foncières urbaines et pastorales*, 1988.

Journal Officiel de la République Française. *Associations: régime général*, 1988.

Kaminski, Philippe. "Des chiffres pour l'Économie sociale: les sources d'information; mobiliser les données existantes et en créer de nouvelles". *Ier colloque de l'ADDES*, 8 June 1983.

Kaminski, Philippe. "Proposition de classement des entreprises qui constituent l'économie sociale". *Revue des études coopératives, mutualistes et associatives*, 37, 1st trim., 1991, pp. 27–34.

Kaminski, Philippe. "Nouvelles données sur l'économie sociale. Enquêtes régionales sur l'économie sociale: une expérience pilote, des enseignements". Xème colloque de l'ADDES. *Revue des études coopératives mutualistes et associatives*, 255, 1st trim., 1995, pp. 40–7.

Kaminski, Philippe and Claude Vienney. "Des chiffres pour l'économie sociale". *Revue des études coopératives, mutualistes et associatives*, 23, 3rd trim., 1987, pp. 35–44.

Kandel, Irène and Emmanuelle Marchal. *L'emploi dans le secteur associatif: du salariat permanent au bénévolat.* Paris: Centre d'Etudes de l'Emploi, 1984.

Kepel, Gilles. *Les banlieues de l'Islam.* Paris: Le Seuil, 1987.

Kouchner, Bernard. *Charité Business.* Paris: Le Pré aux Clercs, 1986.

Lanneree, Suzanne. *Les associations de la loi 1901.* Paris: Editions du Puits Fleuri, 1991.

Laville, Jean-Louis. *Les services de proximité en Europe.* Paris: Syros-Alternatives, 1992.

Lemaire, M. *Les associations du domaine sanitaire et social: première étape d'une évaluation de leur poids économique.* Paris: Ministère des Affaires Sociales-SESI, March 1988.

Le Monde. "Les Français et leurs écoles", 16 January 1994.

Léna, Hyacinthe. *Fiscalité du mécénat.* Paris: PUF, 1991.

Lenay, Michel and Jean Werquin. "Le volontariat, aspects sociaux, économiques et politiques en France et dans le monde". *Notes et études documentaires*, 4780. Paris: La Documentation Française, 1985.

Lucas, Michel. *Transfusion et Sida en 1985.* Inspection Générale des Affaires Sociales, 1991.

Lucas, Michel. *France transplant.* Inspection Générale des Affaires Sociales, 1992.

Marchal, Emmanuelle. *Le développement de l'emploi dans les associations et le phénomène de professionnalisation des activités économiques.* Centre d'Etudes de l'Emploi, 1987.

Marchal, Emmanuelle. *Du désintéressement au marché: les différentes formes d'entreprises associatives.* Dossier de Recherche du Centre d'Etudes de l'Emploi, 33, September 1990.

Marchal, Emmanuelle. "L'entreprise associative entre calcul économique et désintéressement". *Revue Française de sociologie*, 33, 1992, pp. 365–90.

Marczewski, Jean. "Histoire quantitative – buts et méthodes". *Cahiers de l'Institut de Science économique appliquée*, série AF, July 1961.

Margolis, H. *Selfishness, Altruism and Rationality: A Theory of Social Choice.* Cambridge: Cambridge University Press, 1984.

References

Marranche, Victor. *Communication sur les associations.* Comité Economique et Social, Ile de France, November 1986.

Martin, Gérard. "Système financier et associations ou la rencontre de deux mondes". *Revue de l'économie sociale,* 12, October 1987, pp. 49–86.

Masson, Gérard and François Nebard. "La formation des bénévoles dans le secteur associatif". *Recherche sociale,* 123, July–September 1992, 78 pp.

Mayaud, Yves and Gérard Sousi (eds). *Le droit des associations.* Lamy Associations, 1992.

Meister, Albert. *La participation dans les associations.* Paris: Les Éditions ouvrières, 1974.

Ministère de la culture. *Nouvelle enquête sur les pratiques culturelles des Français en 1989.* Paris: La Documentation Française, 1990.

Ministère de la culture. Département des études et de la prospective. *Annuaire statistique de la culture.* Paris: La Documentation Française, 1991.

Ministère de l'Économie, des Finances et du Budget. *Les associations et les administrations financières.* Orléans: Journées d'étude et d'information, 20 January 1990.

Ministère de l'Économie, des Finances et du Budget. "Budget 1993". *Les notes bleues de Bercy.* No. hors série, 1993.

Ministère de l'Éducation nationale. Direction de l'Évaluation et de la Prospective. *Repères et références statistiques sur les enseignements et la formation,* 1991.

Mollat, Michel. *Les pauvres au Moyen Age; étude sociale.* Paris: Hachette, 1978.

Montesquieu, Charles de. *De l'Esprit des Lois,* 1748.

Moulin, A.M., "The Pasteur Institute and the Logic of Nonprofit". *3rd Conference of Research on Volunteering and Nonprofit Organizations.* Indianapolis, March 1992.

Musgrave, Richard A. *Theory of Public Finance.* New York: McGraw Hill, 1959.

Olson, Mancur. *The Logic of Collective Action.* Cambridge, Mass.: Harvard University Press, 1963.

Padieu, Claudine. *Statistiques de l'Économie Sociale, constat et propositions.* Rapport présenté à T. Dreyfus, Secrétaire d'Etat à l'Economie sociale, February 1990.

Passaris, Solange and Guy Raffi. *Les associations.* Paris: Repères-La Découverte, 1984.

Pavageau, Catherine *Croissance et recomposition du secteur associatif.* Paris: Centre d'Etudes de l'Emploi, 1987.

Phelps, E. S., ed. *Altruism, Morality and Economic Theory.* New York: Russell Sage Foundation, 1975.

Philip, Olivier. "Introduction to the International symposium on foundations". *Voluntas-LES* symposium. *Foundations: An International Research Symposium*. Paris, 21–23 October 1993.

Pomey, Michel. *Traité des fondations d'utilité publique*. Paris: PUF, 1980.

Poujol, Geneviève. *La dynamique des associations: 1844–1905*. Paris: CNRS/Centre d'études sociologiques.

Powell, Walter W., ed. *The Nonprofit Sector – A Research Hand Book*. New Haven and London: Yale University Press, 1987.

Radelet, Michel. *Mutualisme et syndicalisme*. Paris: PUF, 1991.

Raynouard, Yves. *Le tourisme social: de l'illusion au renouveau?* Paris: Ten Syros, 1986.

Rosanvallon, Pierre. *La crise de l'État providence*. Paris: Point Seuil, 1981.

Rose-Ackerman, Susan, ed. *The Economics of Nonprofit Institutions; Studies in Structure and Policy*. Oxford: Oxford University Press, 1986.

Roudet, Bernard. "Bilan des recherches sur la vie associative". *Revue d'économie sociale*, 14, April 1988.

Saeys, Guy. *Les associations entre la société civile et l'état*. Paris: ADRAC, 1980.

Saeyz, Guy. "Les politiques de la culture", in *Traité de sciences politiques*. Edited by M. Grawitz and J. Lecat. Volume 4. Les politiques publiques. Paris: PUF, 1984.

Sainteny, Guy. *Les verts*. Paris: PUF, 1991.

Salamon, Lester M., *Partners in Public Service: Government and the Nonprofit Sector in the Modern Welfare State*, Baltimore: Johns Hopkins University, 1994.

Salamon, Lester M. and Helmut K. Anheier. "Toward an understanding of the international nonprofit sector: the Johns Hopkins Comparative Nonprofit Sector Project". *Nonprofit Management and Leadership*. 2, 3, Spring 1992.

Salamon, Lester M. and Helmut K. Anheier. "In search of the nonprofit sector: the quest for definitions". *Voluntas*, 3, 2, 1992a, pp. 267–311.

Salamon, Lester M. and Helmut K. Anheier. "In search of the nonprofit sector II: the problem of classification". *Voluntas*, 3, 3, 1992b, pp. 125–53.

Salamon, Lester M. and Helmut K. Anheier. *The Emerging Sector; The Nonprofit Sector in Comparative Perspective – an Overview*. Baltimore: The Johns Hopkins University, 1994a.

Salamon, Lester M. and Helmut K. Anheier. "Caring sector or caring society? Discovering the nonprofit sector cross-nationally", in *The Future of Caring and Service to the Community*. Edited by Virginia Hodgkinson and Paul Schervisch. San Francisco: Jossey Bass, 1994b.

Salamon, Lester M., Helmut K. Anheier and Edith Archambault. "Participating citizens: US-Europe comparisons in volunteer action". *The Public Perspective*, 5, 3, March/April 1994, pp. 16–18.

Sawadogo, Raouda. *La dimension autogestionnaire de l'économie sociale: mythes et réalités*. Thesis, Université de Paris I, 1989.

SESI. "La clientèle des établissements pour personnes en difficulté en 1989". *Document statistique*, 151, 1989.

SESI. *Annuaire des statistiques sanitaires et sociales*. Ministère des affaires sociales, 1990.

SESI. "La clientèle des établissements pour personnes agées en 1990". *Document statistique* 165, 1992.

Simonnet, D. *L'écologisme*. Paris: PUF, 1982.

Sousi, Gérard. *Le fonctionnement des associations*. Paris: L'Hermès, 1984.

Sousi, Gérard. *Les associations*. Paris: Dalloz, 1985.

Tchernonog, Viviane. *Politiques sociales communales: les modes de gestion des bureaux d'aide sociale*. Paris: LES-Université de Paris I, 1984.

Tchernonog, Viviane (with the participation of Éric Bidet). *Gestion des politiques sociales locales – Analyse du recours communal aux associations*. Commissariat Général du Plan-Laboratoire d'Economie Sociale, 1991.

Tchernonog, Viviane. "The role of associations in the economic and social local development in France. Analysis of the municipal recourse to associations". *3rd International Conference of Research on Volunteering and Nonprofit Organizations*. Indianapolis, March 1992.

Tchernonog, Viviane. "The role of the local authorities in the financing and delivery of social welfare services in France". *Innovation and Employment*, OCDE study series 10, November 1992a.

Tchernonog, Viviane. "Municipal subsidies to French Associations". *Voluntas*, December 1992b, pp. 351–63.

Théry, Henry. *La place et le rôle du secteur associatif dans le développement de la politique d'action éducative, sanitaire et sociale*. Journal officiel. Avis et rapports du conseil économique et social, 1986.

Titmuss, Richard. *The Gift Relationship*. New York: Vintage Books, Random House, 1971.

Tocqueville, Alexis de. *De la démocratie en Amérique*. 1835. Paris: Gallimard, 1951.

Tocqueville, Alexis de. *L'Ancien Régime et la Révolution*. 1856. Paris: Gallimard-Idées, 1964.

Tsyboula, Sylvie. "Foundations in Europe: the view from France". *Voluntas-LES* symposium. *Foundations: An International Research Symposium*. Paris: 21–23 October 1993.

Tullock, Gordon. *Private Wants and Public Means*. New York: Basic Books, 1970.

Turpin, Pierre. "La lutte contre l'assistance pendant les années 70". *Les*

References

Cahiers du CTNERHI, 50, 1990.

Ughetto, Bernard. *Fédérations et associations*. Paris: CNVA-La Documentation Française, 1989.

Ullman, Claire. "Nonprofit organization, public funding and the boundaries of the welfare state: the politics of public funding of nonprofit social services in France". *Arnova Conference*. New Haven, November 1992.

Ullman, Claire. "New social partners: nonprofit organizations and the welfare state in France". *Annual meeting of the American Political Science Association*. Washington, May 1993.

UNAT. *Le tourisme associatif au service de l'économie et de la solidarité nationale*. June 1993.

UNIOPSS. *Associations et activités économiques: approche juridique*. Paris: UNIOPSS, 1985.

UNIOPSS. *Les services de proximité en question*. Paris: UNIOPSS, 1993.

Vaccaro, Antoine. *La bataille de la générosité*. Thesis, Université de Paris IX, 1986.

Vernières, Michel (ed.). *L'emploi du tertiaire*. Paris: Economica, 1985.

Vienney, Claude. "Le comportement financier des organismes de l'économie sociale". *Revue de l'économie sociale*, 12, 1987.

Vienney, Claude. *L'économie sociale*. Paris: Repères-La Découverte, 1994.

Vienney, Claude and Jean-Louis Weber. *La délimitation et l'organisation du champ statistique de l'économie sociale*. Colloque de l'ADDES, 8 June 1983.

Vienney, Claude, Jean-Louis Manoda and Daniel Rault. "Les institutions de l'économie sociale en France: identification et mesures statistiques", in *Economie sociale entre économie capitaliste et économie publique*. Edited by Jacques Defourny and Jose L. Monzon. Bruxelles: CAMPOS CIRIEC-De Boeck Université, 1992.

Villermé, D. *Tableau de l'état physique et moral des ouvriers*, 1840. Quoted in Claude Fohlen, and François Bedarida. *Histoire générale du travail*. Paris: Nouvelle Librairie de France, 1981.

Voluntas-LES. *Foundations: An International Research Symposium*. Paris, 21–23 October 1993.

Vovelle, Michel, ed. *L'Etat de la France pendant la Révolution*. Paris: La Découverte, 1988.

Weisbrod, Burton A. *The Voluntary Nonprofit Sector*. Lexington, Mass. and Toronto: Lexington Books, D. C. Heath and Company, 1977.

Weisbrod, Burton A. *The Nonprofit Economy*. Cambridge, Mass: Harvard University Press, 1988.

Williamson, Oliver. "Transaction-cost economics: the governance of contractual relations". *Journal of Law and Economics*, 22, 1979, pp. 223–61.

References

Wolton, Dominique. *La dernière utopie: la naissance de l'Europe démocratique*. Paris: Flammarion, 1993.

Woytinsky, W. S. and Woytinsky, E. S. *World Population and Production*. New York: Twentieth Century Fund, 1953.

Wresinski, Joseph. *Grande pauvreté et précarité économique*. Paris: Conseil Economique et Social, Journal officiel, 1987.

Zeldin, Theodor. *France 1848–1945. Ambition, Love and Politics*. Oxford: Oxford University Press, 1973.

Zeldin, Theodor. *France 1848–1945. Intellect, Taste and Anxiety*, Oxford: Oxford University Press, 1977.

Special issues of reviews

Après demain
  n° 310, January 1989, Le monde associatif.

Économie et statistique
  n° 208, March 1988, Le monde associatif, pp. 15–45.

La Revue de l'économie sociale
  n° 14, April 1988, Espaces et temps associatifs, 190 pp.
  n° 18, December 1989, Associations et pratiques économiques, 190 pp.

La tribune fonda
  n° 67/68, December 1989, L'association, un management original?, 208 pp.
  n° 69, January 1990, Les associations et l'Europe, 70 pp.
  n° 72/73, May 1990, Pratiques associatives et vie politique locale, 175 pp.
  n° 77, January 1991, L'odyssée des associations, 86 pp.
  n° 87, May 1992, Le financement des associations, appel aux pouvoirs publics, pp. 53–62.
  n° 88, July 1992, Modalités de contractualisation entre associations et pouvoirs publics, pp. 1–57.
  n° 89, September 1992, La vie associative en France, pp. 45–54.
  n° 91, November 1992, Mesures en faveur de la vie associative, pp. 31–56.
  n° 93, January 1993, Pour une éthique des rapports entre pouvoirs et citoyens associés, 122 pp.
  n° 94, February 1993, Les associations dans la décentralisation, pp. 5–13.

n° 98, August 1993, De nouvelles dynamiques associatives locales, 71 pp.

Les cahiers français
n° 221, 1985, L'économie sociale entre étatisation et capitalisme, 72 pp.
n° 260, March–April 1993, Culture et société.

Les dossiers de la lettre de l'économie sociale
n° 3, 1985, Le tourisme associatif et coopératif.
n° 433, Demain l'économie sociale, actes du colloque. August 30–31 1989, Port D'Albret, 32 pp.
n° 492, Ethique et économie sociale, l'inertie ou le mouvement, Colloque CJDES. 8 November 1990, Paris, 50 pp.
n° 537, Les entreprises d'économie sociale face à l'Europe, Université de rentrée du CJDES à Bruxelles, 3–4 October 1991, 43 pp.
n° 562, Innovation et économie sociale, 3ème rendez-vous du printemps du CJDES à Dourdan, 25–27 March 1992, 34 pp.

Dossiers et documents du monde
n° 160, November 1988, Les industries de la culture.

Juris-associations
n° 73, 15 February 1993, Les subventions en forme de conventions, pp. 29–34.

Pratique de l'association
n° 28, May 1988, Les rapports entre l'état et les associations bénéficiaires de financements publics, pp. 4–13.
n° 31, September 1988, Sport et économie – les associations sportives.

Union sociale
n° 50, June 1992, La promotion du rôle des associations, pp. 14–18.

INDEX